NEXT STOP ADVENTURE

BY MATT GAUCK

PIONEERS PRESS
LANSING, KANSAS

PIONEERS PRESS
816 North Main Street #200
Lansing, KS 66043
www.pioneerspress.com

Cover & interior artwork: Matt Gauck
Book design: Rio Safari

Copyright © 2014 by Matt Gauck

All rights reserved. No part of this book may be
reproduced or transmitted in any form or by any
means, electronic or mechanical, including photocopying, recording, or by any information storage
and retrieval system, without the written permission
of the Publisher, except when permitted by law.

ISBN: 978-1-939899-07-1

Printed in the United States of America

June 2014

THE COLLECTION OF STORIES IN YOUR HANDS IS THE PRODUCT OF TEN YEARS OF RIDING MY BIKE A LOT, DIGGING THROUGH TONS OF TRASH FOR FOOD, AND DECIDING "WELL, UH, I GUESS I COULD SLEEP HERE..." THINK OF THIS AS A SORT OF "DISCOGRAPHY" OF MY FIVE ZINES, KEEPING IN MIND THAT I NEVER CONSIDERED THESE WRITINGS WOULD EVER MAKE IT PAST A STACK OF PHOTOCOPIED PAPER — SO THE WILD LEAP TO "BOUND BOOK" STILL LEAVES ME LAUGHING. THE DRIVING FORCE BEHIND EVERY WORD OF THESE STORIES IS MY RESPONSE TO A PHRASE WE'VE ALL HEARD TOO OFTEN IN LIFE — "YOU CAN'T DO THAT."

RIDING MY BICYCLE THOUSANDS OF MILES, LIVING SOLELY OFF OF FOOD SCAVENGED FROM DUMPSTERS FOR SIX YEARS, PAYING RENT WITH DIY, ONE DOLLAR SCREENPRINTED PATCHES — I'VE DONE THEM ALL. EVERY EFFORT WAS PRELUDED WITH SOMEONE REMINDING ME THAT IT CAN'T BE DONE. I HATE NEGATIVITY, BUT IN A WEIRD WAY, I SORTA LOVE THAT PHRASE. <u>NO ONE</u> CAN TELL YOU WHAT YOU CAN OR CAN'T DO, EXCEPT FOR YOURSELF. HOWEVER, WHEN YOU TURN SOMEONE ELSE'S DOUBTS INTO PERSONAL MOMENTUM, THAT'S WHEN YOU'RE REALLY GETTING SOMEWHERE. THAT'S EXPLORING SOME NEW TERRITORY, BREAKING OUT OF SOME KIND OF PERCEIVED IDEA OF WHAT SOMETHING — OR SOMEONE — CAN OR CAN'T BE.

MY AIM IS ALWAYS TO FIGHT COMPLACENCY, TO ALLOW MYSELF TO KEEP EXPANDING — TO TURN IT ALL IN FOR IMPOSSIBLE DREAMS. ALL THE UNUSED PASSPORTS, THE CLEAN HIKING BOOTS,

THE UNEVENTFUL WEEKENDS, THE NEGLECTED HUMAN SPIRIT, THE CREEPING FEELING THAT SOMETHING IS MISSING — THE CYCLE OF THE EVERYDAY — THAT IS THE ENEMY. IT'S NOT HARD TO BREAK, JUST GET OUTSIDE, POINT YOURSELF IN A DIRECTION, AND KEEP GOING. WHAT HAPPENS NEXT? WELL, THAT'S THE ADVENTURE PART...

—MATT

FOR MY MOM, WHO SUPPORTS MY IDEAS
NO MATTER HOW RIDICULOUS THEY ARE

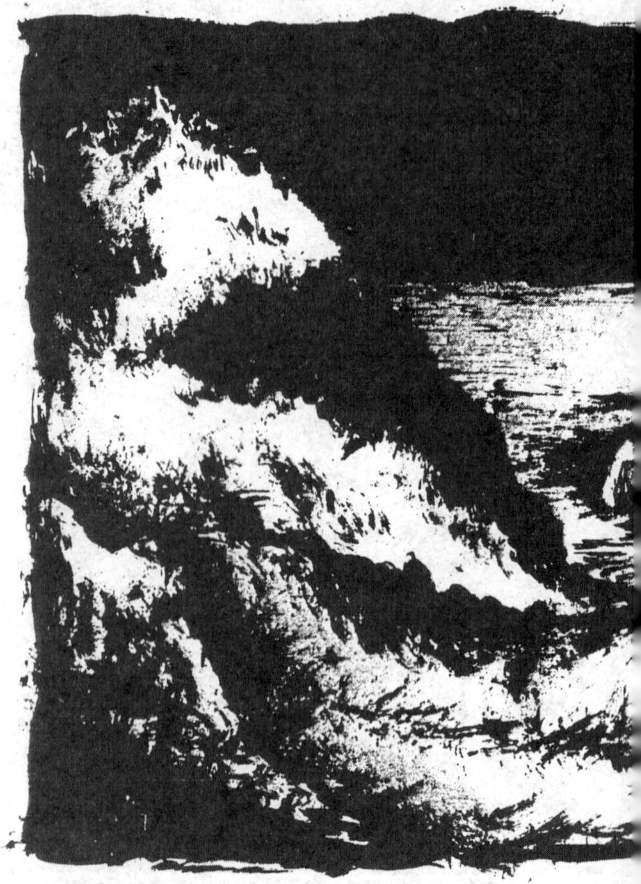

"i am not a traveler, nor an adventurer. things happen to me in my search for a way out."

— henry miller
(black spring)

next stop: adventure!
#one

The Best Idea We Ever Had

THAT PHRASE HAS SEEN more use in my life than I could even begin to explain. And it's true; every new idea becomes 'the best idea I/we ever had.' Someday, maybe the idea generating will stop, and time will slow down: a trade-off of half a life adventuring for the last half comprised of television and working. But...I never wanted that, so it seems like my infinite game of tag with the horizon will go on for years to come.

At the time, this was the best idea we ever had: A bike race with my friend Doug to the midpoint between Raleigh, North Carolina (Doug) and Savannah, Georgia (me). That midpoint was determined to be Coward, South Carolina at the corner of Railroad and Friendfield Street, an appropriate street crossing (based on our means of travel) in an ironic city. On paper, it appeared to be a simple 200ish-mile jaunt across culture-drenched backroads and lush, lively vegetation. Who wouldn't want a spring break like that? Trading a tan and simple beach days for bug bites and lifelong knee problems? I know, I know, it's obvious. Emails were exchanged, a time set for noon on Friday, and I started counting the days until 'go time'.

Now, there are two ways of doing things: the well-researched, buy-the-equipment-you-need, read-up-on-the-subject, 'appropriate' way of starting this endeavor...or there's a Plan B. Despite the fact that 'adventure' starts with the letter 'a', all the best experiences come out of Plan B's. True story: Embracing the adventure aspect, otherwise known as 'a lack of planning,' has evolved into an overused philosophy-gone-excuse that I will forever call my own. "I'll cross that bridge when I come to it." Sounds good on paper, huh?

The Ingredients

At the risk of making this boring, I'll list only the bigger stuff:

- 1 bike! With mountain bike tires. Bought for me by my mom when I graduated the seventh grade. NOT designed for someone, say, over fourteen years old. I was twenty-four. That = bad. Otherwise seen as 'the most obvious problem of this trip.'
- 1 sleeping bag. More on that later. Dang, dang, dang.
- Ø tent. Oops again.
- 2 saddlebags and 1 backpack
- Bananas! One bunch! I may as well list this one as "one mistake"
- 1 jar organic peanut butter (from the dumpster, of course)
- Ø socks! Take that, social acceptance!
- 1 camera

That's about it for important stuff. I had some money as well, and I managed to think ahead and get a mileage counter and another tire tube in case one exploded. You can never be too prepared. This is coming from someone who refuses to wear socks and didn't bring a tent because I 'forgot.'

Maybe the easiest way to explain it is to envision what someone who is about to bike over two-hundred miles *should* look like, and take away all that person's fancy, useful stuff, and then throw what's left, person included, into the trash a couple times. Add a smile, and that's me: A great idea waiting to happen.

So, apart from that, I spent the night prior to 'go time' photocopying the South Carolina map and then ruining it with tons of highlighter. There is nothing even close to a direct route from Savannah to Coward, so I wound up with an eight-road entourage that would surely guarantee me the coveted first-place spot of a two-person race. I folded up that map, put it in my pocket, and went to bed at 6 a.m. Feel free to count the bad ideas present in this text. Hint: There are *a ton*.

Day One: Rocks In My Back And Nudity In My Trash

I woke up after five hours of anticipatory sleep, ate something insubstantial, grabbed my bike, stood outside, and stared at my apartment door for a long time. It was my awkward goodbye with comfortable life and the concept of home. It's an odd feeling, but I've come to appreciate that last glance at normalcy, followed by the excited stare toward the unknown. You live for the fun, uncharted moments. And this was one of them. I snapped a 'before' picture and took off.

I've since read a couple books on the subject of travel, and more specifically long-distance bike touring. They are, generally, very boring, as they tend to focus on the biking part. I don't so much care about that aspect; bicycling simply happens to be the best way to cover distance for free, assuming time to not be an object. And it's not. It's a man-made concept, right up there with the value of a dollar. If I'm rejecting that, then I might as well go all out, right? Right. So I biked a lot. Ate some bananas. Thought a lot. See, these aren't entertaining or insightful stories. We'll keep moving.

Now, South Carolina is composed of winding scenic

roads lined with dense trees and…well, more trees. Sure, it's gorgeous, and I was happy to see it, but, well, if you lived your life with the Mona Lisa on your wall, you'd eventually get curious to see something different. Anyway, these roads connect little dots (complete with names) that indicate a 'town'. In theory. If I learned anything about cartography, it's that just because there is a word next to the dot, this does not mean that anything is there. Case in point: My stop, thirty-two miles into this trek, is a town represented by, and apparently consisting solely of, one gas station. That's it. Things are going great for me.

So, I roll past the locals and head directly for the dumpster. What can I say, that's become my thing: living life as freely as I can while the option still exists. Since it's worked so far, I see no reason to stop. First, however, I filled up my water bottles with the closest thing to water that South Carolina has to offer, which is this stuff called 'brown death' that comes out of the tap. It's awesome. After regrettably downing some 'water', I peered into the trash with fingers crossed. Gas stations, by the way, are rarely good for free food, but I've been lucky before.

Some cardboard, a bag of chips, and me sighing, "Oh great," out loud. I have what some would call a 'talent', what others label 'luck,' and what I refer to as a horrible curse: finding porn magazines. Well, that's not true; it's pornography in general. You name it and I've found nudity there in places that nobody would ever imagine. So, greeted with around twenty coverless magazines abounding with photos of, well, you know, I slammed the lid back down. Only after taking those chips, though. And I did, for the record, consider selling those magazines to weirdo South Carolinians, but decided against that immediately. I'm not about to spread that disease. Not even for money. Maybe for ice cream. Hot weather makes for insane desperation.

So, pornless and laughing, I left for more bridges and mosquito bites.

Me + Tired = Misery

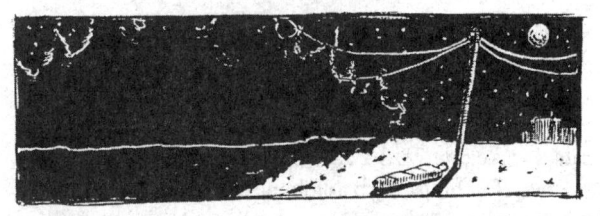

Sleep. Science is still up in the air about the how's and why's of this beast, so far be it for me, some kid on a bike, to stake a claim that I understand it. But I do know this much: Your body cannot be argued with. You actually can fall asleep on a bike. Trust me. So, come 9 p.m., I started thinking that maybe I should settle down. Now, here's where the lack of planning becomes evident. Since it wasn't raining, pretty much anywhere was game, but I'd been going through solid, dense woods for the past five miles. Just as I was debating sleeping in a tree (I'm sure it's possible), the trees opened up to a huge grass field with some factory-looking thing about a half-mile from the road. I pulled off into my new home and found solace under an unused telephone pole amongst the rocks and dirt.

The quality of being able to find humor in bad situations is universally understood as 'positivity.' That's what I call it, at least. A good way to see if you're a positive person is to bike

78 miles, then pull over in a dirty field, lay on some rocks, and unfold what is now appearing to be your little brother's sleeping bag from when he was in elementary school. Oooh. Dang. Sighing with quiet laughter, I pulled the top around my neck, because that's as far as it went. The stars were out in full force, so I considered this mishap to be borderline fortunate.

Day Two: One-Hundred Miles of Solitude

Borderline fortunate, for sure. So, in mid-March, it apparently gets kinda cold at night. Well, I was surprised. At any rate, I woke up freezing at 5 a.m. and forced my dead limbs to do useful things, such as folding a sleeping bag. I saddled up after an on-and-off sleep and managed to bike for about four miles before I absolutely could not feel my hands whatsoever. And I'm still in the middle of nowhere. The problem was that when I was moving, my blood would circulate better, but the wind froze my surface almost immediately. I'm sure that physics could determine a happy medium for biking speed and general temperature, but I didn't have any physics with me.

I was losing hope, so I checked my map, hoping for…well, I don't really know what. Desperate times are very interesting in this regard. Don't go looking for them, but when you're there, make sure to explore a little. The next road I was to turn on seemed fairly close, and without any landmarks, I was running on hope alone. Sure enough, it was about a half-mile on the left, capped off by a gas station. Like, a real gas station. It was great. Heaven is a place on earth and gas was only, like, $2.45 a gallon. After a brief thirty-minute bathroom visit (involving little more than my abusing the hand dryer for warmth), I sat down and wrote a lot until the sun was really, really out. Oh, and I picked up some gloves.

I Guess It Counts As Scenery

There's a lot that you physically miss seeing if you drive somewhere. I think that the comparison is that the slower you are traveling, the more you experience. Crawling on your stomach versus driving. Being on a bike is closer to the 'slow' end, which is nice because it reveals great truths about the open road and travellers past. A hand-carved boat oar? A Stephen King book? At least nine different, un-paired shoes? Three dryers? Relics like these beg nothing but questions. How do these things get here? And, more importantly, why do they remain there? My next fifty miles were occupied with little more than debating the shoe conundrum. Results are inconclusive.

I stopped at some little town to write and got a Subway Veggie Delight (the ultimate touring sandwich; also, it's pretty bad, as I recall). While sitting there writing and barely eating half of my lunch, I observed a three-hundred-pound man playing a slot machine and who was also shoeless. The whole event took on a Norman Rockwell sort of aesthetic, but more than anything, it was just weird. South Carolina. Good times.

I biked a lot more, got to the outskirts of whatever town I was in, and watched the sun hang low in the air while kissing the treetops. I thought about staying put, knowing the next town to be at least twenty-five miles (about two hours in biking time). Do it now or do it tomorrow? Faced with the familiar tradeoff of doing all my homework on Friday night so that the weekend is free, I bowed toward the sun and continued in hot, sweaty pursuit.

Castaway Re-Enactment

This part was awesome. I nearly forgot about it. So, I stopped off at a grocery store surrounded by nothing on all sides, ran around back, and flung open the dumpster. The sun was low and all the bugs emerged to greet it, instead finding me more interesting. Some mosquitos, but mostly gnats. Loads and loads of gnats. I ran to the trashcan, looked inside, and found one single coconut and some grapes. Grapes are straightforward; I took those and put them in my bike bag. A coconut, however…

I got out a bike tool and let instinct kick in. That's fancy-talk for 'I bashed the crap out of it.' Nothing doing. I hit this dumb, hairy sphere on every surface that I could find, including the store itself. I slammed it into the dumpster door a couple times, and after I lost my hearing and pinched my finger, I reverted to 'angry-ape-style' beating.

Finally, I poked a hole in my shirt, went to drink the milk, but actually poured it on my shirt and face. End result? One semi-full stomach, thirty-some gnat bites, and my bike/shirt/hands/face/life = really sticky. Matt: 1; Nature: 0.

Manifest Destiny!

Forcing yourself to bike hill over hills, powered by only Subway sandwiches and bruised bananas, with one Maglite taped to your handlebars on a bike you've owned for at least eleven years: That is one experience I cannot hope to ever describe. You develop faith in the landscape itself, that after some 'proving yourself' period it will then allow you to pass. The pitch-black surrounding never changes at all, and your field of vision becomes a yellowed dot two feet in front of you, shining back bits of rock and broken mirrors. Without being able to see the mileage counter, I couldn't guess how far I'd gone nor discern how far I had to go. This was somewhat hard to comprehend, but when your mind fails, your body kicks in and just goes. And goes. Like running with your eyes closed. Hill after hill, there is something to hope for, and in my case, it was embodied by the pink sky, reflecting city lights on the horizon. Cresting each hill was another visit to the mailbox, waiting for a letter. Ups and downs; hills and disappointments.

At some point, however, it breaks wide open like a dam and the faint sparkle of actual light becomes a reality. That's a good moment. The dim spark burns retinas into believing what life is really about, and you become immersed in a feeling of overwhelming meaning and purpose. It's like you have to go through hell to experience heaven. And, yes, it is, and will always be, worth it. Because there's ice cream there.

Incredible Feats of Multi-Tasking

It was nearly ten o'clock, and upon cruising the main street of Kingstree, the grocery store stood big and closed. Looking up at the sign, a little disappointed (I only wanted a place to sit down that was inside), I hear a male voice ask, "Hey, excuse me." So, naturally, I turn.

Here's the scene. It's dark and we're standing in the parking lot of a closed, unpopular grocery store. To my right is a parked car in the center of the parking lot with a police officer in mid-arrest of a somewhat belligerent, squirming guy. The cop, while applying handcuffs and looking at me, rather than the guy he's arresting, asks, "How far you been riding that bike?"

It's been six hours since I've spoken aloud, and coupled with the strange scene unfolding in front of me, I awkwardly spilled out a response. "Uh...about a hundred and eight miles today."

He looked satisfied and said, well, no, he *declared*, "You know, everybody's got something—me, I run, but my buddy, Charles, he builds cars..." He went on for a couple more minutes while I absorbed the scene. It was funny. "So, where you staying tonight? Hotel?" Hmm. Hadn't figured out that one yet.

"Uh...yeah."

Wait, wait, no. Hotels cost money. The unlocked roof access to the local KFC, however...that's free for the taking. I'm not sure which aspect of roofs makes them safer to me, but they just are. As a bonus, I also found that sleeping near the air vent kept me warm all night (not that my sunburn wasn't doing its part of keeping me hot *all* the time). Consequently, my life (defined as my sleeping bag and self) would smell like chicken-like food crap. I know it's artificial, but it's certainly less expensive than deodorant. Definitely more gross, though.

Day Three: Problems Galore

I woke up on the roof, still, and laughed aloud at how funny I found this to be. The time was around 8 a.m., which is, when you're sleeping 'in nature,' considered sleeping in. It also meant that the KFC was open. Dang.

By some incredible stroke of luck, I got down (bike bags and all) without being noticed, then unlocked my bike and took off. I recall this being a Sunday, because I stopped at a bank's covered porch and was able to charge my phone in order to check my messages and such. Doug, the guy I was racing against, had taken a borrowed phone on his half of the journey. One message awaited from Doug, informing me that he'd already popped a tire and had an awful time trying to get that fixed, involving use of his patch kit and then a new tube. I was sympathetic and thankful that my bike was holding up, but, still, I had been through a quaint personal hell of my own. It's a two-way road. And I still had thirty miles to go.

I left there for Coward and planned not to stop until I was there. The prospect of being 'done' and not having to ride my bike (because I was 'there') was enough to power me through a miscalculated forty miles of dehydrated glory. It was a nice ride, featuring an insane dog that chased me for the better part of a mile and then a huge rubber factory with a memorable scent that chased me for about twelve miles.

I knew that I was close and I finally felt like I was actually able to enjoy the bike-riding part of this excursion. The work of keeping myself moving was traded for the promise of somewhere to sit and laugh about all this stuff with one of my best friends. That sounded great. When I was greeted with the 'Now Entering Coward' sign, I took the obligatory photos, got really excited, and strolled toward the finish line: the corner of Railroad and Friendfield.

I was parallel to railroad tracks already, so I figured that it'd be easy to find this intersection. And it was. Seriously, the third intersection I came to off of whatever road I was on was the designated finish line. And it was in someone's front yard. I didn't expect that. But there was a little public park not a hundred feet away, so I simply went there and sat down.

Things I Hadn't Thought About

The second that I sat down, I looked to the right, which was where Doug would be coming from. I didn't see him. Then it hit me: It would be an incredible coincidence for him to arrive within minutes of my being there. I simply couldn't imagine that happening. And it didn't. Then I turned on my phone to see if he'd called. Bad move.

The message was something like this: "Hey, Matt. Uh, okay, I know this sucks, but I've had, like, three flat tires, and right now I'm five miles from where my bike is. I had to hitchhike to a gas station to try to get another tube and, well, I don't think I'm going to make it. I'm gonna call Hans to see if he can pick me up after this. Hope you made it, though, and give me a call whenever you can."

Hmm.

It's like waking up from a bad dream only to realize that you're still dreaming. Like the super crappy 'trick ending' of a *Twilight Zone* episode. Here's where the main flaw in the 'cross that bridge when I come to it' philosophy resides: Now I'm in a town that has nothing in it except a bike that I'm sick of riding, and I'm two hundred and five miles from home, with no way of getting home except…biking. I don't know how, but that part had evaded me. This wasn't a two-hundred mile jaunt; it *had* to be a 400-plus-mile death trip! I wasn't throwing a frisbee, I was chucking a boomerang, and this was the moment I realized it was heading right for me! Excitement doubles as a pair of blinders. Employing 'the philosophy' once more, I stopped thinking about it, enjoyed the moment, and took a nap.

…And I woke to a three-year-old having his birthday party at the park about fifteen feet away. Parents and everything. There I was, sleeping on a bench, covered in a combination of dirt, sweat, and KFC particles. Ruining someone else's day wasn't on my agenda, so I left quickly. I could easily ruin my own day with some more biking. On the plus side, I was on my way home in this direction. *And* I already knew the roads. Triple bonus because I could sleep on my KFC again! Things were going to be okay! Maybe!

Recipe for Situational Comedy

As painful as backtracking is, that KFC held a genuinely welcoming quality. The sky had turned a troubled blue and it looked like it might rain. Spend enough time doing hard time with nature and you get the impression that she doesn't like human beings. Do I blame her? Absolutely freaking not. On the way into town, I made a couple mental notes of covered places to sleep that came down to the town hall, which had a small but meaningful brick overhang, shading a four-foot square of solid concrete. Comfort was never the issue (which I hope is obvious by now) but this spot put me in the same line of sight of police officers and insane dogs. Despite still being open to the public, the KFC seemed to be the logical choice. One success surely implied another.

Taking the only preventative measure since my unused bike tube, I found a huge piece of cardboard across the street and dragged it with me. The time is seven o'clock; the air was wet and the sky a pale gray. My obstacles were mixed: a ten-foot ladder toward freedom, a seemingly endless string of cars packing the drive-thru lane, (from where the ladder was clearly visible) and me with a backpack, two bags, and a nine-foot square of cardboard. At the first break in the dinner traffic, I bolted toward the sky with everything but the piece of cardboard. One heave and everything landed safely next to the air vent. Scurrying down the ladder and hiding behind the outdoor refrigeration unit, another car passed without problem. Cardboard in hand (sort of), I attempted to climb up again and managed to get to the top while maintaining some semblance of balance by pushing the cardboard over onto the roof. In turn, my face and chest landed on the roof, and my legs stuck out off the edge. Another customer rounded the drive-thru loop and all I can imagine is this person looking up and wondering why half a human is flailing madly off the edge of the roof. Luckily (but more so, inexplicably), nobody saw me. The hard part was done and it was time for sleep.

Two a.m.: I wake up to rain on my face. That's when the cardboard came in handy. My late-night MacGyver gene kicked in, so I hastily folded a tent and then fell asleep almost as fast as I had woken up. Truthfully, it happened so quickly that I barely remembered any of it by the next morning. I stayed dry during the whole night. Oh, and the cardboard is still there for any enterprising campers.

An Entourage of Mishaps

Yeah, as if the entire trip wasn't an 'entourage of mishaps.' The next day was weird because, all of a sudden, I lacked a feasible destination. Going home sounded like backtracking the entire journey. Moreover, my knees had started feeling awful (due to my too-small-for-me bike), which was causing fluid to build up and subsequently become trapped in my kneecaps. It felt like having ball bearings rub against the bone every time I bent my knee, a commonplace movement in the cycling world. That's *bad*.

I tried calling my friend Rob, who I knew was driving back down I-95 sometime over the weekend. Initially, he didn't pick up, and my phone only had one bar of power so I couldn't leave it on and wait for a call. After assessing that I was only about eleven miles from the interstate, I took off to meet it and theoretically hitchhike back south. Hitchhiking seemed like the logical thing to do, despite my having no experience. But, really, how are you supposed to learn if you don't try?

From books, that's how. I've read a million books on successful hitchhikes and I was eager to finally employ this untapped skill set. Four miles into intolerable knee pain and foreboding storm clouds, my back bearings sort of, um, exploded. In bike terms, that means that the wheel stops moving in a straight circle, going askew and rubbing against the frame, and, well, the odometer goes from fourteen miles per hour to about three. Situation critical: dying phone, incredible knee pain, at least seven miles before I can *maybe* get a ride, and now my bike is broken. Oh, and nature thinks she wants to rain.

So I'm walking my bike, getting intermittently passed by cars about every two minutes, and it occurs to me to start hitchhiking now. Why not? It's the same principle, except instead of needing to go two-hundred miles, I only need to go, like, seven! Easy, right?

Ha, right. Three hours pass and I realize that I have become a seasoned pro at walking my bike, stopping to put out my thumb, and then getting passed by cars. Seriously, the same thing happened at least sixty times. All in South Carolina. At the peak of my frustration and right as the thought of spending one more night on a KFC roof hit me, the sky opened up. Well, more like a couple pinpricks, but nonetheless, it was raining.

The only other building I had seen thus far was a 'For Sale' house that this guy in a pickup was "going to, uh, show…uh, yeah, later," (which is why he and his huge truck couldn't drive me seven miles), so the fact that there was a closed-for-Monday church, complete with overhang, was literally a godsend. I figured I would try calling Rob again...

Something Goes Right

...And he picked up. I don't know why or how, but he was only eight exits away from the exit that I would have successfully biked to had the 'problems galore' bomb not exploded all over me. Arrangements were made and, for the first time in three days, I exhaled. And it was all over. Story done. 'The End' drops from the sky and we fade to black. The audience forgets the message the minute that they drive home.

The next thing of note that happened was a long car ride back to Savannah, where I got to think about all the fun things I'd accomplished, how I had actually made it to Coward, survived on a mere four dollars, slept in weird places, and so on. What hit me when I got home, however, was very different. Things were the same again. As in the normal, expected, everyday stuff.

I sat there and, over the course of about ten minutes, I started to miss the adventure, the unknown, the unexplored question mark at the horizon. Most people thought I 'got it out of my system' after this was over, but it's quite the opposite. Eyes open wider, hearts inflate, and life explodes. There is a whole other world over the next hill. The thrill is held within the chase, never in the outcome. A sunset would hold no audience if it were stagnant.

I guess what I'm saying is that I'm never going back.
(But I am going to write about it.)

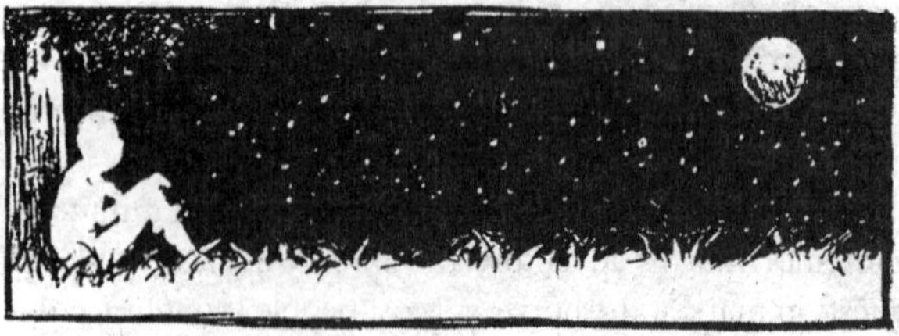

next stop adventure #2

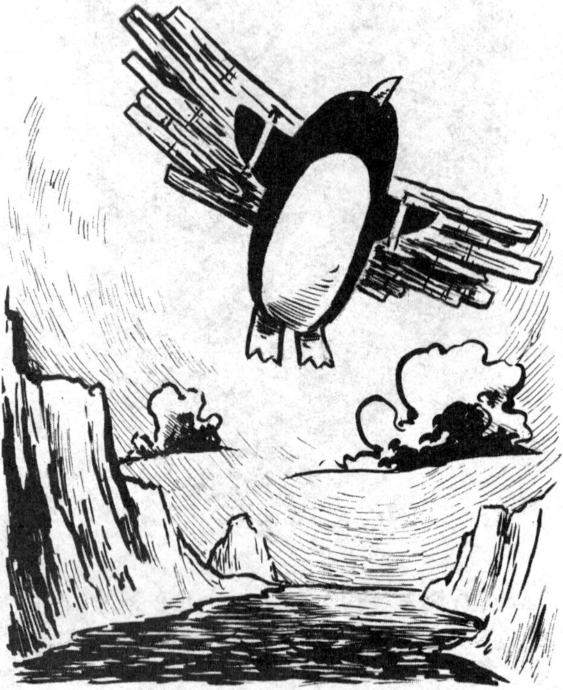

Oregon Dreaming

I LIKE TO THINK that this 'bike trip' idea happened out of necessity. Well, okay, I suppose it *persisted* out of necessity: It was born out of the fear of boredom. The concept of a post-graduation trip is a time-honored tradition, a relic of history I was destined to relive, just as many before me had. While most 'adventure seekers' visit Europe, I felt it made more sense to explore my immediate surroundings, rather than visiting locations that demand a passport. Well, and I didn't have any money. You use what you have, and what I had was a bike, a sleeping bag, and a keen ability to find free food. Oh, and most importantly, I had a friend who had recently moved to Portland, Oregon: the last bastion of do-it-yourself, bike-friendly, art-appreciating, everyone-is-friends, community-oriented life, and, obviously, somewhere I wanted to hang out for a month. Portland is consistently described as some autonomous floating island, hovering one-hundred feet above the rest of the United States. It's technically part of the U.S., but only in cold, mechanical terms, such as cartography and spatial organization. For the rest of us, however, it's an island paradise.

Still, it was a paradise that was about 3000 miles away. Or one huge adventure. Feel free to check the math. I showed my work.

Armed with little more than a desire to visit my friend Nate (and six months to decide that riding my bike from North Carolina to get there, was, in fact, a 'really good idea'), I started dreaming. I probably should have been planning. Oh, well. Having tried both, I can assure you, the dreams are way cooler. "Of what use is a dream, if not a blueprint for courageous action?" Adam West said that in the *Batman* movie. I can't believe I remember that.

Humble Beginnings

Early in my life, I learned that preparatory plans are complete garbage. And I mean that. The friend who tells you she's moving to Italy in two years when she's done with school will inevitably stay in Florida, even after impulsively buying a handful of books on Italian traveling and talking up her non-existent loft space, bragging of the stone work comprising the archway to the garden. I think this is universal: We all know that person, and their stories forever remain fictional beginnings. To be honest, I'm not completely against planning, but it does ruin spontaneity. I'm mostly against *talking* about your plans, and way more into hearing about how they went after they've happened. To combat this, I've adopted the MacGyver school of thought, wherein great plans are born from dire situations and the four seconds you're allotted to concoct them. That was my reasoning when blindly buying a 2004 Road Atlas on eBay, as it was the cheapest option to get a map. (I did consider using my friend's AAA privileges, but that'd be a waste of paper.) It also helped me consider little else until about two days prior to leaving.

For the record, I had already completed a 250-mile trip on a much crummier bike and made it though that just fine. (You just read about that!) So, really, experience and luck were both on my side. I hadn't planned much of that trip, and what I did plan was drastically altered by the time it mattered, so it seemed obvious to 'cross that bridge when I come to it'. Besides, I had an atlas in the mail *and* a place to stay in Portland! Throw your bets down, cuz it's all coming up 'Gauck'!

Flash forward a couple months and an MFA degree later, and that's when you'll join this story. I stood, hands on my hips, looking at all the crap I planned on attaching to my bike, as it sprawled across the floor of my old room at my mom's house. My brother stared at it, too, trying to give some kind of context to a ten-dollar tent, an equally cheap sleeping bag, a bunch of bike tubes, three water bottles, a notebook and pen, and one change of clothes. It made so little sense without the bike in the room.

Four saddlebags and some bungee cords would henceforth hold my whole life together. I feel like that should be a very comforting feeling, but it certainly isn't when you're staring at it on the floor. There is exactly one thing worse than that, and it's trying to fall asleep, knowing you're voluntarily donating your comfortable life for a long time. As I eventually drifted off, I swear I could hear, "I will turn it all in for late nights and impossible dreams…" Majority Rule? Anyone? *Interviews With David Frost*! It kills!

I Didn't Pack Socks ON PURPOSE!

Go time. I stood next to my bike, a blue 1994 Trek touring model, outfitted with my 'life' for the next three thousand miles, and finally realized that I was about to ride the entire gaping distance between North Carolina and Oregon. I recall looking down at my shoes, my trusty, patched-up 'once-black-but-now-gray' Converse All Stars, and thinking that the next time I looked at them would be someplace I'd never been before. That part was exciting.

Leaving, however, was undeniably the hardest part. Of every mile I biked for the duration of this trip (an eventual 2830!), the very first mile was the most difficult. I recognized all the landmarks, relived memories attached to every street sign, and was desperate to combat the reminder that I would not be sleeping in a bed tonight. Furthermore, I didn't know where I would sleep at all. I knew where I was headed but didn't know where I was going. My life was no longer a series of locations, but simply a direction marked 'away'. Oooh. Downer.

Adventure is like that: the butterflies flutter in your stomach for the first one percent of the journey, but then you leave for good, towing all your fears and doubts. Think of it as a trade, with expected and scheduled comfort on one side of the scale, and a tiny, concrete question mark on the other. When you begin to deal expressly with the 'question mark' portion, your personal scale extends in both directions. The lows become drudgingly painful, full of sighs and unspoken regrets, but the highs surpass even extreme excitement and forge new territory in the meaning of happiness. Any kid will tell you that bouncy balls are more fun to throw from the roof for the same reason.

But none of that was going through my mind at this point. I was standing in my mom's driveway, half debating sleeping through the morning sunlight, half looking embarrassed for even coming up with this idea. I must have hugged my mom at least ten times and I failed to rephrase "I'll be just fine" into something that would cull this display of fearful emotion. I remember, and always will, my mom taking a photo with a disposable camera, hiding a tearful face with a cheap, plastic box as I tried to smile and look confident.

I'm only good at one of those. That dull click hung heavy in the air, I straddled my bicycle, and I tried to stop regretting each inch that my pedaling put between my mother and I. To this day, this is one of my saddest memories. That photo never got developed.

Then, while still in the process of leaving our neighborhood, my water bottle holder broke off my bike. The audience avoids eye contact with the screen and everyone shifts uncomfortably in their seats.

I had to laugh. Really, what else can you do?

Day One: The Highlight Reel

I've read a couple of books on long-distance bike traveling and the vast majority is terribly uninteresting because they focus on, well, the bike trip. That is to say, they talk about the bike-riding aspect, the foliage lining the roads, the famous burger place they stopped at in 'Historic Town, USA,' and other vapid minutia. Sorry, but it's true.

I'll sum up the whole thing right now, in their terms, just to say that I did: I rode by some sunsets, got rained on, and saw some trees. See? My point is that I'll only discuss the interesting stuff: the moments when humanity and the plight of the human condition shine through…or funny stories about accidentally finding *more* porn in weird places. Those are basically the same thing.

This trip began from Cary, North Carolina, a suburban panic attack of mini-malls and pre-*pre*-fabricated housing. My intended route was to head as far north as Baltimore, Maryland, at which point I would turn west toward Portland. Simple, huh? It certainly looked that way on my crummy eBayed map. Heading northbound set me on a path through a hilly, uninteresting section of the wild, wrought with trees, forgotten gas stations, and state parks that everyone (the state included) has given up on. I confidently rode by the 'Cars: Three Dollars' sign and smiled at the attendant while easing into one such a park. I had already found some bagels at an early 'bagel shop dumpster' stop, and I walked my bike to a picnic table near the lakeshore to eat lunch.

The odometer read twenty-nine miles, and I sat stricken with the fear of someone approaching me with questions about my travels. At this point, I had no answers. It was fifty more miles to the Virginia border, which would mark this trip being (if nothing else), "Kind of impressive, because I crossed into a different state, which at least sounds cool, right?" Until that point, I was still some kid with a goofy idea and a heavy bike. Heck, I may as well have had my lunch in a Ziploc bag, swaying carelessly in a handkerchief tied to a stick that was thrown over my shoulder. Metaphorically speaking, I guess I did. I always liked that image, anyway.

My food rations increased exponentially in the next town, where I found a bunch of pears and bagged salads. In the trash. To clarify, anything I 'find' came from the dumpster. (Just a technical heads up.) This moment was the first polished ruby in what I was hoping would be a trail of fortune, nestled among the overgrowth of, um, well, unfortunate crap. Science posed the quandary: If I could sustain myself for two years in one town by eating only dumpstered food, then could I do it anywhere? I had found my answer.

I was also lucky enough to be present for the following announcement made over loudspeaker at the firehouse, as I was resting on a neighboring bench: "Request police assistance at the retirement home. They're having trouble with the trash cans." Cool! A group of elderly misfits who called their eco-terrorist gang 'the trash cans'? Could it be? In the ongoing 'green battle,' it looked like the old folks joined up with mother earth! Yeah! We'll plant trees in your sidewalk cracks! Hurl the acorns toward a green future! The revolution *will* be recycled! Exciting, huh? So much so…that I left.

The Polar Opposite Of 'Helpful'

Stovall. The town had a name…but I'm not so sure that the name had a town. Pizza places attached to burger places doubling at gas stations? It'd be like corporate conjoined twins trying desperately to live their own lives but only highlighting the seams. En route to getting there, I passed a house with a Border Collie; she was really pretty. And she chased me. Day one, remember? Thankfully, she only bit the living crap out of my saddlebag and then attempted to bite my moving wheel. My bid for the Nobel Prize this year goes to the genius behind 'the invisible fence'.

The sun was ready to drop as I came across a patch of grass about twenty feet from the road, and I collapsed there.

Sixty-seven miles down. A complete lack of stretching earlier became painfully obvious, as my 'just above the knees' muscles went totally ballistic and locked up. When something that you've come to control quite well (like your leg) gives up on your brain's commands, it's really scary. In the same way that most people can't imagine being unable to move an arm or a leg, I was having a lot of trouble dealing with unrelenting, seemingly muted leg muscles.

The dehydrated state that I was sauntering through didn't help me, either. I've surely failed to mention it, but late June in, well, anywhere, is really hot. Case in point, I'd sweated off all the water that I brought, as well as two 'fill-ups' of my Nalgene. I collapsed, a parched, stiff-legged zombie, with the express purpose to drink some water and try not to throw up. I *hate* throwing up. It comes with the territory of dehydration, though, which makes me hate dehydration, as well. I must have spent an hour continually sipping water, breathing slowly, and planning my stretching routine for the next morning, when a man in a huge truck pulled off road in front of me and rolled his window down.

Detective mode kicked on, and I noted it was an old-model truck, driven by an old-model guy, caked in dirt and with landscaping equipment in the back, screaming, "I've been working / burying a kid I killed." My eyes unperceivably narrowed and I tilted my head, ready to keep up—but not start—a conversation. What transpired instead was the conversation equivalent of talking to a shotgun while wearing a blindfold and being spun around in one of those chairs that spin.

"That your bike? You ride it here? Nice weather, huh? I'm in landscaping, you know, but my daughter…" and other such 'cut-and-paste' phrases. It began as confusing and remained, well, confusing. He had a nice streak about him, though, and ten minutes later I was the proud owner of an extra large pizza given to me as a gift from my landscaping friend. I don't eat sausage or pepperoni (or pizza, really), but when faced with the niceness of a truck driver, I had to be kind. Please recall my dehydration. I picked off the meat, ate half of one piece, looked at the rest, and told him I'd finish it later after stretching for a while. Whew. Situation diffused. Or, wait—detective scenario, sorry. Case closed!

...Until he came back, twenty minutes later, to offer a shower, some potato chips, and then, as a weird afterthought, some advice. "You know, we had a bear spotted in these woods not too long ago...but I don't think that'll be a problem". *Good*, because it's not like I have some huge uneaten, meat-topped pizza wafting beckoning smells in every direction, right? Problems galore, dude. Problems galore. Every car that passed, branch that cracked, and noun that verbed was, in my mind, a bear. That hated me. Bear or no bear, I slept a bit and woke up with a sleeping bag permanently reeking of cheap gas station pizza. Just like my life.

Day Two: The Turning Point! (Well, One Of Them)

My decision to pack up my tent, get back on my bike, bungee-cord a pizza box to my front rack, and leave Stovall for the Virginia border marked the second most difficult obstacle presented in this text. I was, at that moment, exactly one day away from where I started, meaning that if I biked it all over again back south, I'd be in a bed that night and wouldn't have any problems to look forward to (save boring financial ones, which I planned on just 'avoiding' for the bike trip portion). However, if I kept going north, I'd be continuing with my 'Plan A' and one step closer to making this adventure a reality. Upside: adventure. Downside: twice as far from bailing out. I don't think I can explain what gave me any hope in this situation—I felt awful, slept poorly, had a to pack a wet sleeping bag and a wet tent, and had completed exactly one six-hundredth of this adventure—but possibility filled the silence, so I kept my bike pointing north–ish and somehow started moving again.

Apart from some mental roadblocks that I bested, not a lot happened. Biking, in its own exciting way, is boring writing material. I did, however, fulfill a role based solely on my physical appearance. About mid-afternoon, I stopped off in some small town and found an abandoned storefront at the end of the 'downtown joke' this town had attached to the street, and sat there in the shade, eating some carrots, taking some photos, and eventually falling asleep. Totally sprawled out, not five feet from the sidewalk, with no covers or pillow or anything, only a body on the dusty concrete. How cool is that? Do you have any idea how hard it is to fall asleep in front of people, much less total strangers, outside, on the ground, at four in the afternoon? Some aspect of me was really impressed. So this is what having a master's degree is like, huh?

Post-sleep, I poked at a computer at the library then kept biking for another…bunch of miles. After an altercation involving my trying to throw away what was left of that crappy pizza at a laundromat (because the bank didn't have a dumpster) and getting yelled at for it, resulting in my leaving with all my trash—now leaking ranch dressing all over my shorts—because I thought it would be helpful to compact the box as best as possible to fit it in the trash can that I got yelled at for *trying* to use in the first place. I asked if there were any dumpsters close by and got "not for two miles" in response. Are you serious? That's incredible! You have to laugh at times like this. My clothes were ranch-stained with no hope of changing, and now I'm forced to carry the rest of that awful pizza with me for who knows how long…it was funny. Kind of. The pizza attracted a bunch of flies that swarmed around my bike for ten miles at one point. I pretended I was Pigpen from the *Peanuts* comic. It worked really well. Because I clearly was not pretending.

The town I arrived in for 'bedtime' (a.k.a. sundown) was composed of sketchy gas stations and, well, people who hang around sketchy gas stations. It was more of an interstate exit than a town, and I was presented with *Professional Vagrant Checklist Item Number Two: Sleep under an overpass*. I'd already slept in public, so I figured this would be even easier. Here's a fun list of things that are loosely (or tightly, in some cases) connected to that particular sleeping situation, and try to surmise which ones are good or bad: Stagnant air beneath the overpass that never moves and remains ninety-seven degrees, the thirty billion cars that keep passing *on* the underpass (which, as it turns out, was an interstate), the spider that crawled across my head ten minutes into trying to sleep, the four inches of dust that was 'my floor', or, well, anything else you think might happen under a bridge in a nameless Virginia town in mid-summer. The point is, twenty defeated minutes later, I then wandered into a huge field and enjoyed my view of the moon (much more than the 'I wonder if *that* guy saw me' game I had been playing earlier with the passing cars on I-85). I had cell phone service for the first time in my trip, but I chose instead to stare at the stars, looking for an obvious 'thumbs up', or 'yep, you're doing the right thing, Matt' constellation. If you stand on your head and squint, then you can see both, but it took me about twenty-three years to figure that out.

Boring Technical Answer To A Boring Technical Question

A lot of people ask me which roads I used during this bike trip, and I figure that I can answer *en masse* here. Well, everyone, I didn't touch any interstate roads, except for that accidental two-mile stretch we'll get to later in Maryland. It was all smaller highways, mostly ones I found on my eBayed road map and 'had a good feeling about'. Nothing special here, really. It's that MacGyver thing coming in. To make the best of a situation, you have to get yourself into a crappy one to begin with. Hence, the eBay map.

Man's Greatest Invention

I woke up again to the sun baking my once-chilly tent to an alarming forty-thousand degrees. It's the equivalent of having an alarm clock / space heater that lights your pillow on fire when it goes off. Also, you're wearing a sweatshirt and your sheets are made of flannel and in this case are actually a sleeping bag. The metaphor may not translate from the world of distance biking. Oh, well. Try it at home, I guess. Science project!

Guess what I found thirty miles from Richmond? Here's

a hint: It's freaking awesome, it's the greatest invention of all time, AND, uh, it's a pool! Sneaking into pools is always fun, but the urgency of it being a really hot day mixed with a total lack of responsibilities (as well as being in a town that I'll never visit again) makes it *way* more fun. I didn't even try to blend in, which meant 'boxers-only' cannonballs with my camera on timer mode. Upon getting the photos much later, I *almost* nailed it. Almost.

The ride into Richmond was a really disgusting, unavoidable mess. All the roads are huge six-lane expanses of space where I was confident that no one had ever biked before. I wound up going half-speed through this mess, riding along the sidewalks past an infinite number of strip malls, fast food places, and gas stations. I was passing through the quintessential America stereotype. I did, however, get some dumpstered pizza out of this deal, so I can't complain. It's that same American ideology that allots such living: For as much as I hate to see a Pizza Hut on every corner, I will reap the benefits while they're around. If we hit a point in which the U.S. isn't throwing away enough food to live on, I have a feeling things will have changed so drastically that I won't mind buying food. Call me pessimistic (weird!) but I don't think that'll ever happen.

I have been through Richmond at least four times in my life and had recalled the city as being fairly small, with all the 'cool kids' living in the same area next to the college and organic grocery store. I was totally wrong about that, and after a failed library excursion that was coupled with my scouring phone books for the name of that grocery store (Ellwood Thompson's, for those who know), I got awful directions and somehow wound up in the parking lot. Ellwood is great because in the back they leave out produce for the Food Not Bombs group, so you don't even have to hunt for it. There were apples waiting for me! I had also marked out a spot to hop the fence and sleep in the grass near some trees, and the sun was just now setting! Inarguably, this was the most exciting moment of the trip yet. I recognized where I was, I had food to eat, *and* I was set for sleeping! How could this get any better?

How about running into the only guy I know in Virginia inside Ellwoods, getting invited to have dinner with him, sleep on his couch, *and* go see Melt Banana play with Ultra Dolphins that night? I made friends with Richmond kids all night, slept wonderfully, and was presented with vegan pancakes in the morning. Words failed me. So I hugged a lot. Let this be a quick lesson to anyone who cares to learn: Pancakes / dinner / small gestures like that may not seem like much, but these things can make someone else's *year*. I'm serious. Try to help out whenever you can. Good Clean Fun said it best: "If you've got two kidneys, then you have one to spare, cuz' the people who win are the people who share." So share.

Incredible Moments in Vagrancy

I always wanted to name a little segment 'Incredible Moments in Vagrancy,' in the style of an NPR show, featuring things that you never thought you'd do but circumstantial dilemmas justified your idiotic actions. Hint: There's one of those coming up.

I left Richmond after buying a vegan popsicle and talking to my mom on the phone. I also had to part with my bananas, which had inexplicably 'separated' into equal parts liquid and solids, and my pear, which was well beyond disgusting. Oh, and a lot of people, namely cashiers or strangers I spoke with in and around Richmond, told me they 'wish' they could do what I'm doing—biking really far, that is. Why wish for that? I can guarantee from personal experience that I'm nothing special in the biking world. My only 'talent' is a drive to do this, and some free time. Everyone has that! My point is: Don't 'wish' that you could do things. Just do them. Really.

Back to my 'Incredible Moments' story. I came across another Food Lion dumpster (perfect timing) and wound up with a bunch of fruit and vegetables, as well as a small plastic container of unopened fondue chocolate (!!!) with strawberries. Insane! Dessert, on a trip like this? The grand prize, though, was the cake. I unearthed a pre-made, two-foot by one-foot 'party platter' cake with a *Dora the Explorer* icing scheme, and I stared at it for awhile. I had a fork, yes, but I also didn't feel like finding it. I felt like blazing new territory in the world of vagrancy. I set it on the ground, popped off the plastic lid, got on my knees with my hands behind my back, and went at it, eating-contest style. It was really, really funny. I ate a little, but mostly got icing in my beard. I would sooner end this bike trip with funny memories than anything else (hence this incredible moment in vagrancy).

As the sun set, I found a little town designed around another interstate exit, but this one toted a *ton* of strip mall stores, including an unfinished Applebee's that had roof access (and no chance of workers, as it was a Saturday night). Sunday morning would be a breeze—heck, I could sleep in! But I didn't, as there was a hotel chain across the street, so, before I went to bed, I set my watch for 6 a.m. Because that's when the nice lady at the desk told me continental breakfast started. $ Cha-ching! $ If my pupils could turn into dollar signs, then they would have right there.

The next thing you know, the sun rises, I leave my rooftop paradise, bike across the street, walk in the hotel like I own it (that's the key, to anyone who wants to try), go to the bathroom, wash the parts of me that people can see (face, hands, etc.), and stride confidently back to the breakfast area. The next three hours involve me sneaking muffins into my bag while eating a ton, charging my phone, and moving my operation poolside, simply because I can. It was awesome. No one suspected a thing. Well, okay, in my mind *everyone* suspected *everything*, but nobody did anything about it.

For bonus points, I even hopped over the pool fence when I left to avoid going back through the lobby. The punkest distance between two points is a straight line, right? Ha! That's funny. Read that again.

INCREDIBLE MOMENTS IN VAGRANCY!

Pool Hopping

It was another day of biking, with side stories including my wandering around William and Mary College and finding nothing useful because the whole thing is closed for summer (What? I tried to go to school on my vacation?), and then leaving to walk around historic downtown Fredricksburg. Nothing happened. I saw some used books. I tried to draw a tree, but my grip on my pen wasn't as strong due to holding my handlebars so often. That was weird. Disconcerting. But again, I came for adventure, not for drawing. I can draw anywhere.

I came across an abandoned Dunkin' Donuts about seventy miles later (I told you, it was a slow day for stories) and I sat on the curb, eating something dinner-like. (Bread and fruit, basically. Not to be confused with breadfruit.) There was roof access, but the location, in general, was weird. It was like a mall eruption with sidewalks everywhere, mini-malls all over the place, and, well, a ton of traffic, both pedestrian and car, to deal with. It didn't feel right. Furthermore, some cops arrived to make sure that I wasn't causing trouble, doing so by parking ten feet from me and staring the whole time. Cool, it's like I'm on TV! With consequences for my actions! Goodbye, Dunkin' Donuts. And cops. See how I didn't make a joke about the police and a donut place? Creative restraint! Well, not anymore, though.

These roads are the absolute opposite of bike lanes. Northern Virginia is *not* bike-friendly—well, at least not between towns. There was lots of sidewalk riding and getting honked at. This was the first time all trip that the biking riding part was my main concern. I came to an insane cluster of hotels, interstate bypasses, and highway construction. There were *no* wooded areas around or anywhere that looked like a good place to sleep at all, except the hotel, obviously. (Kidding. That wouldn't happen.) Flash forward to my walking the bike *down* the up-ramp of the exit, and then getting underneath all the construction stuff, and finding a patch of desert-like dirt in the center of an exit ramp. Does that make sense at all? It didn't to me, either. And I lived through it.

For the first time during this trip, I left my bike, took my journal and phone, and walked back to the hotel…to hang out at the pool! I'm telling you: Pools are where it's at. Especially when you're not welcome there. I received my continental breakfast timetables, wrote a bunch, and walked back to my desert paradise. This particular night was like sleeping on rocks…rocks that really, really hate you. I squirmed a lot and eventually justified packing my tent up at 5 a.m. I had breakfast in an hour! And Washington, D.C. was only seven more miles! Fret not, for things are going well! Despite back pain and a light-brown-dirt coating on everything I touch.

I locked up my bike, grabbed my toothbrush, and put on my 'yes, I did stay here last night' face. As luck would have it, the breakfast room was not only gigantic but also insanely crowded, meaning that as long as I didn't stand out too badly, this would be really easy. However, I smelled awful and was covered in dirt, two things that most patrons of sixteen-story hotels are, um, not. So I evaded all hotel personnel, grabbed a washcloth from an orphaned housekeeping cart, and slipped into the bathroom. This scene played out exactly like a spy movie, in which instead of killing somebody or stealing a diamond, our protagonist just wants to clean the visible parts of his body in a hotel sink, and then take food intended for paying customers while covertly charging his cell phone. It worked great, probably because I was squinting my eyes in the proper spy manner.

With this new spy motif in full swing, I started pushing

my luck, asking for special breakfast items, demanding envelopes and paper to write letters, hanging out by the pool, and even requesting access to the exercise room because I 'left my card upstairs'. How solid of an alibi is *that*? While moonwalking on the treadmill, staring at the clock reading 8:03 a.m., I couldn't help but feel that I was doing something right.

Burning Bridges That I Just Slept Under

I left that hotel with a ton of bagels, two new pens, and about seven miles to go before I hit downtown Washington D.C. The bike ride was easy and, consequently, boring. So, I'll skip ahead. I made it to the heart of Washington, a city divided into four quadrants, with a billion free museums all over the place. My day consisted of art museum hopping and then biking clear across the historic district to go hang out with the gigantic Abe Lincoln. He was cool. I took the obligatory tourist photos then sat down in the park to picnic with a squirrel that ate some dumpstered starfruit right out of my hand. After that, I visited the library, in the hope of the nation's capital playing host to the grandest of public libraries. Surely an enormous edifice sat waiting for me to use one of its thousands of computers and peruse its billions of books...

...But after five people couldn't tell me where this

theoretical library was, I started to lose hope. However, after *minutes* of wandering around, I accidentally happened upon it: a huge, menacing building, brimming with centuries of knowledge and...four computers? Sitting on top of old filing cabinets? And only fifteen minutes of Internet time? Now come on, that's funny. Our nation's capital has only four computers capable of going online, and there aren't even chairs? I laughed out loud then left.

A very good friend of mine lives in D.C., but she told me she wouldn't be back in town until the next day, so I was on my own for the night. I figured that the worst case was biking back the seven miles to the overpass cluster and sleeping there again, seeing as how downtown layouts generally don't afford many hiding places for a kid and his bike. However, somewhere between the big statues and the library visiting, the nightfall caught me off guard. Dang. I guess I lost that mindful spy persona over the course of the day. Anyway, I started instinctively heading back south, certain that I would 'wing it' when I saw an opportunity. Opportunity found me, however, and I was struck by a huge raindrop right in the center of my head, backed by an eerily gray sky. Dang.

Now, the problem with cities or towns (especially big ones) is that, even on the outskirts, there aren't many trees or anywhere it would be acceptable to envision a tent. When you think about it, there aren't many inviting places to sleep in any given city...well, assuming you're not looking for a bed or a standard roof, or anything like that. I found myself biking against traffic, across a bridge, in light rain that looked to be getting much, much worse. These are the times of trial, these gritty, desperate moments when I find what I consider 'adventure'—the moment in which you always wondered how you might act, the moment when you put faith in chance or god or something and immediately consider how funny it will be to look back on this and laugh, the moment where you pass the concrete support column of the bridge you're biking across and decide it to be a perfectly acceptable place to sleep...So, that means (by my definition) that adventure implies total surrender to idiocy.

I proved that theory when I found myself hoisting my bike over the guardrail and onto an 8-foot-by-8-foot square of concrete that served as a bridge support. The ground was level, but I couldn't pitch my tent because I was literally six inches from the freeway, with only a two-foot high wall between me and D.C. traffic. Which, by the way, there was a *ton* of. I laid my bike down, curled into the tent like a waterproof burrito, and faded in and out of sleep as the rain passed over. I had been trying my hardest not to be seen, trading that for any amount of comfort, and I was doing a decent job, I thought. The rain eventually passed and I was able to sleep without the tent, uncovered, staring at the moon. Just to reiterate, this was the *worst* possible sleeping idea in the world. It was more like hiding than sleeping. I was tucked behind an extremely small concrete wall, already imagining how funny this would be a couple days later. I was sure it would be a lot funnier the moment I wasn't there anymore, that's how 'funny' it was.

I stopped worrying about the cars seeing me and shifted that fear to the forty or so spiderwebs lining the walls and railings next to where I was laying. Though I should have been afraid, I felt some strange affinity for the spiders, as we were sharing the same home for the night. I left them alone and they left me alone. What can I say? Community works.

Gaining an army of gross bugs as allies was pretty awesome, but it wasn't until I managed to pee off the edge while still lying down that I became fully confident in my spy persona not only being back, but also well deserved.

However, as I awoke the next morning, and peered through the gap in the guardrails, I was greeted with bumper-to-bumper traffic. I had no choice but to pack up and lift my bike back over the railing and onto the bridge, where at least thirty cars' worth of an audience was now *all* staring at me, their faces frozen in utter confusion, trying to figure out just where in the world this dirty kid had crawled up from, and, more importantly, why his pants were covered in pee. Yep, today was going to be great.

Day Four: Something Else Happens

That was a really rough morning. I laugh about it, but it was not anything I would ever recommend to anyone. Except anyone who has yelled at me while I've been riding my bike. There's a special corner in hell for them. And trying to sleep there *sucks*.

My day was spent tracking down my friend Allison (someone I am absolutely sure will help save humanity and the world) and playing catch-up with her. I also absorbed some local oddities, such as businessmen riding things like Segways *and* Razor scooters to get to work (what?), a bunch of tourists wearing fanny packs (truly, the 'tribal piercing' of our culture), and the huge economic gap between these Segway-ing businessmen and the hordes of poor people. After thinking it over, cell phone in hand, eating a bagel from the trash, I figured that you can't build bridges out of money…but you can probably make a dam. Looks like no one wins. Sorry, D.C.

The rest of my day was spent making new friends and eventually sleeping on their floor. Notice how I didn't do any biking? I only totaled like five miles today! Awesome! Life pulled a 'sitcom moment' when I went to throw something away at the house where I was staying and saw a whole box of cereal in the garbage, so I took it out, saw that it was three-quarters full, and put it in my saddlebag. Free granola cereal! Come on! It may as well have been a bag with a dollar sign on it! Anyway, the real humor emerged five hours later as I learned that Kirsten had to throw her cereal away because "like, a million" ants had gotten into it. Ha! I think to the average viewer, it just appeared that I was extremely shocked that her food got invaded…but my mind was somewhere else at that moment. Double dang. I'm sure the audience loved that one. I bet people even quote it.

Sick Day! No School!

I went to a bike shop and met a very, um, vibrant guy who told me that Eugene, Oregon was "f—ing beautiful, man" at least four billion times. He also spit every time his mouth moved. He was just really animated. Nice guy. Oh, I also bought some replacement spokes for my back tire. These will become important in California when I break a spoke and then can't replace it because I don't have an extremely specific axle wrench. But that's not anytime soon. I'm not even to Baltimore.

Day Six: I'm In Baltimore

That was fast. My time can be summated in the following, cryptic list: duck pin bowling, free ice cream, an actual place to stay with friends, shower number one, Reptilian Records, passing *lots* of signs for straight-edge movies ('XXX'…get it? No? Yeah, it's a stretch), and, uh, that's pretty much it. Despite being basically homeless for an indefinite amount of time, I still bought three used records and promptly sent them to my mom's house. Somehow, this 'crosses the line', or whatever that film term is ('fourth wall'?) when the illusion becomes questionable. I was certainly confused. When the heck was I going to see them again, anyway? You could make the economic/social argument that 'old habits die hard', in that 'shopping is so forced into our brains, that blah blah haven't you seen *Dawn of the Dead*…', but I beg to differ. Why don't *you* try finding a Madonna record for 99 cents and not buy it?

Two vacation days later, I tried to leave this town and managed to get lost in the more 'project-y' part of town. My list of 'cons' are that I was a confused white kid, biking in circles, who looked exactly like a confused white kid in the Baltimore outskirts. However, on the 'pros' list, it was Father's Day and about 10 a.m. on a Sunday. In short, I was saved by church (double meaning! wicked!) and the fact that anyone who might mess with me was probably occupied by sleep or fatherhood. It was a good choice for a day to leave Baltimore. The secondary bonus to this day was free ice cream I got when I stopped at a cafe, after the following conversation:

Guy: "You bike here?"
Me: "Yep."
Guy: "From where?"
Me: "North Carolina."
Guy: "WHAT?"

And then I got free reign of anything in the store, which was really, really nice of him. I won't forget this, nice 'my age' kid. I'll probably just forget your name, and face…but not your niceness. That has to count for something, right?

Amish Reference Number One

The next day (one of the infamous 'West Virginia' days), was hilarious because I was offered a place to stay in a trailer I could occupy by myself (!) on 300 acres of land (!!) that some really old guy who was talking to me owned (!!!). Crazy, huh? He showed me photos of a barn raising he took part in with some Amish folks across the Pennsylvania border (which was four miles away) and described a long, work-filled couple of days, which culminated in a huge lightning storm that burned the whole thing to the ground. Pretty sad story, really. Conversationally, I couldn't think of anything to cap off that downer ending, save "…dang." I'm quite the wordsmith, huh?

Anyway, after I politely declined his housing offer (it

was about 9 a.m., and what would I do all day?), I made an incorrect turn (surprise) and wound up on the entry ramp to the freeway. Now, normally I don't bike on freeways. This is, in fact, a terrible idea. However, it was only three miles to the exit that I needed to get to, and the entry ramp was all downhill, and really, I loathe backtracking from the deepest chambers of...somewhere...so, any justification to keep going forward is okay by me.

However, the next thing I know, I get pulled over by a huge SUV cop car, who immediately starts writing me a ticket. Hilarious. All is not lost, however, for he insists, after writing the ticket (while *not once* thinking about just offering a warning, which I kept telling him was a 'really, really good idea'), to drive me to the exit I was headed to. He doesn't, however, offer to help lift my extremely heavy bike into his back seat, but instead delights quietly in watching me struggle to lift and shove my bike/life into his dumb SUV. He offered advice like, "Push it...yeah, well, no, harder," which is *not* helpful, nor is it constructive. What it is, for the record, is stupid. A lot like him (ooh! burn!) However, what's a *Next Stop Adventure* story without a plus side, right? Exactly! In pushing my bike in, my chain rolled off the front sprocket (the huge gear that the pedals attach to) and then, as I pushed even harder, the aforementioned sprocket tore across the leather comprising his back seat. It left a hilarious streak of grease and holes on his leather interior. Somehow, he didn't pick up on this part, and I didn't think to tell him. For some reason. Huh. Let's hear it for small victories! Good to know karma is down to get revenge sometimes. For the record, I don't recall paying that ticket. I would have needed money for that, and, well, yeah, you guessed it.

While we're talking karma, this was the day that I got a free doughnut from the Dunkin' Donuts lady who said she didn't have day-olds, but I could just have a 'today un-old' one, and then twenty minutes later I found a whole cheese pizza, which I put my free box of Wheaties on and ate it in a bush. Wow, that sounds ridiculous. What's worse is that my journal entry reads (in extremely excited scribbling): "Today I invented wheat-zza!"

I Want My Forty Dollars

There was another classic moment when I was headed up a long hill with no end in sight, being passed by everything on the road and getting pretty bummed out because of it. There's something demeaning about giving all your energy day in and day out doing one thing only to have people do it for three dollars a gallon and fly right by you. I'm not saying I'd trade it, or anything like that, I'm just stating that having everyone on the road zip by you so effortlessly gets a little old, and makes you feel even slower than you're already going. The last motorcycle that passed me made me think, out loud, 'Why in the world am I not on one of those? What's the point of seeing America this slowly?' which was followed, within *feet* of where I thought that, by finding a twenty dollar bill on the ground.

Furthermore, after a couple more hours, I stopped at a scenic overlook and wound up talking to a nice guy about traveling, family, and so on, and then parting ways with him. I thought that'd be it, but then about two hours later, when I was preparing for a 'now entering the town of…' photo, he pulled over and gave me a twenty dollar advance on the book! Like, the one you're reading *right now*! I'm not sure how much each story I've written is worth, but it had better add up to twenty dollars or else I'm a con artist. Wait, that sounds awesome: Let's do that instead. Forty dollars in one day without doing any work at all but, rather, being my slow-biking, lovable self. It's nice to know that pays off both figuratively and literally. Though I don't like money very much (for long, complicated reasons), I do like genuine gifts. So, California guy who sleeps in his awesome van/car and travels around all the time: thank you. Very much.

Then, I kept going, deeper into West Virginia, shuddering at the homely quality sputtering out of every crappy car that crept by me, or every crap-covered shirtless dude staring me down from the crappiest lawn I have ever crappily looked at. That happened a lot. I am not even joking that I passed a log cabin library, which was a squalid gathering of brush and driftwood held together with rubber bands and shoelaces, and it had no electricity. *None.* They did have books, though. In the same way that thrift store trash bins have books. They're available, sure, but even though they're free, nobody wants to read these. Just because it *can* be bound and published, doesn't mean it *should*.*

The Math No Longer Carries Weight...

This is where I finally reach the point in which my mind had fully acquiesced to biking mode with very little thought given to what I was physically doing. Some things happened. I stopped at some places. I ate some stuff. But mostly, I thought a lot. At one point after a one-sided battle with the

*uh oh

Appalachian Mountain range, I started to develop an intense knee pain, which was the direct result of my stubborn nature, a side known only to emerge when I'm pitted against, well, myself. It's a 'body versus brain' conflict. I want to be on top of this mountain immediately; ergo, there will be no stopping for water or changing gears. My body doesn't so much as put up an argument, but rather stubbornly teaches by example, and afterwards it fails to function when the adrenaline wears off. On the plus side, I did get to watch the sun set from nearly a mile above sea level. It's a slim 'plus side', though.

After a while, the next day allotted me a place to stay right next to a church. This was the first night that it rained all night, yet I remember it more because my knee locked up quite firmly. My reaction was that of a quiet, option-less panic. My odometer read about 860 miles with the glass half-full (and 2140 miles when half-empty), my food supply was decent for the night (but not good for more than two days), my left hand was constantly slipping into numbness from pressure on the handlebars, and my tent smelled like (this is a quote) "super feet". I'm willing to bet that when bank robbers plan the night before about how much fun the robbery will be, it comes as a real shock when something goes wrong. You set your eyes on the path you want to see, and the second that you lose stride and wind up somewhere you hadn't planned, well, that's what being totally alone is like. Happiness itself can be a very good friend, but sadness defines itself as the distance between the both of you. At this moment, the horizon was farther away than I'd ever noticed. I blamed the altitude.

Ten Lousy Minutes

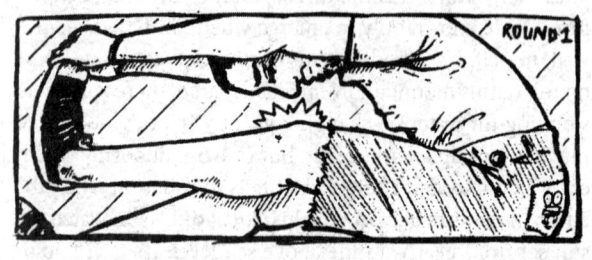

That's how long I biked during the next day. Exciting, huh? I made it as far as a little 'out-for-summer' middle school, wandered to the back, found a plug, charged my cell phone, and (in incredible fits of pain centering around my right knee) tried to enjoy the most boring scenery that's ever surrounded me. What's worse is that I couldn't *do anything* about it (save keep hurting my knee). Sitting idly and unable to improve my situation from 8:23 a.m. until I fell asleep was a monumentally boring experience.

Though the 'half-full' view would be that I was given time to relax and enjoy my thoughts and life in general, the reality was that I wrote for an hour, stared at my knee in disappointment, and eventually recited about eighty percent of *Mallrats*, a movie I've seen like three times, yet was oddly memorable on this particular day. I dreamt of kids enjoying their days of summer as they flew by (much how I once did and was *not* now), in hope that my slow day would follow suit. I even started debating if I should slit my kneecap open to let it drain out some but decided against it, hoping I was building 'positive fluid', or perhaps I didn't want to cut my knee with the same knife that had been spreading peanut butter and cutting black bananas in half. I managed to read a used copy of Camus's *The Stranger* that I brought with me, only to remember about seven pages into it that I'd read this a couple months ago. It's a great book, but a time lapse would've been nice.

What happened next was a bunch of internalized thunder-storming and boat-rocking. My knee was incapable of bending without a great deal of pain shooting through it, I was still extremely far away from everything, and, at 904 miles down, I had no plan whatsoever. However, I rely on happenstance frequently enough that I know that *something* will work itself out, and sure enough, after some phone card usage, and a little map-debating, my brother Zack agreed to drive and get me and take me to Iowa City with him to help move into a new apartment. What followed was a lot of not bending my knee, but rather, hanging out with my brother, dumpstering all the furniture we could find, and then just enjoying the small town that is Iowa City. This went on for a while. Long enough for an intermission...

Something TOTALLY Different

I'll get back to the whole 'bike trip' thing in a moment, but I have another story worth telling. Besides, the concept of *Next Stop Adventure* is an adventure-esque text that generally happens to relate to biking. Keeping with the theme, this next tale involves me riding my bike, doing something illegal, and centers around the concept of adventure. I think I've learned that adventure is when you stop thinking in 'normal mode' and switch to 'I wonder...' or 'what if?' Largely, this type of living and planning is just plain ridiculous. But it *is* fun. And I love fun.

I also love Rainer Maria. Hands down, they were and are the best band of all time. Reversal of Man, Good Clean Fun, Pg. 99, Bad Brains... they all take a back seat to Rainer Maria. Yeah, I know—some list to compete with, huh? This is the only band that I have gone out of my way to collect all their recorded material, including the split 7", the *Old Direction* LP comp, as well as the 1995 record *and* cd. That's just sad. The songs are identical; it's strictly a format difference. Anyway, it takes an unbridled love such as this to kick one's mind into 'all or nothing' mode. Oh, and it certainly helps if you don't want to pay sixty-five dollars to see them play a twenty-minute set at Lollapalooza...

The news was in place. Rainer Maria was playing Lollapalooza in Chicago (where I had recently relocated and was happily living) and it was incredibly expensive. There are two things I hate in that last sentence: One of them is Lollapalooza, and the other one, well, I'll let you gue$$. It was staked out for noon on Saturday at the small stage near Lakeshore Drive. I studied the map on the Lollapalooza website and thought it to be close enough to the barrier that I could probably listen from the sidewalk, then throw a zine at them as they were leaving and yell, "I met you in Austin, at South By Southwest..." Seemed like a decent plan. Heck, maybe I could pull the old, "I'll help you carry that amp in, if you want," routine, right? I mean, I've seen *Catch Me If You Can* twenty times and it can't be *that* hard. So, I set my watch's alarm, fell asleep on my floor, and dreamed of Caithlin asking me on stage to help with backup vocals. Preferably on "Atlantic"...

The next thing you know, I'm looking at my bike, my phone, and my total lack of a real plan (save a map drawn on the back of a receipt) and it occurs to me that maybe I should grab one more thing. The whole night before, I had also been pouring over my old issues of *HeartattaCk*, specifically those in which Mack Evasion had written columns, one of which is expressly about gate-crashing. I didn't learn anything new but left with a good feeling: that maybe it *is* possible. There's one way to find out, huh? Oh, and that last thing I grabbed was my old tour pass from the Circle Takes the Square tour I had last roadied on. It's a small, shiny, laminated card with dates on the back and a key ring hole at the top. It probably measures about four by five inches. Small. But it's extremely powerful, as it turns out…

…Because the next thing you know, I've biked downtown, locked up across the street, did a 'talking on the phone while wandering around the back fence' routine for a second, and then decided I'd give it a shot. My first plan had actually been to jump the fence somewhere, but there really were a lot of guards and the fence would have shaken fifty feet in each direction. It would've been obvious that something was going on.

I needed to be obvious for a different reason. I was important. I was a roadie for a band playing Lollapalooza…and if you repeat the lie enough, then you will believe it. That's what I learned when I took my keys from my pocket and attached them with a carabineer (a touring essential) to the front of my shorts, which was completed with my 'real-yet-fake' tour badge that shone proudly at the front of this loud, jingling mass.

ME, LONG KNIVES DRAWN

At this point, I was supposed to be inside, so, naturally, I started walking there. There was one guard right in front of me. I acted like I'd been awake for too long, like it took an extra three hours to drive the van here, and like I had to hurry back to a merch table I shouldn't have left in the first place. So I didn't even break stride when I flashed my tour badge at him. He waved me in, and I just kept walking past him.

The *second* I got beyond that fence, I then had all the 'band cred' in the world. I walked out from the area I was in to the main courtyard, sat under a tree, and waited about twenty minutes for Rainer Maria to set up and go on stage. In this span of time, nothing happened. (Specifically, no one came up to me, looked funny at me, or, well, paid attention to me. It's almost like it worked, huh?) I noted not to finger-point too much while singing along since I didn't have a wristband, which was one of about four million differences between the surrounding crowd and me.

Twenty minutes later, after knowing all the words among a sea of people who may have all been either asleep or dead, I figured that I'd press my luck until it backfires. The worst that could happen was getting kicked out. And I didn't care to see Nada Surf or any of the other insanely huge bands playing, so I had nothing to lose! Besides, I had to at least say 'hi' to Caithlin again—mostly to give her a zine, but also because there was the off-chance that she'd been trying to call me over the past eight months since we last met so we could hold hands. (I mean, it *is* possible. Not probable, but who cares—I just saw Rainer Maria for free, right?)

As it turned out, there was a guard blocking the entrance to the backstage area, and I managed to hang out there long enough for Kyle, the guitarist, to come up and thank me for singing along. We talked for a moment, ending with my asking if I could say 'hi' to the rest of the band. "Well, yeah, but I think you need a pass to get back here", to which point I replied (loudly, so the guard could hear), "Oh, yeah, I got one", and showed Kyle.

"Oh, cool. Yeah, they're right back there..." I fooled Kyle, I fooled another guard, and as I crossed that 'audience/performer' barrier, Caithlin turned her head right toward me as if to say, "...*Finally*."

Or, realistically, just to say 'hello'. In the end, I gave away a zine, talked to the whole band, offered my services as a pro merch guy (with references to boot!), and exchanged emails and phone numbers. My 'touring with Rainer Maria' dream would ultimately never work out because they broke up; however, I am confident in saying that *had* they toured again after I saw them, I would've been on it. I'm serious. I have phone numbers and emails, people. Heck, the next time I saw them was in Milwaukee (after a bus ride and hanging out on a playground for nearly four hours) when Caithlin walks by, recognizes me, and invites me to dinner with her,

Kyle, and their merch guy (a 'just-out-of-high-school kid' that Kyle's family knew). They even paid for my dinner! Keep in mind that this is my favorite band of *all time*, they recognize me in a different state, dedicated a song to me, *and* bought me dinner at a 'sit-down' Thai restaurant. Yeah, exactly. When I get 'in' with a band, I get *in* with a band. (Writer's note: I am always happy to sell merch, so if you're in a band and need to get rid of ten shirts to an audience of five, then get in touch! Seriously!)

I left Lollapalooza that day sitting on top of the world (well, biking, actually), thanking myself for never eBaying that old tour badge. I probably would've made only six dollars off of it. It's funny how useful things like that can turn out to be, huh? One of the last things I heard as I was leaving was: "Excuse me, can I see that badge again?" Huh. Time to switch 'confidence mode' back on.

"Sure. I'm just taking a little walk. I'm with Circle…" (As I motioned toward the big stage, knowing full well they weren't playing Lollapalooza.)

"Oh. I'm sorry".

Sorry? A guard apologizing? I knew there was some way this could get better, and that was it.

A Postscript Note to Rainer Maria

If I haven't said it enough or ended this movie with the proper 'outro' speech, I'll do it again here. Your band, the creative force that it is and was, stands as the most inspirational, groundbreaking music that I have ever heard. A flurry of compliments will surely fall into a well-worn path of positive reviews over your eleven-year career, so I will state it simply:

Caithlin, Kyle, and Will: Thank you. I *love* Rainer Maria.

Bike Trip: Not Over! STILL!

With this intermission over, I hung out with my brother in Iowa City for about a month or so, a month in which we furnished his apartment with trash, did a bunch of flips on the high jump mats at the track and field center, and found a constant source of free food called 'the Aldi dumpster'. That's pretty sketchy if you've been to an Aldi, but I just can't say no to free corn on the cob and apples every day. Who can? The other best part involved the terrifying amount of Papa John's pizza places, which all seemed to prepare way too much food *every day* only to throw half of them away in the boxes!

Back on the bike trip, I left from my grandmother's house in Bondurant, Iowa after writing a couple letters on my mom's old typewriter (a Smith Corona 110 electric!) and having my grandmother pack me two peanut butter and jelly sandwiches and a Ziploc bag full of chocolate chip cookies. What was once a boy striving toward manhood on an epic bike journey had somehow rewound to an eight-year-old telling his parents that he was going to run away. How Norman Rockwell, huh? I hugged my grandmother, yelled "Yukon, ho!" and left. That's a Calvin and Hobbes joke, not some offensive slang, by the way.

Nothing happened in Iowa. I biked for three days, dumpstered very little, drank *awful* water, and got rained on at three separate times. I also didn't have any knee problems (yeah!) and slept in a playground (in the town where John Wayne was born), a school, and then a weird field...in Omaha! Other high points involve a house with Christmas lights still up in August, an impromptu fireworks show at the school where I was sleeping, and getting really excited going up a huge hill because I heard Rainer Maria being blasted from far away, leading me to do a ton of searching, only to realize that the music was coming from the iPod (that I'd failed to 'lock') in my bike bag. Dang. I went from having a place to stay with a Rainer Maria fan to having nowhere to go and only myself to talk to. It's a rough transition. I don't suggest it.

Omaha was surprisingly awesome. I found the spot where I think all the train-hopping types hang out, a small grouping of trees which would look like an oasis, except that you can see hotels in the background, so it's, well, a small grouping of trees in a field. I slept there, quite comfortably, for three nights.

Omaha provided a bunch of decent record stores, some funny conversations with funny people, and a ton of boring downtown 'things to see'. The *Tower Of Light*? Surely that's some wicked castle thing that houses a superhero, or Lincoln's brain, or something, right? But no, it's a bunch of metal welded together into some shape that's supposed to inspire people. You can't even climb it! I mean, *I* did, but you're not supposed to. Omaha lost a bunch of points that day. It gained them back when I found a book on Einstein's theories for 25¢ and a girl at the record store said that I looked like a "hot Amish fisherman". Huh. You know what that means, right? Exactly: I wound up reading my book on the river that night. Close call.

Awkward Backtracking

I should probably take a moment to describe how decision-making works when you're on such an intense trip, because it's a far cry from the way in which 'normal' thought processes function. You see, when you're in a situation that is...well, 'taxing', we'll say, it becomes easy to think about ways to get out of that situation. I say 'taxing' in place of 'stressful' because, in a lot of ways, this bike trip was a vacation: I didn't once think about my epic student loans, my lack of healthcare, or any one of those daily annoyances that I am reminded of when living my 'normal' life.

However, elements of this trip were not actually great. Knee pain coupled with a lack of food variety and a huge distance to cover will get the gears turning pretty quickly. (Not bike gears, but rather, the brain kind.) Thoughts like, *Why did I ever start doing this?* will surface, and it's awfully difficult to devise a mental list with enough 'pros' that this lonely, slow crawl of a bike trip remains the 'best idea I've ever had'. Perhaps my insane positivity has filtered out the reality that all situations are unbiased, and the experience is wholly decided by your mental state at the time. For instance, if you took a camping trip after you won the lottery, it would be incredible, as you would know in the back of your mind that despite all the rain, the gross food, and the warm brown water you had to drink, that you had still won the lottery. A positive mindset raises the overall morale of the experience, right? The other direction is more telling. Let's say you visit a water park right after a funeral. Things would be awful. All the slides would be overrun with quiet contemplation and all the wave pools flooded with distraction and memory. All the yellows turn blue, the loudness slips quiet, and you snap out of it days later. What could've been a great memory now came with heavy baggage attached. That was my current problem: knowing it'd be fun to reflect and remember the high points, but too weighed down by low points to care.

So, what does that mean? It means that I started this trip because I wanted to visit my friend Nate in Portland, and I also wanted to experience something different and adventurous. Was I going back on my thesis by even rethinking my current situation? Was I giving up on adventure because I was in physical pain? Was this, god forbid, *learning*? Or was this just obvious to me, and me alone, having been the only person there... Clearly, you had to be there, because sometimes that next good idea is getting a ride back to Iowa City from my brother, who went to Omaha to see The Faint play. So, dear reader, do you know where that puts me? Back in Iowa! Yeah! It's easy to be positive when you don't have to ride your bike eighty miles every day and all you do is hang out downtown, go to the library to rent free movies, draw stuff, eat free food from the dumpsters, dig through school trash, explore steam tunnels, kick soccer balls with your brother, sleep on the couch, dance all over the place, school everyone at *Pictionary*, and then accidentally buy a ticket to San Francisco on a Greyhound! Yeah! Alrigh—wait, wait...what?

Broken Things Make The Best Building Supplies

That's a quote. I can't take credit for it (since that would be Defiance, Ohio's work). But it does an excellent job of describing the 'sandlot-sized pickle' that I'd thrown myself into. It was forty-four hours on a Greyhound with my bike in a box from the trash and I was headed to San Francisco to see my friend Andy for the last week that he'd be living there. The plan after that was to bike straight up the West Coast on the famous Highway 1 all the way to Portland. That meant about one thousand (more) miles of biking, which, when you're thirty hours into a Greyhound trip, sounds freaking incredible.

The plan to bike all the way across the U.S. had been strewn onto the floor, but I thought I could still salvage most of it. I was still traveling all over the U.S., just, you know, differently. I pulled out my figurative sewing needle and patched together a new plan from the leftovers. And the next thing I knew, I was walking off the bus, boxed-up bike scraping the ground, in Sacramento, and I was raring to go all over again. I put my bike back together in an alleyway, watched a punk kid get stoned ten feet away from me, and then started toward SF.

First time in California! First time west of Omaha, for that matter! Things were back on track! I was on my bike trip again! My knee only 'kind of' hurt!

San Francisco Math List!

I could probably write a novel about my five days with Andy in SF, but (in an attempt to keep this under a billion pages)

I'll keep it to a math list. Math lists are lists that involve numbers, and occasionally addition or subtraction. I made that up a long time ago and I still love it.

- 4 'borrowed' pears from orchards lining the highway between Sacramento and SF
- 7 avocados, acquired in the same method
- 4 failed ATM withdrawals leading to realize I had …
- 1 suspended bank account, from my card traveling so sporadically (ha!)
- 1 HUGE high-five from Andy (the 'arrival five')
- 2 visits to Survival Research Labs (look this up if you don't know what it is)
- 1 appearance on the History Channel (see: *Weird Weapons of World War II*, about 24 minutes in)
- 32 miles of walking around the city
- 0 miles of biking
- 1 beach visit x 1 dead seal = about 14 eerie photographs
- 5 nights in San Francisco
- 6 days around San Francisco
- 1 birthday, for which Andy got me an ice cream sandwich (an It's-It to those who know)
- And the loudest high-five I've ever been a part of (the 'departure five')

All in all, it was a great six days, and I had the pleasure of leaving on my birthday. Oh, and I crossed the Golden Gate Bridge on my bike because it was on the way! How *Full House* of me! Shoobah-dee bap bah dah! From here, it was me on only one road—Highway 1—that is a heavily biked road (complete with bike lane) from Southern California all the way to Seattle or something. (I didn't care what was past

Portland, honestly, so I don't know how far it goes.)

I do know that you're supposed to bike south on it because then the wind is at your back. Oh, good. Awesome. I'd wondered where my friend 'Mr. Wind', a.k.a. 'The Invisible Force Set Out To Murder Me', had been all this time. Now I found him. Cool. Great. Ugh. Seriously, you can't even spit at it because it comes *right back at you*! At least you can punch the ocean, you know?

Intermission Part Two: Or, Another Wacky Story That Somehow Involves Adventure And Me

This seems like a good place to pause since there's about 720 miles until Portland. I thought I'd switch it up a little with a non-Rainer-Maria-themed story. This one's about life in Savannah, Georgia.

I lived there for two and a half years, and it was brought to my attention one year into my stay that everyone who worked at the hip, indie coffee shop thought I was homeless, because I was only ever seen on my bike with lots of bags and carrying food all over town. All this was merely a result of dumpster diving and the fact that our social circles didn't intersect that often. In short, I was an urban legend! The cool homeless guy who bikes everywhere! Otherwise known as the quiet yet charming introvert! I wish they thought I had a hook for a hand or something, but that's really the only way it could've gotten better. Well, that, or I could view this theory as a prophecy for future events. I chose that one. Because prophecies are cooooool.

Flash-forward to my biking four saddlebags full of soda cans I took from recycling bins to the next town about seven miles away, where one can recycle aluminum for money. Was this what my life was bound for anyway, or was this strictly a result of high social expectations? Could effect precede cause? Did I care? That one I can answer: No. No, I did not. All I knew is that the deeper I waded into the 'freeman' lifestyle, the funnier my life became. I would make about four dollars for a twenty-mile round-trip (including finding the cans) and I only popped a tire once. Economically, it probably wasn't worth it, but I still felt the importance of the act. Sometimes, the story is more valuable than money; the experience is richer than the result. I took this to the limits, though. Here goes nothing…

I made a fake sticker for my invalid school ID so that I could continue using the library and the gym (which is where I showered a couple times). I didn't need to do that—I had plenty of friends who would've let me borrow their bathrooms, and I'm not the cleanest kid in the world, anyway—but I thought that if I was going for a 'freeman' lifestyle, I might as well max it out. I only ate food from the dumpster (Note: This is way, way easier and cleaner than it sounds, and is not very different than my previous lifestyle), I sold what I found in the trash on eBay, I sold textbooks back to the school after kids threw them out after graduation, and I had a really good friend at the local ice cream place (so I didn't have to worry about dessert, *ever*).

I didn't really need money because my student loan didn't demand attention for another six months, and, seriously, what else do you need money for? Clothes? I found stuff in thrift store dumpsters and sewed it to fit me. Food? We covered that, but just for proof: When you're eating two bananas, one avocado, and oatmeal for breakfast every day,

I tend to think that you don't *need* money for food. Basically, if I needed something, I'd 'plan' on finding it in the trash, and nine times out of ten, it would work. If not, I'd go to the printmaking department, work on an etching, print them on free scrap paper, and then sell them to downtown shops on commission!

I know what you're thinking: What about rent? Yeah, that one's complicated…

My friend Andy lived with a couple other guys with whom I was friends, and they let me stay on their couch. However, since I was showering at a gym and brushing my teeth at a library (after sneaking in muffins for my famous 'email breakfasts'), I figured, *Why not?* The wheels begin to turn, and next thing you know, there I was…

…Standing with my hands on my hips, at two a.m., on the roof of a seventeen-story abandoned concrete factory. I could see all of Savannah from the other side of the river, a vantage point taken in by a very select few. The irreparable downside to this plan was the seventeen-story ladder climb that I had to endure to get to the roof. Not stairs, not an elevator, but a series of ten-foot ladders in a pitch-black space that was the size of a large closet. Seriously, though, once it's over then the view is amazing!

I think I slept there only once, but it was awesome. Everything except the ladder-climbing, the mosquitos, and the three-mile bike trip back across the 'illegal-to-bike-on' bridge was great. So was the journal entry stating: "Slept on concrete factory roof, got breakfast in Kroger trash, brushed teeth at library, then worked on graduate thesis for three hours." Classic! In certain ways, I wish that line was pure fiction. It's not, though. Despite all the fun of decimating my professional self, there had to be somewhere else I could sleep.

I think I initially checked it out because I heard it was 'possible' to get on the roof. But it was the downtown Hilton hotel and the biggest hotel in Savannah, so *how* could it be possible? Or easy? Well, believe me, it was a cinch. I spent a great deal of time up there over those last six Savannah months. You take the elevator to the eleventh floor, then the west stairs all the way to the top. After that, you're one short ladder away from touching the sky…or finding a haiku I wrote a long time ago in whiteout pen. I spent a couple nights at that Hilton, and had I been paying to sleep there (which most everyone who stays there *is*), I would owe them nearly six hundred dollars. But it was free! I got extreme bonus points for all the 'hope you slept well' comments I was given when leaving every morning. Ha! I did sleep well! And I didn't even have a bed!

Eventually, a good friend of mine moved out of her place and left the lease with another seventeen days until anyone else moved in. This was great for me, because she gave me the old key and a free half-month lease, complete with working fridge! (I never used it once!) But I did sleep there quite a bit, which was pretty nice. There was a storage closet in the public space of the first floor hallway where I stored things up until I left Savannah for good (mostly printmaking supplies and changes of clothes). That closet was doubly exciting because it yielded a box of love letters from the 1940s (!) and it also got me in trouble with the girl who moved in after I stopped 'living' there. I swear, people notice (and get upset about) the smallest, most mundane things.

"Are you living in the storage closet?"

Jeez. I bet you've never heard of a friendship starting with that line. Our brief relationship certainly didn't snowball into anything more positive. After some poor explaining and a lot of creative lying, I became much more covert in my visits. See, I did learn something. She, on the other hand, did not.

I lived using this method of friend/town/scholastic exploitation for about nine months, which may seem crazy to you, but it seems absolutely bonkers to me. Somewhere in the midst of all that unscrupulous vagabonding, I started clinging to 'day-to-day' living as a substitute for trying to plan my life. No amount of groundwork could have made what I was 'doing' any easier, so I simply awoke each day and decided on that day's direction as it came to me. More than anything, I have fond memories of reading lazily in the park, stopping only to sew up a new shirt, or new shorts, or my shoes, and then running into everyone I know and talking for a long, long time. This was a wonderful period in my life. There were a lot of sleepless nights and impossible dreams…flash-forward to my bike trip, in which some of those impossible dreams were becoming 'impossible realities'…or, uh, something.

Breaking Wagon Tongues On The Oregon Trail

Dang. Biking. Right. Imagine the song "Here I Go Again" blaring across the Golden Gate Bridge and you'll have an excellent idea of what my San Francisco sendoff was like. Loud, rocking, but also leaning toward bittersweet, as I was back to being on 'the only road I'd ever known'. Solitude, dude. Oh, and despite the metaphor, it was really quiet, save the deafening wind and infinite onslaught of traffic.

With eyes fixed intently toward Portland's general direction, I considered this leg of the journey to be the third and last time I would leave somewhere I had stayed for a long enough time to call 'sort-of-almost-home'. That train wreck of a term is based on the fact that I had a friend there; good friends make places worthwhile. If I am able to convey any central theme or purpose across with this collection of stories, I would hope it to be that real friendship, that honest, emotional connection, is an unstoppable driving force that is capable of creating laughter out of the most negative of situations. I started this whole trip nearly two months ago with the intent of getting to Portland to hang out with my friend Nate. I told him I'd be there, and by golly dangit heck almighty, I was gonna do it somehow.

You see, I've seen a lot of cities—at the time of writing this, I've been to forty-nine of the United States (North Dakota, I will find you one day)—and I've started to pick up on the parallels running throughout them all. A city is literally just a couple buildings all clustered together, usually near a river or a lake. Now, unless you're totally bat-crap about history and can spend four hours with your mouth agape while staring at a building where some dead writer used to hang out (or where a former president once used the bathroom), the chances are that you'll find buildings to be only buildings, and cities only cities. If visits are not to be historically significant, then perhaps the shopping prospects can draw in crowds. Or maybe the food is particularly…edible, or something. I guess I can ask it like this: Do you remember all the details surrounding when you bought those shoes, or do you have better memories of when you talked all night with someone you'd just met, huddled around a dying fire, and then walked to the playground to catch the sunrise? Even if the sunrise wasn't there and you both walked back technically defeated but too excited about life and real, earnest connections among friends to think twice about it? Heck, I could barely go to sleep that night, and I laid down at seven a.m.! These things matter! These moments *are* life!

My inability to be brief or concise is spilling into this subject, so I'll try to keep it contained. My friends have helped me become ten times the person that I am capable of being alone, and I thank them daily for that. Friendships mean the absolute world to me: rampant with possibility, boiling with capacity, and overall, able to create (and live out) our impossible dreams. My friends are going to save the world. That's a quote, too, but I would've come up with it, too, after awhile… probably. I'll also probably say it again.

I Think I Derailed My Everything

Right, so, my plan for the next seven hundred and some odd miles was to bike north. How easy is that? It only took me three hours to reach a point from where I could see the ocean to my left, and the next week or so remained more or less the same. The roads look like they were all built on a dare, or that after four months of construction the foreman reluctantly flips the blueprints around and mutters, "Ohhh…" Seriously, it's nuts out there. But, come on, who would I be to comment only on the road architecture. It's also beautiful beyond words out there. I mean, like "adverb-adjective" beautiful. Exactly!

When I'm dwarfed by the natural beauty in the world, I find that I wonder why people live other places, like cities. I hate to play the 'hippie' card, but I swear, it's so inspiring out there. So much so that I came full circle to day one and started to enjoy biking all over again. When you're on top of the world, it sure is hard to look anywhere but up...well, until...ha, kidding. Nothing bad happened. I almost got hit in the face with a vulture, though. True story! It was eating something dead on the side of the road when I somehow surprised it, and when it started to fly up and take off, it swung a weird curve right in front of my face, and I shrieked out loud like people do in movies. (Coincidentally, the movie *The Birds* was filmed in a town that I stopped in the first day of my West Coast biking. These two events were seemingly unrelated but intertwined with eerie parallel...ity.)

California provided all kinds of fun for me to work around. I spent four nights in a row within twenty feet of a 'No Camping Here' sign without any problems. Had I been carrying a gun or walking a dog, I would've been breaking *all* the rules...but things being as they were, I was only a one-third offender. I guess that's why nobody messed with me.

I didn't have to put up my tent, either, because in California (where everything is perfect all the time) there are no bugs to protect yourself from and it doesn't rain at night. Cooperative weather is really the best friend you can ask for from the natural world when you're on a bike trip, and I have to give it to California, because it was being friendly. I think that this is how the trip should've felt the entire time: all fun, no bugs, no problem! And free avocados everywhere. Who wouldn't want that, really? The bugs, just to let you know, have been replaced with blonde rollerblading 'babes', like the kind that I would tip my sunglasses down to look at if it were 1985 and I was John Cusack. Think *The Sure Thing* kind of babes. Boy, zine anonymity really lets you 'say anything'...but really, talk about having 'one crazy summer'— this was one time I knew I wasn't 'better off dead'. No way. I cannot believe that I just wrote that. It should've been waaay earlier.

BEACH + FULL MOON = NO TENT!

Day three of California provided such serial murdering of the English language and appropriate social norms as demonstrated by the following passages taken (unedited) from my notebook: "Got a free sunset—the horizon is my hypercolor shirt tonight—wow, that metaphor sucks and is simultaneously DEAD ON," followed closely by, "...I smell worse, I have rock-hard salt deposits in my shirt, and I just washed my underwear in a sink at the mall."

I remember trying to be covert and real 'spy-op' going in, but when I came out with soaking underwear, I let the whole world see. To clarify, I was not wearing them, but, rather, I tied them to my back like a cape so that they could dry. My life has been pretty public so far, so I might as well air out the dirty laundry as literally as I can. California must have had its seventy degree, weather-regulated, laid-back (falling over) grip on me, because when I got to a supermarket, not only did I just ask the truck drivers out back for free food (which worked), I also wandered inside only to see doughnuts and think, "Sure! Doughnuts for dinner!" Perhaps this is the underlying theme of this trip and my life: immediately accepting the first positive step forward out of whatever situation I'm in, and in this case, the doughnuts were food, I was hungry, and then—bam—problem solved!

The next day provided more phenomenal landscapes coupled with more oddities, such as an old woman next to me at the library accidentally clicking spam email and winding up with tons of porn ads popping up on her computer (she kept saying, "Oh—oh, these words! *These words!*"), which took place in the same library where an edgy youngster had spray-painted his 'handle' on the outside wall that read, 'Coast Bacon'. What the heck is going on? Coast Bacon? Really? You sure about that, kid?

Fifty-six miles later, I was wandering the 'city' of Fort Bragg, walking around a weird field and looking for a place to set up a tent, when I ran across a homeless guy with a radio! Cool! I say 'cool' not because I think it's cool that he's homeless, but rather that I love the idea that the woods are an acceptable home. Squat the woods! Yeah! We shared an odd moment, but I think we both left with quiet respect for each other, which was a nice change of pace. Most people look at me like I'm an idiot, like I'd never heard of soap before, or like I was in the way of their crappy car. But…respect?

Forget The Windows; Let's Look In Mirrors!

A series of extreme hills with summits residing *in* clouds gave me ample time to come up with more interesting theories on distance biking...because, really, I haven't covered this enough yet, right? I remember going to bed the night before and being able to see Mars as well as the moon, their flat cut-out shapes sliding aimlessly about the sky, and thinking how weird it was that I could see *Mars*, yet I couldn't see Portland from where I was. I understand the curvature of the earth, of course, but what I'm getting at is that when you can see something, its attainability becomes completely possible, but when working on faith alone, it's hard to think you'll ever get there. In a way, yes, I'm saying I had more faith in making it to Mars than I did in getting to Portland. It's like running the mile: If you ran it all in one straight line (rather than multiple laps on a turning track), I think you'd perform better because you can see the entire distance the whole time.

Sure, being an artist, I'm stuck in the 'visual people' category; in addition, I think that my brain's distance-computing mechanism is wholly ineffective, as well as my ability to realize that things continue existing despite not being able to see them. This is the same way that children think, which is why 'Peek-A-Boo' is so exciting. When I climb tall things, like cranes or huge ladders, my immobilizing fear of heights is solely overcome by closing my eyes. I once climbed a twelve-story construction crane with my eyes totally shut the whole time. It's the only way I can do it. I realize that math and logic dictate that, yes, I am getting closer to Portland, but if I can't *see* something growing slightly on the horizon, or coming more into focus, then I just don't understand our distance. Cold logic and numbers have no place in such a warm, heartfelt endeavor. I'm sticking to finger painting and hugging.

After some photos of me laughing at gas prices, and then setting up tent outside a town with no food at all, I fell asleep about twenty feet from the highway. I slept with some rocks, which were bent on destroying my resolve for the evening. They won with no contest. Another night of 'not great' sleep. Oh well! About ten miles later, in a town that was given a **bold** font on my map (!), I met two punk-ish girls outside the Holiday Inn (where I was brushing my teeth) who used their 'hotel patron' status to get me free food! We sat and talked for a while, which was an extremely nice change of pace as it didn't involve sweating uncontrollably. They even knew the band VCR! Richmond was over three thousand miles away, but East Coast pride dies hard, and by-dangit-all-heck, we stick together!

Later that day, I wandered into a tourist stop while hugging all five of my water bottles as a woman sauntered by, locked me in with a weighty stare, and whispered, "*Man of many waters…*" directly into my freaking soul. I still can't figure out if I was terrified, lovestruck, or suffering from dehydration and heat stroke. Now I know it to be all of them, in one jaw-dropping moment.

The Only Bike-Related Problem I Endured

You know what that means: no popped tires yet! And it had been over two thousand miles! (This *would* be both the time and place to plug my tire brand of choice…but too bad!) I did, however, incur a broken spoke, which, to the non-biker, sounds akin to small potatoes. This is light years from the truth, however, as a broken spoke on the rear passenger side is the biggest of all problems in the 'spoke world'. The tire relies on the spokes to keep it unfailingly circular (otherwise known as 'true') and losing one makes the wheel go all wonky-like. Remember about a million pages ago when I said something about 'that time in California when I broke a spoke?' Well, here's where foreshadowed future and grim, biting reality merge into one unholy beast I call *problems galore*! I readjusted my tire, went another seventy-eight miles, found a bike co-op, and fixed it. Problem solved! Crisis averted! Taxing endeavor assuaged! Quagmire precluded! Thesaurus overused!

Actually, that co-op is worth mentioning in slightly greater detail, as it merited at least ten photos by me. It was in Arcata, California, and it was officially called the 'Bike Library', housing about ten thousand dormant bikes in various states of functionality. The high point included three road bikes turned into stationary bikes that stored electric current in a battery and were capable of powering anything with an AC plug. I spoke with the owner/operator and he told me that he powered an apartment for year on nothing more than a bike. Even to non-bikers, that has to sound amazing. Because it is. Here we are, dead center of an energy crisis, and we could be harnessing power from simple everyday actions like that? I bet you could power a city block if you configured a gym correctly. Think about it. I kept wondering what I could have powered, had I the means to harness my kinetic energy from all this bike riding. But I also kept wondering why I gave up on physics class, so, well, there you go.

Thanks to him, I also realized how painfully easy it is to ask people if you can stay with them for the night, because he asked if I needed a place to stay and I declined (as it was still before noon), but he offered, "Well, all you gotta do is ask—

like this: 'Hey, you, can this guy stay with you?'" at which point the 'my-age girl' who was browsing bikes glances over to reply, "Well, I guess so…"

Goodbye, Arcata! And goodbye/thanks anyway, potential friend!

Dumpstering Apples, Sure—But Dumpstering A House?

Seems crazy, huh? Though, in keeping with the groundwork already laid by squatters the world over, I though that this was something that could happen. Literally, a 'house' (by my crappy, uninformed definition) is only a place where you can sleep with a roof over your head and with little to no fear of being attacked by an animal. So, in a sense, it's only empty space, right? If I were, say, plotting out which hotels I planned on continentally ripping off (or 'creatively testing their food-related security measures') and I saw a couple model trailer homes, would it really be so wrong to test their doors? And so what if one opened? That's basically the situation, so please come to your own conclusions: Was I blurring the line between right and wrong? Should I have expected a sign that I had gone too far? I love asking the important questions. I did a great deal of interviewing myself that night.

But I also did a great deal of sleeping on the carpet, indoors, with my watch alarm set for 5 a.m., in the event that someone might show up and get angry with me. I'm pretty good at talking someone out of 'let's *not* call the police' situations, but I'm typically not on the ball that early in the morning. (Like the time I came up with a plan as I heard the door being unlocked when Jake and I snuck into a hotel and stayed on the floor of the conference room. I think the plan was solid, since it was only our sleeping bags that gave us away. But that's another story, for another time. Probably later in this book.) This merely put me indoor with my own house and sleeping with no threat of bugs or animals or rain or nothing! However, I did harbor great terror toward a possible run-in with the law, and this far into my trip, I wasn't *about* to fall short of Portland for any reason. So I slept awfully and left at 4:30 a.m. I learned a lot about homeownership that night. And I hated it.

A Straightforward Ace Of Base Reference

At this point, I don't mind writing that not a lot went down from the tip of California to Portland. This is to say: I biked a lot and (since I was so close) I discontinued my streak of checking every dumpster, stopping in all the little towns, and doing silly little things like that. I redefined hope for myself and called my mom while exuding a feeling far surpassing that of elation when I saw the first 'Portland: 338 Miles' sign. That sign is there to tell people that, 'Yes, you can get to Portland from where you are and that's not out of the question at all,' which meant I was going to make it!

And, spread across the next four days, I did. Highlights included turning onto a different road one time and going to Eugene, which was (as my prophetic, spitting homeless friend in D.C. had promised) 'really f-ing beautiful, man.' They have a bike superhighway through fields and around buildings so that you can travel a lot of places while avoiding traffic. It was pretty awesome, all in all. And green—awesome and green. The trees in Oregon are amazing. Seriously.

You could tell that my focus had shifted from riding my bike to getting to Portland because my journal started becoming weird thoughts and theoretical inventions, such as, 'turn a paddleboat into a tricycle, add a the steering wheel from a bus to a bike, make a cupcake the size of a normal cake, use old books from the dumpster for photo albums, etc.' However, I did come up with my 'bike heart' image during this last three hundred miles, so I'd say that it wasn't a waste in the slightest. Oh, that, and I GOT TO PORTLAND!

I Can Stop Riding My Bike (Again)

However, the day I rode into Portland was a weird one. I knew that it was the last day I'd be biking toward something (rather than biking around for fun in Portland). I would be going from straight lines to simple loops, if that makes sense…think Etch-A-Sketch versus Spirograph drawings. I recall, very clearly, passing a dormant and sprawling wine vineyard and watching a thick grouping of 'Northwest' clouds roll over everything in sight. I was still gritting my teeth at hills, but then cresting them only to think, *Oh my gosh, I'm almost there*. I was extremely close, but eighty miles is still a long 'day ride'.

With severe split personality disorder in full swing, I somehow managed to keep my limbs moving and my heart beating. My unfathomable excitement spilled all over my shirt when I finally got to employ my photocopied 'this is where Nate lives' map of Portland. To those who understand, he was living on Northeast 39th, so I made up a route that seemed logical and set out toward his house. Much to my amazement (as well as his), I wound up staring at a house on the corner about 3 p.m. or so, a good two hours before he got off work. It's ironic that I could be considered 'early', isn't it?

I propped my bike against a tree, got my phone out, called Nate, and was told that he'd leave work immediately, as he was equally excited and dumbstruck by my earliness. When I hung up the phone, I sunk down a little bit from my straight-backed sitting position and looked at my inactive phone. It was over! But, wait, it was *over*. I was done.

The feeling was not unlike the last, panicked day of summer before school starts; except, in my case, I hadn't known *when* it was going to be, so it hit me without warning. I mean, yes, I had warning, and I knew four days ago that I'd arrive in Portland soon, but you don't think about it like that. So now, with summer over, I swelled with confusion and remained quiet and close to my bike for the next twenty minutes before Nate showed up. In the flurry of emotion and outpour of desperation, I found myself wishing that I'd enjoyed it all more—I should've taken more photos, I should've thanked more people, I should've called my mom more often, I should've sent more letters to my friends…I was an inconsolable string of pleas, wishing for a life of pre-climax moments, and to do away with the denouement in which I had bottomed out. It's like when a friend comes to visit for a long time and eventually you have to take them back to the airport or train station, and you find yourself wishing that you'd done more with them and that every hour of every day needed a story attached to it. Our hearts mean to say so much more than we'll ever be capable of expressing.

To pen the story written inside me, to quantify emotion and event, to explain the capacity of human life: This is beyond my scope as a writer, as an artist, or as a person. Instead, I hope that the experiences, those rare moments—the 'perfect days'—will silence our talking, engage our every sense, and carve permanent, inescapable marks on our lives.

NEXT STOP ADVENTURE #3

mid-air hifives from here on out!

The Haikus!

All haikus were written between July through September 2005 within two to four feet of my bike. To clarify, I wrote one haiku each day of bike touring, as it's much easier to remember that day by reading a short three-line poem as opposed to a multi-page journal entry. That, and they're funny. To me. Maybe to you, too!

UP AND DOWN N.C.
RIDING THIS ROLLERCOASTER
MY KNEES EXPLODED

NAP ON THE SIDEWALK
SLEEPING UNDER OVERPASS
HOMELESSNESS IS WEIRD

I CAN SEE MYSELF
CHLORINATED PERFECTION
CANNONBALL, SANS PANTS

OH, MOSQUITO BITES
COMPANY IS NICE AND ALL
DON'T YOU EVER SLEEP?

YOUR FANNYPACK RULES
BUT YOU TRAVEL BY SEGWAY
WE CANNOT BE FRIENDS

DOWNTOWN BALTIMORE
WAIT, THOSE AREN'T STRAIGHTEDGE MOVIES
STOP PICKING UP CHANGE!

THESE PAVED ROADS TAUNT ME
BLACK AND YELLOW FOR TOO LONG
SUNSET, I EARNED YOU

FIERY SUNSET
SKIES ABLAZE IN PINKS AND REDS
WHO CARES MY LEGS ACHE

KNEE IS EXPLODING
ONCE WAS A THOUGHT, NOW I'M SURE
LIFE, I HAVE YOU PINNED

CRISP WINDS BRING NEW CLOUDS
WIPE OUT TUNNEL VISION
HOPE BOBS UP AND DOWN

HILLS LIKE FLOWING STREAMS
HOUSING SKETCHY SHIRTLESS MEN
AH, WEST VIRGINIA

BIG REFRESHING GULPS
IOWA — WHAT HAVE YOU DONE?
YOU TASTE LIKE BROWN DEATH

YOU SMELL A WET DOG?
THIRTY MILES, IN THE RAIN
THIGHS ARE GRATED CHEESE

TWO KIDS WITH COFFEE
ONLY GROWNUPS DRINK THAT JUNK
THOSE MULLETS TASTE WORSE

ONE GALLON OF GAS
THREE DOLLARS AND FIFTY CENTS
PEDALING IS FREE!

OUR FRIENDSHIP IS STRANGE
WHEN I TURN MY BACK ON YOU,
THEN WE GET ALONG

TRASH BAG FOR LUGGAGE
SMELLS LIKE URINE ON SWEATPANTS
GO FASTER, GREYHOUND!

A KISS ON THE CHEEK
I RECALL WE WERE ONCE FRIENDS
OH WIND, WHAT HAPPENED?

NO CAKE ANYWHERE
BUT SLEEP AND FRIENDSHIP WILL DO
HAPPY BIRTHDAY, ME

THEY WILL SAVE THE WORLD
DREAMS TRAVEL PRIORITY
THIRTY-NINE CENT FRIENDS

THE KING MIDAS TOUCH
ON DISCARDED TREASURES
MY LIFE AS PROFIT

PROBLEMS OF HARD EARTH
COMPARED TO THE INFINITE
THE SKY IS FALLING

CONSTANT LIVING PROOF
"NO SUCH THING AS FREE BREAKFAST"
YOUR DAD'S A LIAR

FLAT, CHALKY ABYSS
LIMPING TOWARDS THE HORIZON
CARS ARE REGRESSION

LIFE'S BEST THINGS ARE FREE
LAMINATED, I DEFY
ARTIFICIAL LIGHT

OUR VERY FIRST DATE
YOUR TOUR PASS SAYS "MADISON"
YOUR EYES SAY "DON'T LEAVE"

ARMATURE IS WEAK
BUT SO LONG AS THIS HEART BEATS
THE DRUMMER WILL MARCH

FABRIC, HARD AS ROCK
SANDPAPER REPLACES SKIN
MODERN DAY GANDHI

TENT, I WILL MISS YOU
WET STENCH OF FEET AND HOT DEATH
NO, I TAKE THAT BACK

BRAND NEW TOMORROW
THOUGH CLOUDS RUIN OUR PLANS
FRIENDSHIP SHINES BRIGHTER

THE END BREAKS MY HEART
FINDING LIFE WHERE I LEAVE IT
I'VE BEEN HERE BEFORE

The Corn Revolution is Over

"**H**MM...I SHOULD BIKE THERE..."

I swear that if I had a nickel for every time those words have fallen out of my mouth, I'd be able to pay off my student loans five times over and afford a train ticket to whatever city I'd have dubbed my personal 'finish line' that week. However, this is *counter*-counter intuitive. The agonizingly long and disaster-laden bike ride is *clearly* what it's all about! It's way more fun, way more free, and wrought with adventure! What if Lewis and Clark had flown westward? Come on! What if Thoreau had played *Sim City* instead of going the proverbial transcendentalist 'full nine'? Exactly! And Chicago to Iowa City? That's only, like, 240 miles! Let's do this!

At this time, I lived in Chicago, a 'cool-at-times-but-way-too-sprawling-and-treeless-for-me-to-love' city, and my brother Zack was living in Iowa City, the tree-filled, co-op-having, cool-library-housing, hippie-retirement haven that everyone overlooks. And I didn't have a job to deal with. So, ditching 'okay city life' for 'fun bike trip life' was an easy decision. Here's a test: If you hear your housemate's alarm going off through the wall at 7 a.m. and you're still up writing letters or printing patches, then you are officially ripe to go on a trip of this caliber. It also helps to have a bike...or feet. Or whatever. The point is: "*Get outside!*"

My brain was bobbling stupidly with that 'who cares, it's summer' freedom, so I barely glanced at my trusty, crappy eBayed road atlas before deciding I was one hundred percent in for a bike trip to Iowa City. My only other plan / precautionary measure was to make pancakes for breakfast the next morning. Pancakes are distance-biking *gold*. (Well, the edible kind. It's a bad metaphor. My fault.) Regardless, the last thought I had before I fell asleep that night was my stupidly optimistic, infinitely overused, personal catchphrase: 'I'll cross that bridge when I come to it.' Good planning leads to good plans, but *no* planning leads to great stories. I stand firmly on my choice.

I fell asleep. Then I woke up! That means pancakes, D.I.Y. round bread! This trip was going to theoretically *rule*! But... well, of all of the monumental disappointments I'd been privy to in my twenty-six years, having the power die in our kitchen two minutes into pouring the batter ranks *really freaking high*. This mishap set the stage for the remainder (read: 'ninety-nine percent') of my Iowa Doom Trip. I made four half-cooked pancakes from residual heat, which became wet sawdust flooded with maple syrup. Awful. Not even fun. So I brushed my teeth and attached some crap to my bike...

The Crap: A Math List

I swear that I can't write a *Next Stop Adventure* without a math list.

- ➡ 1 extra shirt, zero socks, and only the pants I was wearing (Technically, this totals four outfits, if you flip the shirts inside out. I refused to count 'being shirtless' as an outfit. I am not a total moron, thank you.)
- ➡ 1 bike, a 1992 Trek 660 series, to those who care (All I see if a blue thing with two wheels.)
- ➡ 1 sleeping bag that smells like 2 feet and has been to 49 states (North Dakota, where ARE you?)

- 1 tent that smells like ten billion feet
- 3 bagels
- 1 jar of peanut butter
- 3 water bottles, which should've been 9 or 15, or anything more than 3
- 1 hand-drawn 'map' detailing how to leave Chicago on bike, based solely on guessing road bikeability using Google Maps
- 240 miles to bike (according to math)
- 287 miles to bike (according to reality, the bitter mistress she is)
- 2 days to bike it
- 1 brother waiting with two arms open wide

That's all I had going for me. I attached this to my bike with some bungee cords between two rear panniers, carried my bike downstairs, and started southbound. To retrace a sentiment that I've set forth in prior scribblings, I'll remind you: Bike riding is fairly uninteresting. I biked through some sketchy parts of southwest Chicago, drank some water, and immersed myself in full to the whitewashed blandness of the Midwest. Fun hint for travelers: If it doesn't touch saltwater, then it's probably booooring. (Don't get me wrong. Anywhere *can* be fun. If you miss that point, drop this right now and go outside.)

It was just an uneventful bike ride. The first couple hours were pretty awful: no shoulder, way too many cars, and I could *not stop* spitting mouthfuls of poorly mixed pancake batter. I have *no idea* how it was possible, but I'm certain I spat up nearly thirty pancakes' worth of that crud. Yeah, I called it crud—so what?

At the 100.35 mile mark, I decided that the corn field alongside me would serve as a decent sleeping place. I made a list while in my tent of some pluses and minuses—as well as a haiku—and the plus side stood tall with the promise of two letters awaiting me in Iowa City (since I had given my brother's address to a couple of my friends). Yet the minus side provided a very compelling argument, as my tendons in the back of my legs were, um, killing me. Uh oh. No matter how I tried to spin the fact that I was halfway there, the list still added up to a negative. My glass would've been half-full but my water bottle was all-empty. This is my life as a convoluted trial in optimism, otherwise known as 'problems galore!'

I awoke with zero water in my water bottles yet morning dew all over everything. I was also in the middle of the extremely rural, flat-as-an-undercooked-pancake that is Illinois. Yet it appeared that I was surrounded by a cloud, something I thought I knew to be impossible, given my altitude of 'zero'. This *Twilight Zone*-esque weirdness perfectly framed the bizarre goings-on of that morning...

My plan was to get water at the absolute first place I saw, and since I was in the epicenter of nothingness, I was actually concerned. My worry vanished in about seven miles when I came upon a two-story building that resembled a small, extremely crappy motel. The door on the far end of the front side had a 'Come On In' sign, so I Nancy Drew-ed the conclusion that this was the office. Offices have employees. Employees need water to life. Therefore, offices have water. Nancy and I are geniuses. More her than me, but still. A small dog appeared in the window, so I took that as a cue—and walked in.

My eyes got real wide, as the room I just walked into was someone's apartment, not the office I was expecting.

Furthermore, there were piles of 'stuff' all over the place—visual non-sequitors such as a bag of open dog food perched atop ten phone books and old socks or a broken ashtray seated on the TV set with a VHS tape bearing the gripping title, *How To Surf The Internet*. It was unopened. And there was no VCR (at least, not one near the TV, as far as I could tell), much less a computer.

I purposefully cast myself in an 80s camp slasher movie and thoughtfully asked, "Is anybody home? Hello?" I love pushing my luck. One of my all-time favorite things to say is, "Well, at least it can't get any *worse*," and then look around stupidly and expectantly for a lightning bolt or a swarm of bees. Anyway, apart from the dog, I received no response of any kind, so I went right for the sink with water bottles in hand. I immediately noticed a plate of tomatoes with a half-inch-thick cobweb coating the entire dish, a mold that I am incapable of describing. A new thought entered my head: What if this *was* someone's apartment and the tenant was dead? It would explain the stale smell and the yellow, unmoving air with its quiet hum of fruit flies... this was *actually* getting weird. It seemed extremely feasible that this hoarder of a tenant was crushed by their boxes of useless crap, and I was going to be the one to find them. I filled one water bottle, took a sip, and came two inches from barfing up my entire spinal column. The water both looked and tasted as though it were tea steeped in musty polyester pants, the kind you find in the thrift store dumpster but don't take because you don't want your backpack to smell like... well, like the apartment I was standing in. Ugh. I felt like drinking toothpaste. But I didn't. There's a warning on the label... evidently, for people like me.

I grabbed my water, fed and watered the dog (no, not like that), and left. Quickly. Keep in mind that it's 7:10 a.m., sunny outside, and that despite some extremely tender leg muscles and tendons, riding my bike for the next ten hours sounded much, *much* better than staying in this 'motel hell.' I needed no convincing from the chainsaw-wielding, pig-headed guy—my imagination was plenty. (P.S.: If you've never seen *Motel Hell*, that last sentence won't make too much sense. Forget the internet, go find it on VHS someplace, that's how it was meant to be enjoyed.)

Outdoors, I rejoined my bike, sat on a bench, and recounted the weirdness in my journal. Fifteen or so minutes passed and an old man wandered over, quietly asking in a dead-sounding gurgle, "Can I help you?" Some deft coercing earned me even more tap water (hooray), which was beneficial to my body's physical well being, yet little else. So I left. I'm good at that part.

Looking in Mirrors, Not Windows

What followed was biking. Real, actual, 'wow-that-sounds-*so-nice*' biking on lightly used two-lane rural routes connecting farmland to farmland. This environment and inviting atmosphere perfectly defines the purpose of riding a bicycle. At the risk of getting a nosebleed on the soapbox I'm about to climb on, it's days like these that make me wonder how or why one would prefer to drive anywhere. The nice weather and general feelings of excitement, positivity, and potential always remind me of being a kid. You sprint outside first thing on Saturday morning with no plan but the intrinsic knowledge that you simply *should* be outside. I fear that if I ever lose that feeling, I'm in trouble…

That sentiment is synonymous with summer—specifically, one that follows an awful, introverted winter. I *love summer*. And spring. Oh, and fall. To be fair, I like winter too, that's when I get all my drawing done. Hmmm. Anyway, this *Calvin-and-Hobbs*-ian clinging-to-childhood approach brings together just about everyone. You can see it in their eyes, it shows through their step, and it shines brightly in their speech. People who feel this way never search for friends but simply 'find' them. I smile at these people when they're biking around me, and they tend to smile back. They remind me of the reason I ride for such long periods of time. If you're reading this, the chances are that you 'get it', which means I owe you a huge thank you. It's friends like you who made me want to ride my bike away from boredom and into the mouth of excitement. Friends that double as signposts reading, 'Keep going. It's worth it.' So, really, thank you all.

Having said all that, I hope it's obvious how I feel about bike riding. This becomes really important in a moment. Now, after another day of riding, I was seated in Clinton, Iowa, a town that smelled like, 'burgers on a grill extinguished by a bucket of tepid red wine,' but, as I sat outside of a Target, shifted to, 'the smell of a generic cafeteria lunch, specifically hot barf, macaroni and cheese, and Dr. Pepper poured all over burnt toast.' I *hate* that town. Well, my nose does. I should note, this town reappears in my life some two years later, when riding a freight train through it, and identifying our location based only on the smell. Read about it later! In this very book!

On A More Tangible Note...

I was still fifty miles from my brother's place and my leg tendons were *killing me*. I could actually *feel* it when it moved: It slid up and down like an unoiled, sandy piece of rebar in my leg. My initial intent for taking this trip was, please recall, to see my brother Zack. So, when I talked to him and he said his friends could pick me up—I mean, the choice was obvious!

At the great risk of making my inability to actually 'complete' one of these bike trips public, I did bike nearly two hundred miles, but leg pain is dang hard to argue with. So is more time to spend with a wonderful friend. This has never been about the bike ride itself. It's the feeling and thoughts, the dreams and plans—*those* are the intended results from unplanned, seat-of-your-pants trips like this. Even when you fall short, I guarantee that you'll 'get there.' So, I arrived in Iowa City partially defeated in the world of distance biking, yet rich with accomplishment in the realm of potential.

I recount these stories so that they may become vague blueprints to anything you see fit. I have been told before that *Next Stop Adventure* comes off as inspirational: turning my monologue into a dialogue, a game of inspirational ping pong, only getting faster, rocketing back and forth. Hopefully, my physical failures will stand as concrete proof that, really, anyone can do this. Heck, I barely do it! And to keep things ending with exclamation marks—to retain the energy at full, Good Clean Fun / Latterman gang vocal levels—I promise that the last bike story will end on a proper, accomplished note. It's only fair.

Go!!!

Bottom Feeders Unite: Everything I Need to Know... I Pulled Out Of Your Trash And Put In My Mouth

Of all the activities I've been part of over the course of my life, I feel like dumpster diving has been the most devastating, in a positive way. What was born one night after a coming home from a show, as Doug and I stood outside a closed movie theater and both wondered, "So, wait—where do you think the popcorn goes...?" has now snowballed into a full-on addiction complete with environmental justifications. I am at the point where my initial response to seeing a grocery store is to go around the back.

This text is simply some collected experiences penned with the hope that the inspiration to try it yourself would be given, like an eye-opening chain letter that you found in the trash. That being said...

I'd never heard about dumpster diving; this is to say that the idea came to me before I'd read about it even being possible or something anyone would *do*. The idea really did begin that popcorn evening, but it quickly moved onto the dollar store, the bagel place, the thrift store...the idea was: 'If they sell it, then they probably throw it away.' And that's true! Video stores? Movies! Grocery stores? Groceries! Thrift stores? Everything!!!

One of the biggest moments in my personal trash history was our first visit to the bagel shop. We found, as anyone could guess, tons and tons of bagels. Obviously, this makes sense—one could even predict such a thing—yet my face lit up like fireworks when we pulled from the dumpster three trash bags full of bagels. It was amazing. It actually works. In fact, there were enough bagels to bring them to an art and craft fair downtown, set up a small table with a sign reading, 'Free bagels! Tips welcome!' and feed, like, thirty people over the course of two hours. It was basically a bagels-only Food Not Bombs, another thing I had never heard of, having grown up in a small town. I was taking tips, but the tips were all for the 'raise money so that Doug and I can drive to Vermont and see Botch at Krazyfest' fund. Twenty-two dollars later, I was pretty sold on dumpster diving: It fed the hungry, saved some space in a landfill, and, in this case, got me one step closer to jumping on top of people during that awesome part in "Saint Matthew Returns to the Womb". I freaking *love* that song.

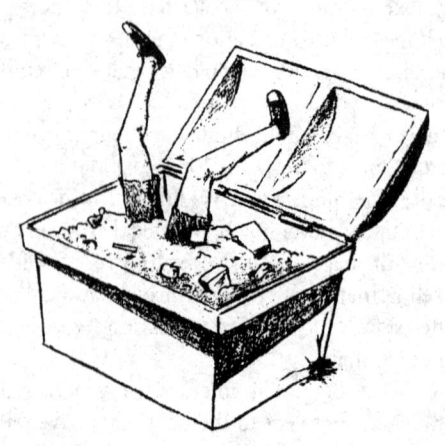

It might appear to you as 'careless' to give away food from the trash. Well, in my eleven years of trash food, I've never gotten sick from it, so...I don't care. So there. Eat it. Literally. I really have never gotten sick, though I have gotten sticky from donut glaze or stained from bird poo or exploding juice. However, I use this awesome thing called common sense when eating 'waste,' meaning that moldy fruit does *not* go in my mouth. Sure, I'll disregard the expiration date, but that's pretty arbitrary in the first place. Printing a date on something containing a horrifying amount of preservatives says little regarding food quality and stands to remind us all that this food *should* go bad at some point (despite the fact that it won't burst into moldy nonsense at midnight).

My 'tips' could be summated as such: Wash all fruit and vegetables, don't eat anything that's open, eat pizza anytime unless it has meat on it (go ahead and avoid meat all together, especially when you're shopping inside), and lastly—share it all! There's beyond plenty of food, so give away what you don't need. The dumpster gods operate on karma alone and your givings will be reimbursed threefold (at least). Oh, oh, oh—the last tip is to eat a clove of raw garlic every morning. Super anti-bacterial when raw, this junk saves lives. I'll stop short of transcribing the Wikipedia entry on garlic, but I promise you: Garlic is *great* for your heart, stomach, and body.

Thrift stores were a surprise on the 'totally free stuff that I would've never imagined would be free' front. A huge part of me had always assumed thrift stores to be 'down' (using and reusing everything, never wasting a single item donated, the proverbial 'last stop before the landfill'), but reality is painted a darker hue. It seems completely random as to what gets trashed and what gets resold. Quality may be a factor. But it certainly isn't *the* factor.

I proved that when I unearthed gems such as an inflatable raft with zero problems, a ton of great books (including

Into the Wild, *The Electric Acid Kool-Aid Test*, and *Invasion USA*, which may be a movie, but who cares), and a food dehydrator still in its box! (I sold that one on eBay.) Oh, and this one time I found a box of one hundred unused two-foot-long glow sticks. Double oh—I also found a life-size cutout of Sarah Michelle Gellar as Buffy the Vampire Slayer. Who in the world would donate that? Or own it? Anyway, the thrift store is a veritable wacky-as-crap grab bag of random free stuff—clothes, books, and cooking utensils typifying the mainstays—but I would go into this realm expecting the unexpected.

Another place that is the seldom investigated and always overlooked is the storage unit dumpster. Fifty dollars a month adds up quickly and people may eventually give up or forget about it—and their stuff hits the trash. The other bonus here is inherent in the service that self-storage provides: It's a place to put your stuff that you don't want to get rid of because it's worth something, yet isn't important enough to keep within earshot. There are things like record collections, weird furniture, or boxes upon boxes of toys from the eighties. Potentially, there are boxes of VHS tapes from the same decade awaiting me to find them…but our paths have not crossed as of yet. *Yet*. The best time to check seems to be after the beginning of the month, since rent is due and that's when stuff starts moving around. Take what you need and eBay the rest! Or give it away! I don't care!

In cities, people move out and void their lives of short-term useful stuff like canned food, a secondary TV set, et cetera. Actually, this happens everywhere, but your likelihood of benefitting from it is greatly increased by the social density of a city. However, college towns afford a one-time shot at 'tons of useful crap' at the tail end of May. Futons, bikes, food, food, food, books (which often can be resold to campus bookstores for shocking amounts of money), and, well, all kinds of fun. If you're looking to furnish an apartment, this is your best bet. It you're looking to make money by selling stuff online or at a yard sale, or trade bike parts for records or something, this is also your jam. Heck, I can't think of a single reason you shouldn't check college trash come the end of the year. Trust me on this one. Once I found a handheld metal detector! However, after two years of frisking people and identifying metal objectives, I ultimately threw it away. So it goes…

I Can't Believe This, Either: The Only Story I'll Ever Write Containing the Word ▓▓▓▓

This story is a whopper. Everybody has one: that over-the-top ridiculous coincidence you couldn't plan, make up, or even hope to plan or make up, and this is one of mine. It's hands down my best dumpster story. Way better than the time the night shift guy caught me and Doug standing, inside the dumpster, knee-deep in donuts at Krispy Kreme. (We locked eyes, didn't say a word, and he offered a bag of donuts in quiet admonition. We win again!)

So, this one time I was biking around Savannah at, like, 3 a.m., and I decided, since I was passing near it, to check the dumpster at the video/magazine store. Much like a corporate chain bookstore, this particular shop threw away all their coverless magazines monthly, and every so often you can find *Maximum Rock'n'Roll* or design magazines like *Print* or *Adbusters*. I stopped by, threw back the lid, came across some magazines, but was immediately intrigued by a huge cardboard box that was both taped up and really heavy. Double bonus! My assumption was that the coffee shop that neighbored the magazine/video store had trashed a busted coffee maker (one made of metal that I could recycle for free money).

In the dim 3 a.m. light of this cobblestoned alley, I thought I saw tea labels under the tape. Maybe this was twenty pounds of old tea and teapots! This box held all my dreams and hopes! A veritable morass of good fortune condensed into one box—and I found it!

At this point, I assumed that whatever was in the box was wholly necessary to my worldly contentment, so, regardless of its contents, it was coming home with me. A crude balancing act and a half-mile on my bike got me home by 3:30 a.m. and I threw my new purpose in life on my bed, grabbed something pointy, and ripped it open. Thoughts of endless chocolate bars, pounds of Corey Feldman/Haim VHS tapes, heck, suitcases of money—it was all potentially my trash-reality! I pulled back the cardboard and…and…and…

…Slumped down to my knees, eyes as wide as beach balls, and glazed over at my new collection of damaged-in-shipping dildos! Fake penises everywhere! Something in the ballpark of seventeen brightly and oddly-colored artificial male reproductive organs, all somewhere dented or dropped or imperfect in some way, sitting on my bed looking awkward (as my sheets were Batman-themed). Furthermore, I'll happily admit that I'm not really paving any new ground for the sexual revolution, which is to say that I had (and have) no use for seventeen sex toys. Heck, I can barely do *anything* with seventeen of the same thing: toothbrushes, shoes, staplers, you name it. There was even a shattered penis pump, as well as this hilarious item designed to resemble a mouth... That one cracked me up. It even had fake stubble on the chin! I love that kind of detail, because what it made up for in mouth detail, it lacked in 'eyes', and instead just came to a flat plane. Like half a human face after a sawblade accident! The point is that I didn't need any of this, and, moreover, I could only assume that (against all reason) everyone I knew and respected would show up at my door at this exact moment. Why? I have no idea. Would it really have been that big of a deal? No, most likely not. However, getting the surplus of dildos off my bed and out of my life was the most crucial purpose in my existence.

This is precisely what I did. I boxed it back up, ran to someone else's dumpster—a nearby restaurant—and negated the past hour of my life. There are times when I wish I'd kept them for practical joke purposes, or to enliven some of my penpal relationships, but more often than not, I'm one hundred percent okay with my decision. The story was totally worth it. Oh, and to retroactively apply some logic: It turns out that the video/magazine store housed an extensive and sizable 'back room'. I had no clue, but now I know. And so do you. We all win!

More Incredible Moments in Vagrancy!

It's been a hard-fought downhill battle to underachieve these incredible moments in vagrancy. To turn up my nose to hygiene, the concept of cleanliness, and good ideas in general: This is no task for the meek. Or perhaps I'm aimlessly justifying some of the stupider moments in my life. And these are two of those instances.

One time after biking my Sunday afternoon dumpster route—a fifteen mile string of backroads that connect four grocery stories in Savannah, Georgia—I came to the Food Lion on the *far* southside and pulled a 'kind-of-frozen-but-on-the-way-out-because-it's-97-degrees' half-gallon of ice cream. It was melting! Panic sets in! Gears start turning and the next thing I know, I've transformed an ice cream carton into one big Push Pop: a hard, firm squeeze on the sides, and an entire half gallon of ice cream went shooting toward my face. A lot went in my mouth, a ton went all over my hands, and, inexplicably, all of it got in my beard. It was extremely worth it. It you've never eaten something with the intent of being messy behind a grocery store, I suggest you try it sometime. It is liberating. I'm all about destroying some socioeconomic lines. (Or free ice cream. It's one of those.)

The second moment isn't story-worthy, but it found me eating some organic peanut butter out of a glass jar that had shattered, while inside the dumpster itself. This is only 'incredible' because I would find a bagel, turn one hundred and eighty degrees, dip it in peanut butter, and then pick out the bits of glass…all while standing knee-deep in the Kroger megadumpster. From your waste we eat! Prying back your metal skin, we make a feast of your guts! *Trash can*nibals! *Yeah!*

I read this in the liner notes of a Zegota album: something about bike-riding as a radical act, choosing the pro-earth option as opposed to driving, polluting, or wasting gas…I feel the same way toward dumpster diving. It's basically extreme recycling, like pirates stealing the neglected trash-booty from landfill barges. Think of it this way: If you choose the route lined with trash bags, half-eaten everything, and tons of porn, then you can be the last line of defense for the earth in a smelly, seems-like-it's-not-getting-much-better battle. Perhaps it's best stated simply: There are free things being thrown away right now and you can go pick them up, use them, not pay for them ever, and this way it doesn't go to waste! Seriously, how do we *not* all win? Exactly! Now get out there, go around back, and liberate some awesome stuff!

Some fun places you could (and should) check out are grocery stores, bakeries, juice factories, catering places, office supply stores, thrift stores, anywhere that's going out of business, libraries, colleges (especially around graduation), bookstores, REI, camping places, self-storage units, art stores, bagel places, donut shops, and, well, I'm sure you've figured it out by now: If they sell it, they trash it. Looking for distributors works well, too, as a little phone book and Internet research can really pay off. It's also a good idea to check the address on whatever you just ate and return with your backpack. Then send me a postcard about whatever you found and I'll trade you something. Well, probably. Ha!

Odds & Ends from the x912x

Nine-one-two? That means Savannah, Georgia, a town known for thousands of plague victims buried beneath ninety percent of downtown, really heavy music, cockroaches swarming everything (just like the end of *Creepshow*), and more than anything, my three-year home that provided ten years of stories. Living in a town so dense and wrought with 'old money' tends to either invite you in if you can afford it (and if you're reading this, you can't) or to reject you—

meaning, you reject it back. All the fancy hotels and their amenities begged to be unlawfully 'borrowed.' We'll swim in your pools, eat your breakfast, sleep on your roofs...but you're never getting our money!

Our plan was in action as we rode across the bridge, heading toward the twelve-story hotel on the north side of the river. We'd soaked up sun at their pool and picnicked all over their everything, so why not sleep in their hammocks? Surely not because it's a bad idea.

And yet, after a late night ride back over the bridge as I laid out my sleeping bag on an outdoor hammock, it occurred to me that my warm body and blood-filled pheromones had fully polarized and I became the mosquito magnet that I was born to be. Helpful tip: When you're camping or sleeping *en plein aire*, bring something to put in your ears that *isn't* every mosquito on the Eastern seaboard. That idea—my reality for seven hours—sucks. (Pun very much intended. Thank you, thank you.)

Being woken up by landscapers wasn't that bad, or even awkward for that matter, and neither was waking up to realize that my friend Andy didn't sleep at all that night, but instead consciously swatted mosquitos for the better part of the evening. The grandest logjam of them all asserted itself nearly two hours later as I reached into my rear saddlebag and expected donut holes from the day prior. Instead, my greeting was around four hundred fire ants trekking about my food, bag, bike, and now my arm and shoes. I trashed the donuts, submerged my bike bags in the Forsyth Park fountain, and sustained eight or so fire ant bites. My right hand inflated to a comical *Simpsons*-esque proportion and my foot fattened up so much that I couldn't get it back in my stupid shoe. Lacking the adrenaline shot I needed to help drain myself naturally, I instead sliced up some garlic with my pocket knife, purposefully keeping the blade wet with garlic 'juice,' and stabbed both my feet and hand a bunch to 'bleed' it, later packing it up with the cut garlic. Did this help? Well, I didn't get infected.

Am I recommending borderline self-mutilation for the sake of a 'quick fix'? Um…no. But I did get a wicked scar and a totally un-heroic story to couple it with. Lessons to retain from this idiocy: Avoid fire ants, eat more garlic, don't put your bike on top of ant hills for any amount of time, and stab yourself only if the ends justify the means. Oh, and never pay for anything at hotels. The more expensive they are, the harder they fall…

Homeless, Not Hopeless

This one takes place at a dead time in my personal history, not due to a lack of things happening or anything along those lines, but rather because it was before I rode my bike much. I won't debate or argue the assumed equation 'Matt = bikes'—that's fairly on point—but there was a time when I skateboarded and walked everywhere, and this takes place in that unstirred lapse of my life. I can say now, in my uncharted sea of retrospective knowledge, that if I had owned a bike at this point, I probably wouldn't have a better story, and it certainly wouldn't culminate with a broken foot and explaining to a cop why my I.D. had blood all over it…

Doug and I were *really good* at email. I mean, we talked daily from one dorm room in the mountains to another four hours away in the Piedmont flatness, and we tackled both surface-level nonsense and weighted thoughtful nonsense as well. The majority of conversations centered on taking theories and ideals offered in Thoreau's *Walden* and how to apply them to the 'modern world' in which we ate trash. Over time, a plan formed: more an experiment than anything solid, but even at our young, hyper-idealist state, we knew the results would make for good discussion. In short, it was a plan that would assure us each a good story (stories being our currency of choice).

The idea was, and is, very simple: You leave your room/house/job with only a backpack and no money whatsoever, and stay 'outside' for the entire weekend. The *idea* of this excursion (in theory) was to learn that you could live without things that you thought you need, like a tent, sleeping bag, and, atop the pyramid, money. Furthermore, inventive ways around prescribed living would be McGyvered and unearthed. And, really, wouldn't it be nice to know that *if* we hit that tipping point in which we were stuck on the streets for a bit, then we'd be slightly more confident that we wouldn't starve? Exactly! So, on Friday after class, I put my Poison The Well hoodie (that should effectively 'date' this tale, huh?) in my backpack with my sketchbook and a pen. That was *all*. And I left my room.

Now, stating that I did some 'hard time' on the streets would be grossly unfair and painfully naïve. This was Boone, North Carolina, a small college town with a citywide bedtime of 10 p.m. and *nothing* resembling crime (save frat parties that get out of hand and some great urban legends about murders in the library crawlspace). But having nowhere to sleep in an urban area is similar, no matter where you are.

I wandered around downtown for a bit while brainstorming the food situation. The only successful dumpster diving I'd done at this juncture was popcorn at the movie theater and bagels at bagel places. I roll my eyes in retrospective embarrassment at how I had checked restaurant trash. You'll find only half-eaten leftovers mixed in with napkins, empty Lysol containers, and the unusable parts of meat or vegetables. In a word: gross. In two: revoltingly inedible. In a ton of words that I'm not going to bother counting: A good rule of thumb—dumpstered wisdom, if you will—is that anywhere serving cooked food is probably a *bad* place to try and find edible sustenance. On the 'so-rare-I've-never-seen-it' off-chance that they cook an entire entrée mistakenly, you'd still need to cross your fingers that they don't eat it and that, upon trashing it, this particular meal gets its own germ-free container. If I found something like that, untouched and still warm, then I'd assume it was poisoned.

Back in grounded 'reality,' I came up empty-handed and -stomached. The great loophole of the Homeless Not Hopeless project is that fasting for two days isn't hard. Keep in mind, though, that we were in search of stories. I still didn't know to check supermarket dumpsters yet, nor would it have mattered as the only ones I knew about had compactors. So, naturally, I walked in the 'out' door of the dining hall ten minutes before closing and staked my claim as the king of all neglected French fries—and ate all my subjects!

I emerged full and pretty content, too. I'd never done that before: going straight for neglected-but-not-trashed food. I stand in firm and wholly unmoving opposition to wastefulness, so playing 'cleanup eater' helped solidify my street cred, too. Or something.

I left and it was dark. Moments ago, the town seemed dormant and positively *inviting*, but once the sun gives up for the day, the warmth retracts and you're left with an uncaring, cranky giant. The familiar becomes intimidating. Think about it: Daytime means you can hang out in libraries, climb trees, play on playgrounds, lay in the grass…but try to do these at night and you'll get in some weird, troublesome situations. Having nowhere to go during the day is seen as 'carefree' whereas the same situation at night is considered 'threatening'. Go figure. Given this dilemma, I piddled around aimlessly in the twenty-four-hour supermarket, justifying the concept of staying awake walking the aisles until sunrise, at which point I could legally fall asleep anywhere my head would fit. However, tiredness is not one to be argued with, so I left, wandered around back, and started giving the roof my bedroom eyes.

There was no ladder, yet there sat an air conditioning unit designed to resemble the Aggro Crag while burping odd noises wildly, which coalesced into a gentle, mechanical whisper, beckoning, *"Maaatttt...cliiimb meee...and sleep on the roooooff..."*

When the 'Crag' talks, you listen. So now I'm on top of a Harris Teeter, excited that this will most likely be an okay place to sleep. Rooftops emanate safety in the sleeping department. I always figured it was because nobody can see you, much less wake you up by stealing your wallet, calling the cops, or biting off your ear. Or, well, whatever. The point is that rooftop sleeping is (occasionally) *great*.

I walked over to one side of the roof and lay down by the two-foot retaining wall (the part of the castle you'd duck behind during an arrow attack). I put on my hoodie, stared at the moon, and smiled myself to sleep, fervently wondering how Doug was doing...

...Uh oh! I woke up! Something was poking me in the face, and it was cold, wet, and seemed to pelt me intermittently. Rain? Really? Ugh. A moment of panic set in. I have no idea why, but I recall thinking that I had to get off the roof *immediately*. So much so that instead of walking back to the air conditioning unit, I eyed the ground, guessed I was about eleven feet up—crawling over the edge, hanging off the corner, doing some 9.8 meters per second math in my head—and let go. At 3:20 a.m. In the rain. And the dark.

It turns out that it was over fifteen feet down and I managed to land badly, cracking my right foot and, trying to 'roll it off', forced a rock into the palm of my hand. This is a common skateboarding injury, so I was used to it. But this one was a *bleeder*. Broken foot, bloody hand, tired, cold, in the rain, and my bed—indoor and safe—was just across town... have you predicted the cop-out yet? Did I publically undercut my own credibility? Did I *care*? At that point, I didn't. So I went home.

The aforementioned police run-in was a non-event. He stopped me because I was walking at 4 a.m. looking sketchy, which I understand. I looked like trouble: a bloody, limping wreck, but on *my* side I looked like a privileged white kid who wanted to be 'homeless' for eight hours so that I could brag about it to my friends. I wanted to use these successful experiences to prove a point. I didn't know exactly what it was, but I was sure that this was the way to figure it out. I would single-handedly level the playing field, open closed eyes, break open closed ear drums... but it's hard to see straight when you get blood all over your idealism...

I came back defeated, but instead of remaining down, the choice was made to learn from this. I'd think things through a bit more, such as not getting into sketchy situations unless I *have* to. In short: Be smarter and understand the 'cause→effect' relationship. And it worked, because every night I've slept in an 'unconventional' situation—KFCs, under/beside bridges, both abandoned and totally occupied buildings—I've come out on top. It's all been smiles and personal hi-fives since that first debacle. Homeless not hopeless means more now than it ever did back then.

Independence Day!

I sincerely hope that you're sitting down, as this story... well, it ends like I had hoped it might, meaning it's a distance-biking story with a happy, 'successful' ending. It's bizarre, I know, but the overriding *purpose* of this bike trip was (in keeping with my established themes) a total failure. Once again, I will smack my forehead in hilarious disappointment. So, get ready.

In retrospective rationalization, I think that *this* particular bike effort was the seed that germinated into my 'long rides for life' journey. If events in one's life read like a book, major shifts being chapter breaks, this bike ride would read as a preface. A really awesome preface, and yet one that I forget about because it was all contained within twenty-six hours... not nearly lengthy enough to merit retelling, right?

On the evening of July 3rd, 2001, I was quietly considering the upcoming holiday. I'm not one for anything resembling political discussion, so a weighted debate or diatribe on the concept of cultural freedom is best used on someone else. My abilities excel on a much smaller, personal scale. This is to say that I defined 'independence' within my own life that evening in as many ways as I could: parental freedom, financial freedom, social freedom (that last one basically means not feeling as thought you're directly relying on anyone). I don't think that this is a fair idea (as it goes against communities and friendships, two organizations I put a ton of faith in) but I also like to know that one can retain the 'self'. What is a group but a collection of individuals, right? Well, anyway, I wanted to rely on my bike and me while keeping doors propped open in the event that I needed something. I also happened to be visiting my mom's house in North Carolina, which meant that meals and beds and roofs and clean clothes were all free. (Love-based exploitation can still feel like exploitation!) And, lastly: the almighty dollar, the green paper fence we fight daily, yet never consider burning... rejected also! Even if it's only for one day, realize that you can make it twenty-four hours without buying anything.

The three pillars stood in place, and on this Independence Day, I would declare my personal independence from money, parents, and, well, normal processes of functioning life. I took money out of my wallet, put air in my 'bought-in-eigth-grade' mountain bike, and brought a backpack filled with a hoodie and a water bottle. No sleeping bag! No money! No plans and nooo problem! Apart from, rather obviously, my plan to bike around downtown Raleigh with a bike fit for a ten-year-old on some dirt hills. Whatever! I had fireworks to catch! Somewhere!

Actually, I did have some extremely tentative plans. That night, while checking that my bike was still in real working condition, I happened upon the local library dumpster and dredged up about fifteen books: mostly hardcover James Michner nonsense, and at first light of this discovery, it occurred to me that I could sell them back to this weird bookstore on the other side of downtown, a nasty, gross drive, and an abysmal bike ride…why not? It gave Independence Day a directed purpose while leaving the day totally open for 'whatever.' Perfect! I went home and slept, excited for the ridiculous possibility tomorrow brought.

I'm awake! Backpack on and water bottle filled, I turned down 'free-because-my-mom-bought-them' bananas. Not today! You can take that kindness and run it up a flagpole! With my tattered metaphoric rag flying high, I hopped on my bike and headed toward Raleigh. Within the first ten minutes, I had already made enemies with the books on my back—specifically, their weight.

On I rode, stopping at nearly every dumpster that could

be interesting and coming up pretty empty-handed…until I crested some hill near the Gold's Gym and dollar store and wacky recycling dump-thing. "Dollar store," I thought, "surely I'll find something in your trash to break my unlucky streak and then get tons of food at every dumpster from here on out." A great deal of 'travel success' relies on breaking a luck streak—bad, specifically—but it also goes in the opposite direction. Fingers crossed, I tossed back the lid to find…

Potato chips! One bag's worth! And beneath that, an oversized VHS tape with…oh…uh…naked…oh…right. Great. The porn streak continues: My talent for discovering naked people exploiting sex goes nearly unmatched, to my knowledge. If you are better at finding pornography than I am, then congratulations. You should not, however, care or flaunt this…talent? No. This is a curse. A glossy, overly-tanned curse.

Take chips. Leave porn. Keep biking. Pass things; things pass me. Boring. I stopped at a handful of grocery stores that eventually allotted me four banana nut muffins. Not bad luck, but certainly less that I've become accustomed to.

After over thirty miles of bike riding and water drinking, I could see the bookstore on the horizon. What began as five pounds of books (or maybe 'a backpack-full' is more on point) now felt like four hundred pounds of concrete, sweat-laden and sticking to my back, and so the bookstore meant relief beyond anything I could fathom. I rolled up to the sidewalk, dismounted, leaned my bike against the glass storefront, and headed in. And by 'headed in', of course I mean 'jammed my wrist on the handle since when I pushed it, the deadbolt caught, and the door didn't go anywhere save into my face.' Of course.

In my personal effort toward independence, I tripped on the simplest 'given' of this holiday: Nowhere is open! They're all off being independent! Ahhh! Irony is a dish best served out of a sweat-soaked backpack. Disappointment not being something I care for, I laughed it off, put the trash books—orphaned, smelly literature—in a box, sat it outside their door, and scribbled a message of both freedom and neglect. 'Free books—I don't want them! You might!' The independence theme shone through like a beacon of apple pie and TVs and red, while, and polluted blue! And I was still rejecting the lot of it!

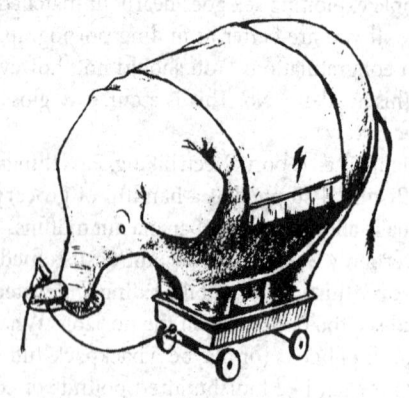

SELF-PROPELLED TRAVEL FOR LIFE!!!

The bookstore plan had set, and the sun was following suit. Now, I just needed to find a place to sleep and some dinner to eat. I ate my chips, left my muffins untouched, and headed downtown. During the ride toward the city, it also occurred to me that it was Friday—the first of the month! That meant that art galleries get 'down' for a couple of hours and throw free food at you and act confused if you don't eat it! Looks like I would be breaking my 'light-brown diet' streak with vegetables and fruit! We'll topple their houses, put bricks through their windows, but the pyramid remains! In this case, I'm referring, rather poorly, to the food pyramid. Another institution that I'm bent on sticking out my tongue at. I digress. Again.

After a bit more backtrack-biking, I was downtown again, surrounded by art galleries that were literally hurling food into my mouth! I enjoyed and harshly judged their artistic efforts, and I ran into a couple friends of mine. (Friends with floors and couches I could stay on! But I didn't want that—not today.) Doug, however, did offer that a building that once housed five stories of something was not only abandoned, but only 'maybe locked.' It's worth trying! Why not? I hope this decision doesn't fall too far outside my staunchly independent paradigm...it was only advice, so...I'm still okay! And I retained the freedom to choose that I *would* try to find this building, which means that the day must go on. These colors run deep! Or bike deep! Or something something!

Five wandering miles of flashlight-less sidewalk biking dropped me outside the building in question. It was five stories and it was very much abandoned, as evidenced by untended grass and cracked windows. Yet the entire fourth floor's lights being on challenged this. There weren't any cars in the parking lot or even near the place, so I assumed the possibility of a timer for lights that someone neglected. Sure! Plausible.

I didn't own a bike lock, as I only owned a Giant brand P.O.S. I was riding that didn't merit a lock, so I searched for a place to hide it in the bushes. While I'm sure that my bike would have been fine, my daylong attachment to this steel beast had morphed into a form of Stockholm syndrome. Well, more like Linus of the *Peanuts* crew. (My bike is his blanket in this case.)

I found the unlocked and broken door, and decided to just bring my bike in with me. It was extremely dark in this building but I managed to find the stairs and not bang my bike into too much. My unnerving fear of the fourth floor lights being on had become a belief that an entire floor of hungry cannibal squatter-folk were waiting for a ripe idiot to crest their horizon. Ergo, I was *unbelievably* quiet on my stair climb, something hard to do when you're shouldering an entire bike up five flights of stairs. Crossing by the fourth-floor door, I think I actually held my breath, standing fully prepared to literally *fight* for my freedom! Or at least throw my bike and run!

However, I made it to the roof access in one sighing piece and I immediately propped the door shut with some two-by-fours and cinderblocks. Me, my bike, a half moon, and the roof—what sounds like a sitcom was my present reality. I sat toward one corner and as 9 p.m. rolled around, fireworks started from, like, seven different directions! I had a 360-degree view of colored, bursting madness: a metaphor for both American history and, in my corner of life, personal liberation. Even if it is small-scale independence, at that moment, it meant (and means) a lot to me. As the displays faded, I fell asleep with no covers, shoes on, and a backpack for a pillow. I slept great.

The next morning was somehow exactly what I wanted it to be. I woke with the sun and with three ravens bouncing about fifteen horrifying feet from my head. I think the ravens wanted my bran muffins. I ate one and split the second with them. It seemed fair.

I climbed down, bike and all, at about 7 a.m., and stood next to that abandoned building with such a feeling of accomplishment and possibility. It's similar to the moment when you realize that you don't die if you fail to eat everything on the food pyramid, or when you don't visit the dentist for a year or so and it turns out that you're just fine. The realization summates as this: There are hundreds upon thousands of ways to live your life, these ways of doing things you've been led to believe have only one approach or outcome. Not true, and in order to understand that, you must live it. Start small. Bike somewhere you had only driven to, sleep in your kitchen, make music with trash, sew up a hole in your shoes instead of buying new ones...and when you accomplish the small stuff—then go big! Get bus tickets to towns you've never heard of! Sleep anywhere the moon can rise! Get rid of an ear infection with garlic instead of a doctor's visit! It can be done: I'm walking, uninsured proof!

The day that I proceeded to live was right from a movie. It seemed like it cut straight from action to next action without pause for anything. I think I actually lived a montage of things one can do alone and remain extremely happy and satisfied with life. I biked to the used bookstore, bought *Of Mice And Men* for a quarter from the 'crazy crap for a quarter' wall, then took it to the Rose Garden and read the entire thing. I also had picked up two vintage postcards at the bookstore, so I wrote two friends, then left. The NC State library provided a great view of town from the seventh story, and as I neared the 24-hour mark from when this all started, I began biking back toward my mom's house. A visit to the art museum elicited an hour-long conversation with some guy from New Jersey—a flurry of ideas, staunchly different backgrounds, and ultimately agreeing that following your dreams and personal goals is the essential ingredient to a fulfilled life. If you allow it, you can have some really incredible conversations with people whom you would never expect to.

As I talked to this guy in the art museum, I shook my head in astonishment that he felt the same way about so many things—love, artistic creation, travel, inspiration—and he was a forty-something married guy! The conversations that I always think should happen at punk shows (yet rarely do) can be found anywhere! Most recently, I lost myself in excitement as a fifty-year-old limo driver told me his dream of living on a boat in the Caribbean. For some, these dreams are horizons—a mark to run toward, to give motion and drive to their lives—but to others, those willing to hold their breaths and hope for success, they understand that we stand on horizons each day, and that no one fears heights but only falling.

I left the museum and idly bounced thoughts and plans about my head all the way back to my mom's house. I failed to sell the books I'd found, making my one concrete plan a total flop on paper; yet, the overarching concept behind this Independence Day shined brightly.

The divide between 'real' things and 'physical' things has an obvious contrast: friends versus money, plans versus nice bikes, laughter versus…well, anything for sale. It's these 'real' things that I'm finding. These carve the definition of adventure—the excitement of possibility rumbles like a battery, shooting current through the frail conductors of our bodies. While all my adventuring is typically solo journeying, it is imperative to understand that my capabilities and aspirations are sustained by truly incredible friendships.

So friends, thank you.

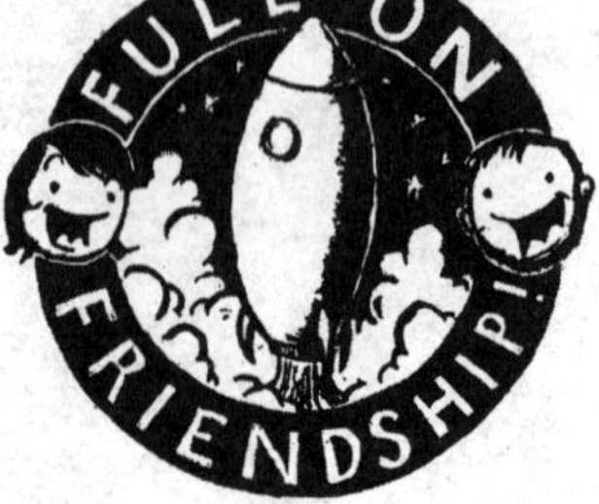
FULL-ON
FRIENDSHIP!

NEXT STOP ADVENTURE IV

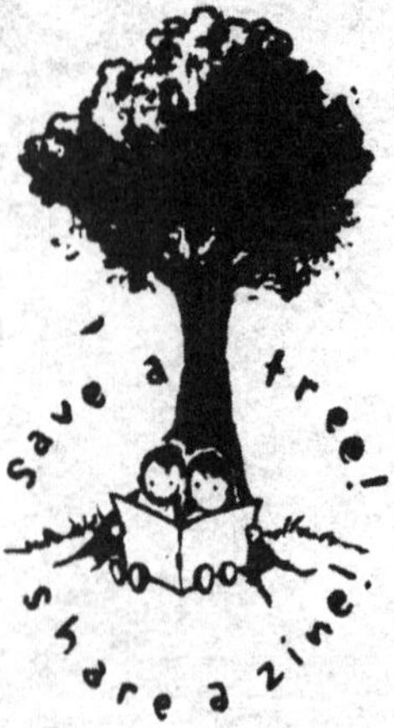
save a tree!
share a zine!

The Downside To Research: Or An Over-Thought, Under-Informed View Of Self-Publishing Today

WHEN ONE STARTS TO understand the process in which our environment is used up at the cost of selfish, human traditions, one has a much harder time morally justifying using those same processes with this new-found knowledge. Thanksgiving becomes a trying, difficult ordeal once a member of the family has extended the effort to learn about the life that the turkey led prior to the table, thereby turning dinner into an argument over the sanctity of life, both animal and *homo sapien*. Much in the same way, dumpster-diving bike enthusiasts cringe at the idea of buying new gear when used gear is unavailable, as they know that there is an ecological impact to their action, yet circumstances will not allow another option. It is in this vein I find myself cringing at the idea of writing another zine. My teeth grit at trees falling for this form of expression…I mean, all I'm doing is telling a story—something best done audibly, in my opinion, say, over a picnic, or biking, or while riding a train, or over a fire. And yet, here I am, debating just how small I can make the type to save space, reminding myself that I dumpster, recycle, and reuse a *ton* of paper, and that really, it's very simple to get ecologically friendly paper options as well.

Perhaps the more destructive element lies in a broader field. By writing a zine that covers well-worn territory on the subject of bike travel coupled with do-it-yourself ethics, am I really *adding* anything to the creative world? Is my brain simply recycling concepts, altering them from ideas into actions, only be to rewritten as ideas once more? Like the snake eating its tail, I will forever walk this line separating new ideas from gears spinning wildly out of control, circles upon circles upon circles. Is it possible to damage the mental world and to send a Trojan horse into the collective unconscious, masquerading as a new idea? Does the world *need* another story about me (or anyone) riding their bike longer than they should? What about riding a train for an absurdly long time? Does it even out the impact since neither of the aforementioned involved me polluting for travel? Biking produces no emissions, and the train was going that way *anyway*....

The Internet has backfired by providing too many options and ideas, and by disseminating too much information to too many people. Prior to email and chat rooms, I could be content knowing that no one I knew had tried to ride a bike such a silly distance, and the idea of 'secret camping' was my own invention. Self-confidence was born of the capacity to think freely, without the stress of money or the reality of our defined world. Everyone has that moment of pure creativity and brilliance, in which something emerges clear from the ether and you claim this new idea as your own. Now, though, all ideas are not only accessible on the Internet, but they likely have newer words to simplify talking about them within their dedicated online communities. What was 'secret camping' has become 'stealth camping', a common term among distance cyclists.

I don't mean to say that biking is 'dead' because 'everybody does it' or that 'everything is dead because everyone's done it.' I'm stating that we should never stop moving forward within ourselves. Beyond irony, beyond post-*post*-post art forms, well beyond our current capacities to see the world as we see it, there are larger dreams appearing as pinpricks in a dark sheet, but shining like the sun right behind it. My goal in bike touring, in travel, in painting, in *living* is to try to find routes to these new ideas. New situations serve as catalysts to electrify the brain, to kick-start the frontal lobe into full function, to create a new color, to define a new sound, to conceive art beyond all comprehension. Every person with a beating heart is capable of something new.

In short (which it's already too late for), I offer this collection of stories as a rough blueprint to be interpreted any way you see fit. Inspiration is simple to cross-apply; just because I chose a bicycle to put my effort toward, it doesn't mean you can't take an inspired turn for your cabinet-building, trapeze artistry, or opening up your third eye. The point is to do something. Find something that you have a real passion for and push it well beyond the edge of comfort. Opportunity isn't a wandering ghost, sliding in and out of your life at random; it's more like the window in the room where you're sitting. It may be nice to look out, but once you're on the other side of it, the chances are that you won't be looking back. Instead of life as a trail in the woods splitting into two paths, reinvent the model to include all dimensions, time, and space. Life as a three-dimensional field, extending infinitely in all directions, endlessly, and make your choices based on this. Science has proven the universe to be expanding, and our realm of possibility acts the same. There will always be new ideas, the catch being that you will never find them on the Internet. You can find inspiration, maybe, but the rest is up to you. A healthy model of the Internet might be an image of a famished snake, desperately choking on its own tail, inching ever closer to paradoxical oblivion. You get bonus points if you picture this in a swirling toilet bowl. Bob

Clark's terrifying and brilliant 1976 slasher *Black Christmas* said it best: "The calls are coming from inside the house!" That metaphor is a bit more esoteric, but what can I say, I love that movie. It's just like having a wart removed!

Summer Is The Best Holiday Of The Year

Seriously! If I learned anything from school (ha), it's that summer should be a holiday every year no matter what. I am officially claiming summer as the *Next Stop Adventure* holiday, which means I own the longest holiday on the planet. Cool. It starts whenever you feel like it's warm enough to bike around without wishing you'd brought a hoodie, and ends when you can't stop laughing because of what you accomplished.

Each winter I get a little stir-crazy and start to dream up schemes, scams, dumb inventions, and basically just start drawing long arrows across my atlas. Come summer, I do my best to connect all these little travel plans with one major theme, and eventually everything goes wrong, yet something really incredible happens anyway. It's like aiming for 'Plan B'. As I stood at the airport in Portland, Oregon with the summer of 2008 sprawling in front of me, my furtive made-up plans scribbled on paper, and a one-way ticket in my pocket, I got 'that feeling' in my stomach. Like the writer penning the novel with no clue where it's headed, I had my beginning and wasn't concerned with the ending. I'd cross that bridge when I came to it. I just quoted myself! Lame!

I flew to North Carolina, where I saw a wonderful friend get married and then played catch up with tons of other friends who now call Raleigh 'home'. It wasn't terribly adventurous (unless you're horrified of people), so let's skip ahead. I needed to get to Staunton, Virginia, which is in the mountains near the northwest corner of the state, and my beloved bike was over 3000 miles away in a storage unit with everything else I owned. I brought a backpack (one I made from an old tablecloth, and way more legit than it sounds), one extra t-shirt, a different pair of underwear, the usual pen with paper, cell phone, and two books.

Anyway, with no self-sustaining means of transport, I scoured Craigslist ads for someone heading to Virginia and settled on a sixty-year-old man driving to Richmond at 7 a.m., because that sounded awesome. Also, it was crazy cheap, which is the prevailing denominator for the adventure lifestyle: 'free, or super cheap'. That's the way we do things. Well, that's the way I do things, at least. If you're on Team Cheap, then welcome to the inclusive 'we' pronoun!

There's something inherently embarrassing about convincing your mom to drive you to a random address to meet some old guy to get a ride to a different state when it's obvious that you are bringing a backpack and clearly have no real plan. I know I'll be fine, but how do you translate that to your mother? I'm sure astronauts say the same thing, "Don't worry. It'll be fine," when they have no definitive clue about the outcome. These are totally unplanned events, pivoting and hinging on chance and luck, yet capable of branching off into a new set of circumstances in one moment. You can only plan the choice directly in front of you; everything after that choice is floating, wandering nonsense. This is the same logic one would use to impress that they were a 'seasoned pro' at reading *Choose Your Own Adventure* books. Can you be *good* at luck? If you make your own, you can. That's my personal take on luck and one that I'm trying to force into reality, thereby making it 'fact'. Anyway, it was with puzzled courage that I told my mom I would be fine, as I climbed in a 7000-year-old man's pickup truck. I got bonus points because the address where we met up was a mailbox denoting a plot of land—not a house, nor anywhere livable, but rather an entitlement, part one of a multi-step plan that eventually results in a home. Hugs are exchanged, phone calls promised, and windows rolled down to guarantee eye contact. It really never gets any easier for me; I imagine it is all the worse for my mom.

There's a funny thing about having supportive parents: They want you to do anything you can dream of in the beginning, yet as you settle on your goal and show momentum toward starting it, the excitement turns to unmoving concern. On some level, everyone wants to sail around the world or bike across the country or climb a mountain—to do something—and most friends and family will feed that notion. "You *should* bike across the country! How cool would that be? Oh, I wish I'd done something like that when I was younger…" The responses sound automated, a generic reply born from imagining just how fun a journey like that would be. Yet as the plans settle, the ambiguous becomes grounded, the timelines become set, and attitudes turn to, "So...are you really going to do this? Have you thought about 'whatever'?"

I'm sure that it's hard on parents and friends, but let's be supportive. If you have an idea, something you *really* want to do, then learn what you need in order to do it and just go for it. Most things are possible, and I assure you that everything in the world is more fun than a job for the whole summer. If you care enough about doing something, then you'll figure out the money and muster up the guts to do it. *Nothing* is that hard. Mom, consider this a 'thank you' for your supportive spirit, even in the face of totally haphazard nonsense. I love you so much!

But Then Again...

"Do you like music?"

When asked such a broad and obvious question, I think it's best to lie and answer 'no'. How can anyone not like music? Otherwise, you might find yourself well over an hour into one of *nine* CD-Rs recorded by the old dude giving you a ride with his nephew on keyboard (a kid, I'm told, who is about my age). Oh, holy freaking crap. Songs like "Ain't Goin' To That Hardware Store Again" with lyrics that are verbatim to the title and set to a 'wonky' electronic backbeat, composed of everything from computerized drums to boops and beeps to saxophone emulations. (Actual excerpt: "You were a jerk / You weren't nice / Didn't help me at all / Not going to that hardware store again / Not going to that hardware store again." To try this at home, murmur these lyrics like you've just had the air knocked out of you and these are your last emissions into the world of the living... Yep, you got it.)

If ever we could coin the term 'demo-button-core', then the time is officially upon us. I'm not sure what kind of response he was expecting, but apparently I wasn't providing it, as he would listen to a song for a minute then jump the next track, perhaps searching for our common ground through music, doing it in a way akin to shooting stars with a slingshot and expecting to hit one on the first couple tries, and realizing that this might be much harder than you originally thought. The feeling in the air was embarrassed accomplishment. Yes, this man had recorded a *lot* of music, elements of which were creative, but when played for an audience (me) who knows people in 'real' bands (um...sort of), his D.I.Y. songwriting just seemed so small and amateur, and I'm afraid that my repeated, unoriginal compliments caused him to realize that. This went on for at least a hundred miles, at which point I stopped talking and managed to fall asleep. That would be my first good idea in this text (perhaps the only one).

I was headed to Staunton, Virginia to hang out with my friend Nelly, a penpal-gone-friendship friend, and after the ride with the old man I was left in Richmond. I figured that it wasn't far and that I could hitchhike for the first time. Logically, I should have been dropped off near the highway heading toward Staunton, but I didn't know where that was and I wanted to give the appearance of *not* hitchhiking to this guy, as I find the best way to avoid concern and problems of that nature is to stretch the truth. So, I said that a friend was picking me up at Ellwood Thompson's, a local co-op grocery store, which was untrue, but totally feasible, so...almost true? That's where the power of lying resides—if it *could* happen, then you're golden!

I ate a banana, bought some little fun foods (snacks), backpacked them, and looked at my map until I decided I knew where to go. Then I walked about two hours in over ninety-degree ultra-sunny weather. The downsides are now making an early appearance: My backpack is a homemade one-strap messenger bag, which is great for big loads but distributes weight very poorly over, say, a very long walk. The scoliosis doomsday clock moves two minutes closer to midnight…kidding. I already have a slight case. *Slight*.

Hitchhiking Realities Versus Theories

Reader's note: The backbone of my hitchhiking writing was developed much like a scientific theory, in that I'll be asserting claims developed from assumptions about hitchhiking and then disproving all aspects of them with real experiences. This is, in fact, a very scientific process. Well, it's about to be.

When learning any new skill, you base 'facts' off of what you know to be true, off of knowledge ascertained from, well, wherever. Many times, like this one, I had hitchhiking ideas based on movies like *The Sure Thing, Thrashin', The Wizard, An American Werewolf in London,* and that one Aerosmith video from when I was in middle school. The point being that I had nothing too useful. However, all '80s movies indicate that hitchhiking is a total cakewalk: a short ten-minute window of eye contact and thumbs-uppery and then you're on your way. Depending on which movie your logic is from, you'll likely end up with some *crazy* stories, too, involving tons of money, unforeseen romances, or something happening at gunpoint. Culturally, I think we can all agree that, weird idiosyncrasies aside, even if you've never hitchhiked, you know exactly what to do. In theory.

Inexplicably, I caught the fourth car that passed me at a weird onramp in Virginia. I stood there for all of two minutes and was whisked away a whopping seven miles down the road by a well dressed guy in a nice, extremely air-conditioned BMW. Take notes here, as we'll be examining every possible combination of human traits in about five rides—like the *Extreme Ghostbusters* cartoon series, in which they replace the 'three white, one black' previous *Ghostbuster* racial makeup with 'one Hispanic male, one black male, a white goth girl, and a Russian kid in a *wheelchair*.' Unbelievable. That's fiction, and yet my findings fall more in line with that ultra-PC version of life than they do with 'reality', the mirrored labyrinth she is.

Following a sixty-six-degree, seven-mile joyride, I found myself waiting at a *huge* onramp with about four hundred yards of stopping space, which meant that the 'look back pity glance' was working in my favor. Twenty minutes and one white SUV later, I had a ride with a well-to-do lawyer who regaled me with stories of his college days spent hitchhiking to the beach and back. For a brief and fleeting moment, the class war had ended and we spent twenty miles laughing about our common ground as individuals of the same human race. I hated his vehicle and his salary; he detested my homemade bag, carefree beard, and artistic temperament. Yet in that dim light of commonality, we found a shared smile, and rode it out for a couple exits.

The universe gifted me with a thumbs up after that, because the lawyer came back to pick me up *again* and drive me for another twenty miles! Despite confusing the 'ride count' tally (is it three total or only two? Two-point-five?), this was a great gesture and one that afforded a lot more talking, reflecting, and (above all) meaningful glances that seemed to read, "Hey man, I understand..." He was not unlike the co-worker who also secretly loves that one Rancid song and pinpoints this in our quiet time together. Picturing the Venn diagram of our lives with the skinny almond in the center that contained 'hitchhiking, college-educated, white male,' I thanked him too much and waved goodbye. The next thing I know, I'm in the middle of nowhere with *very* little traffic. Hmmm. This might get harder. The road to hell may be paved with good intentions, but the road of good intentions is really hard to catch a ride on.

Back in the 'theoretical hitchhiking world,' I was stuck wondering, *Do I stay here, despite very little traffic, or do I walk to the next exit? Do I need a sign? Do I smile more? More eye contact?* The core dilemma of hitchhiking is that literally any car could pick you up. *Any* of them. When one, or say, three hundred, pass you, you're stuck wondering what you did wrong, and since you have all this time to think about it, you do just that. It's *that* exciting, seriously.

The internal debate concluded and I decided that the onramp situation was too 'few and far between' to get me anywhere besides annoyed. However, it is worth noting that a guy driving an eighteen-wheeler offered me a ride, which was *so* hard to turn down (as he was heading back east) because, unbeknownst to non-hitchhikers, the cab of a truck that size *is* the inside of a spaceship. Whirligigs, gizmos, things that light up and go '*boop*'...exactly. I almost went all the way back to Richmond to ride in that thing. The whole moment pulsed the line: "Roads? Where we're going, we don't need roads...."

After politely refusing the spaceship ride, I briefly walked to a state road where (at least in Virginia) hitchhiking is technically legal, unlike on the interstate, which is what I had been doing. For about an hour I stared at stuff, mimicked my shadow, and watched people leave the one gas station without looking at me. I was so out of it that I didn't even notice when 'awesome shirtless dude in white pickup truck' threw it in reverse and offered me a ride. The bonus to this ride was that he was headed quite a ways down the road, with the irreparable downside being that we had to 'stop by his house for a second to get this thing.' Amazing! Not sketchy! Calmingly normal! (None of these words apply at all!)

The aforementioned ride put me on a couch in a single-wide trailer, television blaring, baby screaming, and a cast of six or so people meandering about. The air smelled stale and flat, like inhaling chalk dust. The entire moment felt like old moldy carpet and wood paneling. Me being me, I did my best to be nice and wound up petting the dog for a nonstop thirty minutes, purposefully ignoring reruns of

Family Feud barking from the TV. When I got the word that we were ready to go, I smiled at the puppy and said something nice, the noticed that my hand had turned charcoal black from his fur. That's my official 'green light' on the 'yep, it's time to leave' board, as well as the 'bathe your dog because it's getting out of hand' front.

To make a steady stream of rides into a more concise, simpler narrative, here's what happened. The shirtless sketchy dude who insisted on looking directly at me every time I talked (yes, especially when we were driving) dropped me off on his way to an anger management / marriage counseling class, the title of which was code for 'Chill The F-Word Out' class, and I was immediately met with two cars stopping back to back. All of the sudden, I had the choice in the matter. Do I go with the young mother and five-year-old daughter, and be extra cordial to them both, and help to replace a possibly negative stereotype about travelers and punks with the friendly 'really sweet, artistic bearded guy'? Or should I choose the other ride, because, well, it was about ten feet closer and blasting better music?

Distance won out, I went with the 'alone guy,' and he drove me over two hours to exactly where I wanted to be, a Sunoco in Staunton, Virginia. Okay, to clarify: I didn't want to be at that gas station *per se*; however, it was in the right town. I got super bonus points because he (1) had air conditioning, (2) was a short-ish and super-ripped bouncer at a strip club in North Carolina (note: neither of those are bonus points, they're just facts) and (3) we talked for a long while and he eventually said, "Man, I'm really glad I picked you up". Can you beat that? Well, maybe…I mean, think of the fun stuff I could've helped to teach that five-year-old. Oh well. I got where I wanted to be. A gas station.

In closing the hitchhiking part of this story, it's worth noting that after a long two-hour talk while discussing plans, ideas, and life experiences, it's really strange to get out, shake hands, and then realize that you probably won't see this person again. I've gotten to know this person well, and the second the engine cuts off, then it's just over, we go back to the roles we were playing before, never really remembering the conversation, but recalling that it was meaningful.

Staunton!

The mark of a true friend, in this case, is the one who doesn't bother asking (or rather, knows not to ask) how you got to where you are. As far as I could tell, Nelly smiled and thought, *Hmmm, he probably just appeared here.*

I also found that my 'true friend' side came out, because instead of bragging and talking about how crazy it was to get up there, we talked about what we've been up to since last time we saw each other, all the projects we've been working on, and made dinner, and laughed a bunch. Way better than travel bragging.

Someplace Else Is Where I'm Always Trying To Get To: Or 'The Ground Is Made Of Lava' (So Keep Moving)

To-Live-A-Lie-Records-sponsored fastcore math list: 2-3-4-go!

➡ Greyhound from Virginia to Indianapolis
➡ Hitchhiked to Bloomington (thumb only! no sign!)

- Hung out with everyone at Microcosm Publishing
- All of the sudden, I was on tour with Microcosm
- Wandered across the Central Midwest area reading to people, eating everything not bolted down, and breathing vegetable oil from the RV powered by, well, you guessed it
- Had so much fun
- Greyhound part two: Chicago to Omaha

The Cyclical Nature Of Nebraska

How is it that I wind up in Omaha so often? I'm willing to bend my thoughts and logic to allow for some magnetic pull that's polarized my body's molecules so that I'm gently drawn toward eastern Nebraska. It's my personal magnetic north. It could be selective gravity…in physics, that's how it works—anything with mass pulls on anything else with mass, and it just so happens that the Earth is the biggest thing, hence, we get pulled toward it. If you have two particles in a vacuum, they will pull on one another, depending on how close they are (as well as their mass). I don't see why selective gravity would be any different, with the exception of about six billion reasons that would give my physics teacher an aneurysm. Maybe Omaha is some kind of portal to hell… like a black hole, but with weird religious nonsense backing it up. Or it could be where most nationwide public transportation ends up wandering through.

The point is that the plan was to meet with my friends Andrea, Mary, and Chris 'Two Thousand And Spaight' to get a ride to Onawa, Iowa to detassel corn for a month. I'll get to that in a moment. For now, I had a full twenty-four hours to kill in Omaha, so I wound up sleeping the night (well, the remaining single-digit morning hours) in the bus terminal and finally ventured out around 8 a.m.

Something weird happens when you're in a new town in the morning without any real place to be or obligation to oblige. My bookend was the next day at about noon, so that's twenty-seven hours to do anything I could think of. Literally *anything*. It's the freedom allotted by traveling and the reason that traveling *is* as fun as it is. It's due to a combination of mental distance from your 'expected' actions and a realistic distance (measured in miles) from home. If I lived in Omaha, there's no way I'd be up that early, and if I was, I would check my email, screen print some patches with an '80s movie playing in the background, cut up some fruit to put on soy yogurt and granola…boring stuff. Well, no, that's not fair—it's boring stuff to *read* about, and it's only semi-interesting to me. I like screen printing patches and eating fruit, but it's very normal. And that's the core of traveling: It's best defined in the negative, as what it *isn't*, such as not knowing what you'll do that day, where to get free food, where the nice kids hang out, where the good views of sunsets are, where abandoned buildings are, what times you can sneak into museums. Let me put it this way: If you were to be a visitor in the town where you now live and you'd never been there before, what would you do differently?

Since this new town was sprawled out in front of me, I went into wandering mode and played (read: crawled, jumped, did flips) on the excessive amount of 'corporate art' sculptures dominating the plazas of downtown. The majority of the 'bustling downtown' gives the appearance of a zombie movie set, devoid of movement with no one really around.

The lights change on cue...but for whom? It's like the beginning of *Day of the Dead*, but less messy...so it's like that scene at the end of *Night of the Comet* (minus the fancy car). Beyond the feeling of being recently abandoned, the rest of the town is laid out like some messed up playground with tons of roads running through it. I mean, what other town can you think of that has two huge slides integrated into the central park area? It's so much fun and it's actually a great way to meet other people in Omaha. Take note: Community-building by way of fun seems to work in Nebraska.

My day was spent finding books in the library dumpster, befriending the owners of the one punk record store in town (side note: I bought a Grimple CD there and the dude there was *so* excited that I picked it up, which sort of fast tracked our friendship), reading by the waterfront, and meandering to this weird park near the state line. I think it was an exclusive golf club (pun!) and for some reason (read: 'fear') they allowed me to fill my water bottles in their fancy bathroom.

Sundown is when things get more interesting because of the dilemma that the perception of public space changes when nighttime takes over. This is to say that laying down in a park during the day is considered lazy and enviable, whereas doing the same thing twelve hours later is homeless and troublesome. (This is much like flying a kite, because during the day, it's commonplace; at night, it's a surefire omen that something is terribly wrong.) It's a tricky line to be completely defined by the amount of light shining on the situation. Makes me wonder if homeless folk in upstate Alaska would sleep better during the unending sunlight. While it's too bright to be hassled, it's also too cold and desolate to want to be there.

Anyway, all theory aside and back in Omaha, I took a page from the 'embrace the nature of private space' while using some age and race and class privilege to spend the time between sunset and about 10 p.m. hanging out at a hotel (that was technically across the state line in Iowa, but I did walk there quite easily from Nebraska). I wrote letters and recollections about the day I just lived and coupled that with ideas about why traveling was still a good idea, promising to turn that into a zine at some point, which is now what you're reading. When I finally left, I didn't have a definite idea of where I might pitch my tent (or not). I wasn't sure where to go, so I gravitated toward an unfinished hotel that had rooms aglow with light reflecting off of shrink-wrapped furniture, yet the parking lot was mud and two-by-fours.

This may be obvious, but my personality (contrary to all detectives of the world) is such that if I see a brand new bed in an unoccupied room, I think, "Oh, perfect!" I would never consider that the door would be locked to prevent someone from stealing the new flat screen TVs adorning the walls or trashing the bathrooms for the fun of it. I wanted only to sleep and read there, and so when I opened the door and was met with spinning, loud whirling lights and alarms screeching toward the moon, I realized that I had to leave. The funny aspect was that my reaction was, "Ahhh, man," as I exhaled and rethought my plan, slowly walking off and dodging puddles. Had I been stopped by security or police, the logic would have undoubtedly been my only defense: "Put yourself in my shoes—that's WAY better than my tent!"

Luckily, I didn't have to engage anyone about this. I meandered to a standalone storage unit (the kind that look like a boxcar on a train) and erected my tent in the weeds, falling asleep quite promptly. Thanks, Omaha. Again.

Blastbeat Powerviolence List: Go!

- Got up!
- No cops!
- Walked into functioning hotel (the one with letter-writing) through backdoor; proceeded to eat breakfast and surreptitiously charge phone / hide my tent / be less obvious / oh, who cares at this point
- Walked back into downtown
- Met up with Andrea and Chris and Mary
- Drove away to detassel corn
- Omaha story *over*! (Cymbal crash! We're done! Put out the 7"!)

The Fine Line Of Explanation

So what have we read here? Some would read this as a story that sounds too much like 'a travel punk zine', which (in most senses) is very correct. There was traveling, I listen to punk, and the format I've chose to disseminate this yarn of a tale is a 'zine'. The themes of free food and public transit are explored, as well as the slight 'grifting' of hotel services for my personal gain. And this narrative unintentionally exudes the sentiment that if you're traveling, then you're doing something important. What worries me is that this type of story will be so embraced by some, while shunned and mocked by others. To address that, here's my theory:

Have you ever heard (and loved) a song by some band so much that you memorize the lyrics and see the band play it live—the crowd singing along with passion, excitement and timelessness filling the room, and you find yourself hugging your neighbor simply because they were there, too? Well, what happens when you find out that the particular song you've come to love and respect is a cover song, penned years ago by another seminal band of another era, or originally played by a band that was never credited at all? Either way, the effect is the same: taking an idea and altering it enough to confidently put your name behind it. An example is making a mixtape for someone. Someone else's hard work and countless hours of toil are borrowed without permission to express something you're (nearly) incapable of expressing yourself. Why do we get famous quotes tattooed on us rather than smartly worded comments we have come up with ourselves?

To me, the answer to all scenarios is the same. Amidst our years scurrying about the earth and flittering between safe and dangerous experiences, we hit on essential, shared moments of meaning and simplicity. We find times when the excitement of being alive is undeniably obvious. You can't help but smile or cry or yell or react in *some* way…

The band that covers the song winds up loving that song more than they did in the beginning. It means everything that it meant to the creator, and even more is gained by replaying it and taking the lyrics out of context and into another (perhaps knowing that those lyrics helped a band member cope with a personal hardship). Mixtapes are seen as well-planned gifts denoting thought and time spent, not haphazard collections of someone else's originals. And we get tattoos (well, I know I do) because they mean something important, as their weight carry these carefully chosen words that mean more *because* I didn't come up with it. All of this comes under the banner of 'appropriate borrowing', a concept I am quite aware of (and content with).

So... Zines?

Consider the evolution of the Internet, mass communication, and recording ability. Does a song mean less to you when discover it *is* a cover? Then what's going to happen when you find out that the original you just wrote has identical chord progression to a song by some other band that formed across the world in 2007? It's independently inventing something that already exists. There's a kid somewhere in the world who is looking at two bike frames and imagining what would happen if they were stacked on top of each other and welded together. In her own life, she has invented the tall bike, and to her, it means everything. The problem with the Internet and billions of hours of video online is that she can have that idea, get excited about it, and then see her idea parading around her computer from ten years ago. The moment that happens, it crushes idealism, innovation, and creativity, all in one technological mishap. It sucks! It really does! The more that the world inadvertently reminds you that you're not original, the less likely you are to try to be creative. I know people who consider certain movies to *be* their lives, as the characters perfectly mirror their own experiences through some glossy treatment while set to music. I mean, how many possible experiences *are* there in a 'life', right?

To link this back to my original point, I write, and will write, this zine as an inspirational landmark to both myself and, secondarily, to you the reader. I didn't write it so that I had 'written a zine.' Instead, this exists because these stories happened and that means something to me. I reread these occasionally to revisit my life, and I offer these stories to be enjoyed and pulled from by anyone else in the world. Take my singular view of a special experience in this adventurous, meaningful heap of words, and then make it your own.

In the simplest terms: Your life is exactly that—yours. Do anything you want to with it, since when you live the experience, it belongs completely to you.

This Is What Happens When You Meet A Stranger In The Alps

The idea was (as most good ones are) birthed in a moment of unhinged clarity. Here we are, three of my friends and myself, in western Iowa and a rad three-day music fest (Mauled By Tigers) this coming weekend in Chicago, a measly 497 miles to the right. We have nowhere to stay, no means of getting there, and all we have in on our collective backs is one tent (that comfortably fits two, *maybe*), four sleeping bags, and two changes of clothes each. Oh, and water bottles. We definitely had water bottles.

Anyway, seeing The Ergs!, The Bananas, Japanther, and Chinese Telephones (as well as potentially getting to see our friend Adam) sounded like too much fun; thus, excitement and question marks outweighed logic and foresight and we peered eastward, dreamy with hope. Then, we acted on that peering.

We drove about two hours into Iowa to my grandmother's house, ate dinner, looked at old photos, and climbed on rusty farm equipment. I can only speak for myself, but I had a blast, but that's probably because I got to see my grandma. No complaints here: She rules! As dawn met us the next day...okay, I lied through my face to my grandmother about why we were leaving our car in her driveway, claiming that some friends were picking us up to go visit Chicago, when (in reality) the plan was hitchhiking.

Two of the four of us had never traveled by such loose means and I wound up spearheading the charge, claiming blindly, "This will totally work! Just keep your spirits up and we'll have a blast!" which, mirroring my assertion, was true. I would never consider myself a leader; however, in this particular instance, I somehow rose to the top as the captain, likely because the whole expedition was my fault in the first place. Also, I revel in being 'the talker' during hitchhiking situations. I'll pass the time with 'Joe average motorist' using my two listening ears and an unending stream of 'no kidding' and 'oh, wow.' Feigned interest being a superpower of mine, coupled with insane optimism, I assured my cohorts that we'd be picked up in no time.

After about two hours on a small rural highway in Iowa, a woman picked us up in her pickup truck, assuring us that if we were willing to come home with her for a home-cooked meal, then we'd all be on our way to Chicago tomorrow! She was heading there anyway! And she was really good friends with David Letterman! Wait, wait, wait. Um...oh. I see.

We stopped at a grocery store somewhere west of where we started (net miles gained: negative seven) and followed her inside. A speedy meeting was held in the produce aisle in which we decided to ditch this woman and her home-cooked plans. You see, her nephew worked at this particular grocery store, so I approached him, a young hair-cutted lad of sixteen, and asked if he thought his aunt would actually take us to Chicago. This proved to be a good move on our part, because he sighed out a short "Nah…She's not going anywhere." Ceremonial nods and thanks were given, and we parted ways knowing quite assuredly that we would never, ever see each other again. Then we broke up with our captor and beat feet on the pavement toward the interstate. The goal was now clear: *Get out of Iowa, and do it quickly*. (Also, double-check the sanity of the next person to stop and pick us up, as they may have swallowed their own brainstem somewhere along the line.)

What followed was another series of rides that bridged little gaps between west and east. As I remember it, there was an ex-armored-car driver (who refused on 'legal grounds' to tell me how much money is transported in them), followed by two really sweet 'our age' kids from Iowa City (yep—four people in the backseat for an hour!). I've spent some time in Iowa City, which helped a lot in the 'getting around' realm, and we ended up staying the night with a friend of my younger brother's (thanks, Brian! You've saved my life *twice* in the Midwest!) and managed to remain both well-fed and healthy, thanks to vegan brownies at the co-op and free bread from the cool guy with the garlic tattoo and Saves The Day shirt.

Also of note was our hitchhiking approach. Keep in mind that we totaled four people with one backpack each, which may sound like a lot, but most cars on the road during the day are one person driving alone, so we *can* all fit. Five people would be ridiculous, but four was just fine. Andrea and I would typically work the 'front end' of the onramp with a cute cardboard sign, while Mary and Chris were fifty feet further with a 'second chance' sign that got a couple laughs.

While it may not have been the deal breaker for drivers, keeping spirits and laughter up was really important. If you break out the negativity, then there's no going back and it's infectious. Yes, it's getting cold; yes, this does seem ridiculous; yes, I'm hungry and sick of eating gas station bananas, too; *but* that's obvious to everyone and complaining isn't helping anyone. I must admit that Chris, Andrea, and Mary were super positive during the entire length of this trip, and this has been archived on video, as Chris was insistent (and I'm *so* glad he was) on taking video with his digital camera after every ride we had. If I can stress any new point here, it's that keeping a record of some kind (and video is hilarious, if you can manage that) is super fun. Having watched this years later, it still pulls me back to those moments, and reliving them is hysterical. It's all the fun of a yearbook, minus the awkwardness and 'first-one-to-sign-your crack' type comments. It gets a big thumbs up from me (and the hitchhiking pun is very, very intentional).

Day two started with a ride from a priest (in confusing crossword clue–terms, it might be a 'hodge') who dropped us off in the center of a cloverleaf with no exits anywhere. In short, what I'm sure seemed helpful was all kinds of difficult, and we had to walk about two miles to a rest stop (where, in keeping with the name, we rested) and our journey seemed to... well, stop. A somewhat mute janitor indicated to us through scribbled letters that our chances of being picked up were pretty small and that he'd witnessed folks get stranded for days on end. We thanked him as much as anyone thanks the messenger of bad news, and we plotted.

I nearly talked myself into a ride from two nice older women who had the room and were headed directly to downtown Chicago, but once they realized that I was gently asking for a ride (rather than simply being nice and giving helpful directions), then they seemed horrified and disgusted. This is a textbook example of someone being captivated by my joke-telling and warm smile, then flip-flopping in seconds at the very idea of a free ride.

I offered, "We're actually heading there ourselves…we just don't quite have the means…" This was followed by her comprehension of my proposal, the realization then shifting her expression to sheer horror.

"Those dirty kids are criminals! Criminals demanding our car!" The words were absent, but the interaction spoke quite clearly.

Beyond this, the ideas started flowing out, and the creativity cork had long been lost because we were saying, "I'll go ask that trucker a million questions, and while I'm distracting him, you guys climb in the back of the truck, and then I'll whip around and join you when he goes to the bathroom. Cool?"

After trying to warm up to every stranger that we saw, Andrea decided to wander off to the front of the pull-in ramp, theorizing that one smelly hitchhiker has a better chance than four when starting a conversation. Moments later she came back, as if she'd 'found' a ride laying there in the ditch. The quintessential Vietnam vet headed all the way to North Carolina agreed that we could come, so long as we could fit his enormous tree trunk carved to resemble Jesus into his trunk. And at this point, I wasn't about to let an ill-sized wooden religious figure prevent me from seeing The Ergs! play, so I forced his two-thousand-year-old legacy into the back and we piled in. It was a straight shot to Chicago, with one stop off to get gas station food *on him* (because of the military's retirement benefits), and mere hours before the show started.

His story was easily the most interesting, which rounded out our hitchhiking cliché of a war veteran. He sat hunched forward with a little dog on his lap, a little speed in his sock (um, okay), and a truckload of sketchy war stories (coupled with conspiracy theories about the United States and its involvement in the one-world government / Illuminati / Freemasons / Chase Bank. He kept telling us that he was going to write a book, and that if it ever got published, then we would know he was dead. I'm not sure how this information reads here, but at the time it sounded genuinely scary.

We were dropped off on the South Side of Chicago and he proceeded to show us photos of him as a young soldier in Vietnam, followed by his camp, his friends, and then one or two images he'd taken of dead Vietcong soldiers. This was disturbing—not the images themselves, as they were so blurry and yellowed that they simply read as 'outdated'. However, it was the normalcy in which he presented the photo album—our reaction to seeing a dead body alerting him that maybe it wasn't an everyday thing—that was bizarre. It may have been a perfect endcap to the two days of free travel.

A quick bus ride and two train rides later, we were seeing The Ergs! and, singing along, I couldn't help but wonder about everyone else there. Most of them had biked a couple blocks to bob their heads and sip their beer… they came to watch bands play. But five hundred miles for about twenty minutes of music? That's worth it! A hundred times worth it! Had I biked there from my old house in Chicago, I wouldn't have a story at all. We win! And that's only *half* of it, because the car was still in Iowa and all my stuff was in storage in Portland, Oregon! No plans: Here we go again!

INTERMISSION

Too Funny To Tell

A couple years ago when I still lived in Savannah, I made up a concept called 'stamp fund' that (to me) was freaking brilliant.

Problem: It costs money to send letters to friends by way of the U.S. Postal Service. Problem #2: Many youths of the day don't care about small change and frequently drop it. Solution(s): Any and all change found on the ground or in couches would go to purchasing stamps. Simple, right?

It made for a great way of remembering to write friends, instead of the classic, 'I owe them a letter, but...' And it was a great way to get involved with writing political prisoners for free! And (though I don't know this first-hand) I imagine that, as a vegan prisoner, it would be funny to know that clumsy fast food patrons paid the postage on incoming mail. Well, it's funny to me. In short, this was all a reason to put change to good use and hit two cops with one bouncy ball, as it were.

One discovery of mine was that the best place to expand your stamp fund quickly was the drive-thru lanes of fast food places after hours. (I suppose you could go while they're open and I wouldn't stop you.) Often times I'd find well over a dollar at one BK, KFC, McKEY DEEZ, or whatever oily hellhole chain fast food place resides on the outskirts of Your Town, USA. I mean, it's free money, right?

Over time I incorporated this into my Sunday dumpster run, and while the bike ride rounded out to a nice four hours, I would profit in both money *and* food, so I was in the red. Or the black; I always get it backwards. I strongly suggest you try it at some point, even if it's an afterthought late some night. The worst case is that you find nothing; the best case is that you walk away with a dollar. I found a buck-sixty at *one* McDonalds once! I got bonus points for rearranging the signs, too.

While devising these extra-long 'dumpster-and-stamp-fund' routes, I got to know well the bigger, more suburban streets in the south side of Savannah. This also turned back my sleeping schedule quite a bit, so that 4 a.m. became bedtime and I had very little choice in the matter. As these puzzle pieces fell together, a plot soon emerged…

On a humid Thursday night, my friend Steve, who had been shooting scenes for his senior film project, called me in a slight panic around 2 a.m. "Matt? You're still awake, right? I need a favor…"

As it turned out, he had gotten the okay to 'borrow' an office building way down in south side Savannah between the hours of 9 and 2 a.m. However, the janitor had not returned to lock the doors again, thus securing the building from, well, whomever you lock out of a building that early in the morning. They couldn't track down the janitor or any key holders and therefore could not safely leave the building, as it would remain unlocked all night and ripe for destruction should the wrong parties discover the open door and total lack of cameras.

"…Would you mind biking down here and sleeping in this building to make sure that nobody messes with it?"

Ha! Explore and sleep in a huge office building at night with no security or cameras? Are you kidding me? I told Jake (who is famous for sleeping even less than I do) and we both biked down Abercorn for about six miles to meet up with our new temporary squat. Handshakes and thank you's were exchanged, the door closed at our backs, and we surveyed the grey monotony, wondering where to start.

A preliminary search revealed two floors with about nine separate offices—all with locked doors—and one elevator. The tone was that of the first act in *Home Alone*, in which Kevin realizes the whole house is his and the rules no longer apply. Therefore, we rode bikes on both floors just to do it, and even rode into the elevator and back out on the other floor (not because we wanted to, but because we *had* to). When presented with lemons, I don't give two craps about what you do with them, but you *can't* ignore them. That's for sure.

Getting on the roof was a simple (but necessary) act. We accomplished this quite quickly using an indoor ladder and a submarine-looking hatch in the ceiling. The downside is that office park roofs are uninteresting. We toyed with the idea of taking the office for our own, defending it with spears and rocks from the roof, yet ultimately decided that the idea was beyond pointless. However, during a zombie attack, this would be our stronghold!

Back inside our options seemed to halt, as all the doors were (as expected) locked. I took notice of the double-door entrance to a laser hair removal clinic, because the bolt was completely exposed in the center of the two doors. There was no deadbolt—that was obvious—and it was locked simply with a handle lock, the kind where you push the little button in on the end of the metal dealy. Fundamentally, this was the introduction to lock bypassing staring me right in the face. I happened to have a laminated tour pass in my backpack (from the last Circle Takes the Square tour) and it was flimsy enough to bend slightly, yet firm enough to move a sliding piece of metal. A thirty-degree angle, pushing up and pulling the door at the same time—and the telltale 'click' silenced the room. We were in a laser hair removal office.

I wandered to the back room, sat in the chair, Jake picked up the laser, and we debated how cool it would be to have lightning bolt bald patches on our armpits, or never having to worry about eyebrows again. Ultimately, we decided to raid their fridge, instead. Jake drank someone's unopened POM juice, I helped myself to Oreos and something left over from a birthday. There was a great deal of 4-ounce containers of Aquaphor, a healing salve that is great for tattoo aftercare. Me being a guy who had friend with tattoos, I grabbed some. I also may have accidentally dropped some stamps into my backpack as well, but who could really say at this point? Memory is unreliable, and facts can only be derived from the direct experience; so, reading about it is, in truth, a form of fiction. The point is: free stamps! Oh, and we borrowed a classy diagram of the different types of pubic hair lasering that one can request, such as weird stripes, heart shapes, or triangles. I won't go into my theories on physical attraction, but one thing that kills it for me would be naturally occurring hair being deformed through sketchy cosmetic laser blasting, resulting in a stupid 'Wingding' (you know, that dumb font no one uses) object seated on the crest of a major erogenous zone. I mean, I thought braces were stupid, so if you think I'll have any less spite toward hair manipulation, think again. However, we did get free stamps, if I haven't driven that point into the ground enough.

Since the door trick had worked, we assumed that it would work on other doors, too. The next stop was the office across the hall, which was a computer testing facility of some kind. Again there was a quick success, and we beelined straight for the kitchen area. There was more juice, some raisins, and some other food. To be perfectly frank, we ate because we were bored, not because we were hungry. Ha! Subjectively speaking, I do understand how it could be considered 'mean' to eat someone else's food, but, at the same time, the story easily outweighed the cumulative $4.80 that we probably consumed. Couple this with how often office food is forgotten and left to spoil, and I'm considering us blame-free. I am the jury, the judge, and the executioner. Free food, your time has come!

Jake went to work borrowing long computer cables from storage and then doing his best to actually get us in noticeable trouble by using one of those label maker guns to label half of the nouns in the office space. Things known to most as 'The Printer' now read 'Matt's Wang' and other such intelligent slogans. While he took vocabulary into his own hands, I marveled at the copier that lay before me. For once, I could copy everything I needed with no fear of respite or authority—and yet, I had no zines with me. I did have a small sketchbook, so I copied some drawings only to make them larger, but that was it. Oh, and being party animals, Jake and I photocopied our faces, because, well, when life give you lemons, you throw them at jerks.

A tense moment arose when headlights whipped across the room and we realized that a car sat idling outside the front door. Jake and I have similar mindsets, so our hive mind was throwing out excuse ideas left and right: "The door was open and his blood sugar was dropping," and "My keys somehow fell under the door—I know, how crazy is that, right?" as well as, "Oh, us? Yeah, we work here. Interns. Crap hours, right?"

As the lights stayed frozen, we stood inert and squatting, rapidly discussing the possibility of just hiding. "I mean, what's the possibility that they're coming to *this* specific office? One in nine, right?" Numbers and statistics and probabilities raced through my head as we watched a figure get out of the car, walk right up to the front door of the complex, drop off a stack of newspapers, and then leave. As the car pulled out, we immediately rejoiced, as if we had done something well and we had *planned* it that way. Instead of credit given where credit is due, we were just throwing credit left and right for no reason whatsoever, which is just as good to me. "Yeah, walls! Way to be in between them and us! Jake, nice job *not* running to the front and waving your hands like an idiot!"

Ultimately, the door tricked worked two more times and netted nothing terribly interesting, because the two places we *wanted* to get in—the scuba magazine and the dentist—used different kinds of locks, and were immune to our poorly thought-out plan. Around six in the morning, we went back into the main area, laid down on the thin, overly-walked-on carpet, and took an hour-long nap.

Follow me for a moment here: Imagine that you're a late-twenty-something dude interning at a scuba magazine (maybe as a copy editor or ad salesperson) and you're arriving to work on a normal Friday morning. You show up around 7 a.m., walk in the front glass doors of the office complex, and immediately see two carefree-looking people laying down asleep on the ground with bikes next to them, inside the building. That's the scene. I expected some reaction, and yet all we got was a quick, "Good mornin'!" and he trotted upstairs.

I glanced at Jake, puzzled, and he mouthed, "*What the…*" as his eyes followed the new member of our office park sleepover. He didn't know it, but this guy unwittingly took the torch from us and was now officially manning the building, so we picked up our bikes and rode off in a tired haze of morning sunlight. The next six miles were spent debating if the guy was bothered by our presence, thinking it to be 'something people do'. I still don't understand exactly what transpired…but, if I failed to mention it, I am sure that I got free stamps.

Trying (And Failing) To Get This Out Of My System

In past zines, as well as real-life conversations, I mention the band Rainer Maria. An interesting byproduct of this has been that curious readers such as yourself will hear about this band that's come to mean so much to me and then wonder what they sound like, what they're all about, and things like that. Growing up, it irked me that older punks refused to listen to 'new' music, eschewing contemporary sounds for older ones, such as Minor Threat, Black Flag, L'arm, Neanderthal. These were bands that I could never see because I heard about them too late (even though people still listen to them). Having said that, I very much *like* those bands now, yet occasionally I fear being lumped into the 'it was better back then…' mentality when I get nostalgic about Pageninetynine, Circle Takes the Square, Reversal of Man, and, of course, Rainer Maria.

I feel some inner need to write this as my one marked attempt to do my part for the illumination of non-listeners. Think of me as a non-religious, musically-themed outreach center with a specific focus on one band from the Midwest. History is comprised of snippets we're been told over and over again, coaxed into believing as way of proving it. Written history has a place in the world, and if something meant the world to me, I am well within my limits to write about it as factual, meaningful history. And thus, here is the Rainer Maria interlude.

My options are to give a lengthy biography that would likely bore anyone who isn't me, or to instead give a super speedy rundown of the main points. I hereby commence my ultra-concise Rainer Maria listening guide:

Kyle Fischer and Will Kuehn were in a band called Ezra Pound named after (of course) the poet. Kyle met Caithlin De Marrais in a college poetry class, she plays bass, and Rainer Maria forms, named after (of course) a *different* poet. In 1995 in a basement, they record six songs on a four-track, put them on a cassette tape, photocopy an image of someone's mouth with herpes on it (my guess is from an old health textbook), and send it into the world (or, more accurately, Madison, Wisconsin). Caithlin and Kyle are both singing on the recordings, successfully pulling off that 'two singers screaming / singing different-but-similar things' approach quite well. Then they put out an EP with Polyvinyl, which started their lengthy career with Polyvinyl Records.

Over the course of eleven years, they put out twelve recordings, with two additional songs appearing solely on comps. The arc of their career started with 'half yelling, half singing, dual vocals', progressed to 'more matured, kinda yelling, singing much better dual vocals', and eventually crested at 'wow, Caithlin can really sing now, and Kyle got really, really good at guitar.'

Most all of their recordings are available online (demo tape included!), but I bet that you can find *something* of theirs used at a local record store. Here's the speedy breakdown:

Demo tape (1995)
Rainer Maria EP (1996)
New York, 1955 7" / EP (1997)
Past Worn Searching LP (1997)
Look Now Look Again LP (1999)
Atlantic EP (1999)
Hell And High Water / Paper Sack 7" (2001)
A Better Version Of Me LP (2001)
Ears Ring EP (2002)
Long Knives Drawn LP (2003)

Anyone In Love With You (Already Knows) CD / DVD (2004)
Catastrophe Keeps Us Together LP (2006)

In addition to these listed, there was a *Direction LP* comp released by Polyvinyl in 1997-ish (the Rainer Maria song was "Soo Young"), a split 7" with Hal al Shedad from 1998 (the Rainer Maria song was "Pincushion", definitely one not to be overlooked), and then there was an acoustic version of "Life of Leisure" from *Catastrophe*… from 2006, that I believe was a promo for their new record (released to radio stations and whatnot), *maybe* at SXSW. Lastly, evidence on YouTube seems to point to an unreleased song titled "Name Like Poison", which appears to have been played live on their last tour, though never recorded. (Additionally, Kyle released a solo album with a song in which Caithlin sang, effectively making it a Rainer Maria song.)

To me, their music meant passion, which has always been my most important and scrutinized attribute of music: If you can play your instrument well, have a great stage appearance, maybe even have top-notch merch, that's awesome; *but*, if you're lacking passion, the drive and heart-born energy to play, to create, and to get up in front of an audience of six to six-hundred people and bare yourself, then the band doesn't mean anything to me. Rainer Maria did that. They played from the heart with music birthed from necessity to express an emotion. A friend once told me that he'd gone to see a play and joked that 'the actors all though that 'acting' meant 'yelling", which (beyond being hilarious) is true. The same applies to music—if you're in a band and you yell the lyrics, that implies meaning and value, but it's simply not true. Rainer Maria started their career with shaky, uneven yelling and singing, and the emotion was raw and obvious. Pure, heartfelt energy. Over time, this skill was honed in, and on-key, melodic singing overtook the panicked screams and yells; yet, the message remained.

Finding somewhere to start listening is a bit daunting given the progression of this band, though most agree that *Look Now Look Again* is the best balancing act of the two divisions, yelling and singing. Instead, I suggest that you fiddle around on the Internet or in the record store and do your best to replicate their final set list, featured (and signed!) here.

I write this in the hope that this band might live on as inspiration, their message and meaning barreling out into the cosmos for years to come, inspiring those who choose to hear it. It's not heavy and it's not super fast, but it is raw, honest, brutal at times, and above all, thoughtful and meaningful. I encourage any interested parties to listen as you will, and I hope that Rainer Maria can go on to inspire someone else out in the world. Thank you.

Back To Real Life: Where Things Sound Like Fiction!

To pick up where I left off: We had just seen The Ergs! play (as well as a ton of other bands), I got a free CD, we stayed with our friend Adam then with our friend Rachel, and then we needed to leave Chicago to return to the car (back in central Iowa, about 350 miles to the left). Because contemporary planning is boring and requires mental faculties that I simply don't have (or that I choose to ignore), we opted to hitchhike back, the first part of the plan being to use the city buses for all they were worth.

In short, if you have two dollars, you can get *really* far outside of Chicago and well into the suburbs. You only have to know which buses to take. That's what we did, and at about 1 p.m. we exited at the stop that 'seemed nearest to the highway', which entailed a good four-mile walk that provided ample time to kick rocks, swat at weeds, get passed by cars, and absorb vitamin D pouring down from the sky. I often wonder about roads like that one (a two-lane road with '45 mph' signs and no sidewalk), and I'm curious if anyone has *actually* walked on that road. Yes, I'm sure someone has, but it's strange to consider, as this certainly hasn't been designated a 'good area to walk', especially since it only leads to the highway, and why would you walk there?

The mind wanders as the body wanders, and eventually we made it to an on-ramp that was perfect. However, the downsides were that most drivers were people who work in Chicago and live in the suburbs, meaning that we were probably going to get a ride only to the suburbs. Initially, we turned down one gentleman who was going only a couple miles, and then about fifteen minutes later took up someone else for the very same distance, for no particular reason. Interestingly, I managed to 'public speak' (self-defined as 'coercing or leading thought and action through speech.' See also: 'manipulating') him into going an extra twenty miles! All you have to do is continue the conversation about whatever your 'mark' is interested in, and then get more and more excited until you pass his exit, at which point you say, "Oh well. We'll just keep going—so where were we?" It works, it's brilliant, and I certainly didn't invent it.

The next three hours involved another long walk to a rest stop, in which I did my best to convince a chartered bus going to Des Moines to let us on, which failed, because it was a bus full bunch of middle-aged women returning from France who thought it was just funny that we didn't have rides or transportation in general. I interpreted their total lack of 'we're sorry' to mean 'this *is* class war!' and so, lacking the brick, I threw their bus only dirty looks. Soon thereafter, two heavy-metal dudes (who were missing the distinction between 'good' grindcore and metal and 'really, really bad' grindcore and metal) gave us a ride to a gas station that was actually 'in' a town. This was helpful because we traveled further west, but it was *way* off from keeping us on a road that facilitated state-to-state travel. In short, with the sun dipping toward the dark horizon, it was looking like we'd need a place to sleep. A pissed off older Midwestern dude gave us all a ride to a different gas station three miles away, and this put us within a rock's throw of the city center of Rochelle, Illinois.

After buying six twenty-five cent granola bars and filling up one Nalgene bottle, we discussed finding the train yard to give the whole 'freight train riding' thing a shot. This was a classic scene of book-smart youth trying to cope with how something can look one way on paper, yet very different in reality. To the crew-change guide's credit, the instructions could *not* be any better, and beyond that, it's common sense about how to climb onto an unmoving train. A brisk hour-long walk put us at the mouth of a huge cornfield, looking up at the small gravel hills that comprised the track base and staring at two freight trains with no understanding of what was about to happen. They were steel behemoths stretching to preposterous lengths with a large brick wall behind them. It was yellowed and dusty, lit like a prison yard, and they were belching loud metal noises and mechanical hissing.

This was overwhelming, and so we stared and whispered (taking over-the-top precautions, as we believed that sounds would echo indefinitely in all directions and give us away). You can read the texts all you want, but when you arrive at a spot to 'catch out', it's really, really confusing. There are no arrows but only intuition and a lot of, "Well, I think this one is pointed that way, so that probably means...."

Twenty minutes of debate later and a steam whistle blew, the train nearest us rolling westward, highlighted features flickering from the moonlight. As it left, we realized, "Dang it! *That* was our train! And we just *looked* at it!" Now understanding that the remaining train was indeed facing east, we started to decipher the code that lay before us. Close track means west and far track means east. Done. Over the next forty-five minutes, we debated, "Should we go around the wall? Should we hide for longer? What if we take the eastbound to the next town and *then* get on the west bound? What if that's the last train that's coming tonight?"

Luckily, fate made up our mind as another train (a double-stacked hotshot, to drop some lingo) pulled in and stopped. In a blur of backpacks, half-filled water bottles, and lots of gravel dust, we were up there choosing our cars wisely while not wanting to miss the takeoff due to collective indecisiveness. So we ran for the car directly in front of us, despite it not having much of hiding/riding space. Imagine an eight-inch tall coffin-shaped space just large enough to fit a person lying down, but with no room for arms folded over one's chest. It was like conserving cardboard when trying to ship a person.

In keeping with the community we'd built, we stayed

together. Andrea and Chris rode the 'east-facing, backward-riding' side, and Mary and I were on the 'wind-in-our-face, west-facing side'. In short, Andrea and Chris got sunrises, while Mary and I got sunsets.

The excitement was not unlike arriving at a surprise party painfully early. It begins with a tense 'Any second now!' and then slowly lurches to 'Yep...any second...' But when it *does* start up, the shock comes as if you'd forgotten why you were sitting on rusty metal at 2 a.m. in a field in central Illinois in the first place. That awkward burp of forward motion as we stared at the gravel underneath and watched it slide by—we were moving! And we were going really, *really* slowly! Inertia can eat it; this train was going places!

Old Factory Olfactory

The first hour of riding this train was amazing. It was exactly what I had seen in documentaries, read about in zines and books, and heard from friends. It feels like riding in the back of a pickup truck but with more to look at, since there's no road or cars or billboards or anything anywhere. The landscape actually feels a bit like the European countryside. The surroundings became only trees, deer, the moon, and a smell probably like a tool and die shop in the 1800s. Everything seemed dirty, but not gross, only a long trail of subdued colors scooting across the countryside.

We laughed a ton, took photos, and called everyone we knew who would be jealous. I did leave a message of nothing but ambient train-riding noise for my friend Kate, who correctly deciphered it with no help and sent back a flurry of exclamation-mark ridden text messages. After the initial shock wore off, the 3 a.m. hour wore *in* and we fell asleep. Due to the space, we all crammed in together, Mary and I sleeping like cats with our feet pressed on each other, like some weird shape one would make if crouched on top of a mirror.

Since we had no idea where this train was actually going (except 'west'), we planned to get off at the next crew change and figure it out there. That spot turned out to be Clinton, Iowa, a town that I had biked through a couple years back (remember?) and is utterly forgettable, save for a putrid stench that has seeped into every inch of concrete and mortar erected in city limits. The town smells *freaking awful*, a smell that defies description save the assessment in my journal of it being "hot barf and cooked red wine". Disgusting. So, I was two-hundred percent sure that we had passed into Clinton and paused for the crew change. It looked like we'd rolled into some futuristic Orwellian city, with bright orange and yellow lights throwing harsh shadows in all directions and all buildings appearing to be windowless steel columns. The train came to a slow, hissing stop, and we decided that Mary and Chris should get off at the next crew change, which was only twenty miles from the train yard to their car. It was at this point that we were actually deciphering how the crew change guide worked. So we hunched down and did our best to look like anything but people hiding on a train.

Somehow that worked, and we picked back up and kept riding westward. After more nap-like sleep, it was about 7:30 a.m. and we were coming into the smallest, most neglected train yard that I've ever seen. The sun was doing that thing where it's 'up' but you can't see it anywhere, so it feels like a cloud has settled on everything. Despite being 'open', I didn't see anyone anywhere. But when we pulled to a stop, Chris and Mary *bolted* off into the woods, while Andrea and I lay down and got rained on for thirty minutes.

I will openly admit: Being rained on while you're wearing only a hoodie and old pants and no socks totally sucks, especially when you're sitting on flat, unmoving steel with a light dusting of gray, extra-fine dirt on everything. It's an exercise in comfort, or weighing comfort against a free ride with amazing views, gentle rocking back and forth, and about a hundred hours to read or think without the temptation of the Internet, DVDs, or running fruitless errands. Think of it like a moving study hall with plenty of time to do whatever you want within a certain spacial confinement, staring off into the distance for hours on end, and if you drop out and leave early, then you'll probably break both your legs and be stuck in the middle of Wyoming.

As a side note, Chris and Mary managed to get a ride from a trucker at one point, followed by a ride from an ex-military guy about our age who 'drove around because he had nothing to do,' and took them *right* to my grandma's driveway. In terms of their 'crazy journey', Chris and Mary's story ends here. Meanwhile, Andrea and I are still face down, absorbing rain with winced expressions and hoping to get moving again soon.

The rain kept coming, and after a tense hour spent trying to not care about getting soaked, our train started forth once more, and then the rain wasn't really that bad. I tightrope walked over the coupling, and sat on Andrea's side, since our backs were now toward our direction of travel, meaning we didn't get rained on half as bad. Somewhere during this part we went over a bridge that seemed to be about a hundred feet off the ground, and it was a 'train only' bridge, much like the one featured in *Stand By Me*. I will forever remember that part as the most incredible sight on the four day ride. It was so close and so feasible to fall off, that it seemed fake. In a country that's increasingly putting guardrails and fences on everything, it's oddly refreshing to know you can still fall off a bridge and blame the architect. Maybe. I suppose you can't blame anyone when you're dead. Huh.

Time Travel

From there on out, the stories became simplified, bite-sized mini-stories. During the second night, the wind was so bad that it almost used my sleeping bag as a sail and took me out with it. We didn't get rained on once after that earlier shower. Over the four days, I rationed my six twenty-five cent granola bars into full meals. I read all of *The Jungle* by Upton Sinclair and I tried my best to write legibly in my journal (which was largely impossible when we were moving). Crew changes still happened about once every six hours or so, and while they were stressful, we weren't as worried about it after we passed through the infamous 'North Platte' yard. (The word on the street [rail?] is that virtually everyone gets pulled off there, though we had no problems, despite our total lack of knowledge or cover. My theory is that since we pulled in around 3 a.m., darkness and bad lighting were on our side and nobody wants to do anything at that hour.)

The next day as we were sitting in the middle of nowhere for three hours, I called the freight train customer number from my cell phone (listed in the front of the crew change) and, using the number printed on the freight car coupled with some basic lying skills, I learned that our train was headed directly to the north Portland yard, which we didn't know at all at this point. This train was pure luck! Initially, we had a one-in-three chance that it was going to Portland, as the line had branched into three tracks at the North Platte yard: one leg heading to Seattle, one to Portland, and one to Los Angeles. And I'm not even that lucky of a person!

It's important to understand our devotion to this particular train. We could have easily gotten off at another crew change spot, found water, and then returned to scout out another ride west, but we already had this one. Andrea and I were down to trade comfort for a guaranteed ride to Portland, and we made a pact that no matter what, we were on this thing until the end. Temptation directed my attention to puddles and lakes that reflected a cool, 'you know you want some water' look. It was awful. With two days left, I was getting *really* dehydrated, and my lips and finger tips were almost cracking. I had half of a Nalgene left and was doing my best to ration it out to last forever. We constantly passed half-filled plastic bottles of water thrown alongside the tracks, but I couldn't figure out how to jump off, get one, and then jump back on to make it back to my stuff. Instead, I accomplished a second life goal I always wanted to: drinking my own pee!

Yep, I Mean It

The difficult decision here probably indicates that there are two kinds of people in the world. I had the choice to 1) finish my normal water then drink my own pee by itself, *or* 2) pee in my water bottle to add to the water (thus diluting it). Scenario one yields, in terms of volume, less foul-tasting water, but *much* worse taste; scenario two is more gross-tasting water, but not as bad. Fearing that the urine alone would be awful, I opted for the latter and diluted my half-full Nalgene into an almost three-quarters full Nalgene. The game is afoot! I say from experience that there is *no going back now*.

Andrea gave me a piece of minty gum in hope that letting it sit in the water would alter the water's flavor to make it palatable, but all that happened was that the gum gave it some weird metallic taste. I didn't like gum before, but now I can't stand it. Over the course of the next two days, though, I drank my watered-down pee (which was probably about like normal pee, as I didn't have that much water in me to begin with). The last sip was probably the grossest thing that I've ever endured, though I was laughing as I drank it, because, really, that's a funny story. It is of note that it didn't rain *once* for the last three days, so I couldn't catch rainwater.

On the last day, we broke open a can of vegetable soup and tried to slowly sip the broth, which was...well, who cares, because we lived. We saw a bobcat walking in Wyoming or Idaho, and then upon coming into Oregon, we spied a couple homemade tents and some people waking up from a night of sleeping 'wherever.' We locked eyes with them and they were so pumped to see us on a train—ah, only in Oregon. Well, no—much more likely in Oregon.

One difficult aspect of train travel is deducing where one actually is, as there often aren't mile marker signs or things like that. We looked at grey boxes near crossroads to see which dinky little town we might be near. Coming into Portland, we stopped about five miles short of the yard, but we didn't know that then. We ascertained that we had stopped, and that there were businesses near us and blackberry bushes everywhere.

We sat for about an hour, wondering if we should hitchhike into town or if we were in bus distance. Eventually, the excitement of relying on ourselves again instead of a machine, we left the train, I filled my empty Nalgene with blackberries, and then cut through the bushes to the road (blackberry bushes are *super* sharp, by the way). It turns out we were on 168th Street, which is only one-hundred and forty blocks from the Whole Foods on Burnside! Bus ride! Let's go! The best part was that we spent two dollars to travel five miles, when we had spent zero dollars to travel 2,093 miles before that. Actually, if you count the bus fare from Chicago to the start of the hitchhiking, then it's $2.30 for about 2,200 miles. That's like 9.6 miles for a penny! *A penny*! That's 960 miles for a dollar! Apply this formula the next time you find some spare change on the floor or in a couch. Your earnings could buy distance! It sounds like a stupid infomercial, but you have to admit, those results speak for themselves!

In the end, we got off the bus, found some water, sat at the windowed bench in Whole Foods, ate some fruit, and, well, we were in Portland. Andrea got a ride to Seattle from a friend of hers, and I unearthed my bike from the storage unit that had been holding it all summer. I didn't know anyone with whom I could stay that night and wound up sleeping in a park in Southeast, which was really an awesome game (read: 'incredibly crappy and unbelievably frustrating chore') of dodging the sprinklers when they came on in stupid intervals between midnight and 5 a.m. Interestingly, about two years later, I lived in a house that overlooks that park, which makes me laugh.

With the train journey over and nowhere to live in Portland, I realized rather quickly that I had put myself into a stupid situation. You see, the train (as cold and uncaring as it is) had provided a home for four nights with no problem. I have good friends with less sympathetic house visitor policies than that!

When I woke up early from my extreme speed-sleeping in the park, I tried to go to the library, only to find that it didn't open until the laid back, west coast hour of noon. So I went to a Fred Meyer grocery/everything store and sat reading a book for a long time. It was sad, this being the town that I thought I wanted to arrive at for the entire summer thus far. Heck, I'd already moved everything that I owned into storage here, so I basically *was* living here, but at this point, the city was 'rejecting' me.

Days were spent wishing that it would stop raining. (It rained for four days in a row—not light sprinkles and wafting bits of precipitation, but *rain*.) It was awful, as my down time is usually spent in parks, reading, meeting people, and playing, but bad weather wrecks all of that. Faced with few options and a sinking feeling that I had made a mistake, I invented fun ways to sneak into the movie theater (mostly to get out of the rain, and also because it's the only place open late at night that has a roof and won't demand that you buy something). My favorite ploy that wasn't grabbing the exit door when people leave the side exit was the classic having a piece of paper in my hand while talking on a cell phone as I brush past the ticket-taker and pausing only for a quick 'we did this already.' I couldn't believe that it worked, but she was a high school age ticket-taker and I was someone acting intimidating on a cell phone.

I even tried biking up to Seattle, but on the day I left it started pouring—like, Old Testament rain—so much so that I couldn't see anything, and because I was only twenty miles outside of town, I reformatted my plans and came back. Was Portland commanding me back? I was offered a couch to sleep on from a friend of a friend, which was great because the couch was on the porch and I preferred that to being indoors. Porch rooms are where it's at! I suggest moving your bed to your porch tonight if you have one. If not, maybe shut yourself in your bedroom window to hang halfway outside. On second thought, maybe don't do that.

In the end, I wound up getting a ride with a super rad kid I met at the Zine Symposium (he had a homemade tattoo of my bike-heart image from *Next Stop Adventure!*) to his house in Seattle where I biked around, read stuff, and then had a birthday at my friend Larry's place. A whirlwind of Craigslist-ing and Internet-ing later, I had a cheap apartment to look at with a random roommate to meet, and I had to get from Seattle back to Portland and all I had was my bike. You know what *that* means. No car, no tent, no 'real' plan—no problem!

Bike Trip!

Upon completion, each one always seems like it will be my last. I assume that the feeling is brought on by the general pain in my knees paired with an overall 'life exhaustion' and need to sit down on something more comfortable than a bike seat. However, in keeping with my borderline split personality disorder (a.k.a. 'inability to make up my mind permanently about seemingly anything'), I always wind up going on another bike trip, be it days, weeks, or even years later. And thus, here we are.

It's easy to reinvent the wheel when writing about a bike trip. Basically, if you imagine what it's like to bike through green, leafy wilderness in the Northwest, you'll correctly picture 95% of the trip. The stories worth relaying happen during the non-cycling parts, like the Where Do I Camp? puzzle, and the So…Food…? dilemma. I will skip the descriptions that I'd fail to illuminate, as I'm certainly not a poet, and I'll instead describe the funny parts. It is worth noting that biking alone at an early hour of the morning through the woods is quite a leveling experience. If I can get lost on paved roads while the sun is out with maps at my disposal, just imagine what it would be like to experience a less forgiving environment—say, uncharted waters over eight hundred years ago, or wandering the desert. I bet that Christopher Columbus would flip his crap over Google Earth...and not because of his megalomaniacal slaughtering of foreign culture. Ooh, historic burn!

My friend Larry offered to drive me a bit beyond downtown Seattle so that I wouldn't have to deal with traffic and the awful things that ruin the fun of bicycling in most cities. He also gave me *four* Tofurky sandwiches, which was the nicest thing in the entire world. (For reasons unknown, I agreed to mustard; however; it is a taste that I have always hated and I ultimately regretted the decision for the remaining 190 miles.)

The weather held at a stable 80 degrees with no rain, and the entire first day went off without anything happening at all, save for a lot of biking. My journal notes the largest bra that I have ever seen discarded on the road's shoulder. That sounds like a pun, but it's not—just a huge, huge bra. Beyond this, I missed a turn that wasn't labeled well and went up the steepest hill one can bike without having to get off and push, only to ride six more miles and then stop in some family's front yard to ask the kid mowing the grass where the road I needed was. "Back down the big hill, before the gas station..." *Dang.* The plus side is that enjoyed riding down the hill, which was almost worth it. It's the same paradox of sledding: fifteen minutes of walking up a hill for fifteen seconds of flying down it.

Besides that debacle, the only other issue was finding a place to sleep, and since I was without a tent this meant finding someplace covered (or at least hidden), since wind and nature crawl all over you when you have only a sleeping bag. The sun set and I was coming up to the outskirts of some small town. I spotted a school to the left, and, being summer, I figured it was a safe bet. It had a *huge* baseball complex and three fields for various sports, so I followed the fence from the main road and lay down on the backside of the school.

However, it was colder than it should be in early September, so I wrapped my feet in plastic bags before putting my socks on when I went to sleep. It wasn't close to REM sleep, but I did get some rest, and, come the next morning, I was ready to do the same thing again. I had traveled a little over 100 miles, so I had about 90 left, which sounded super easy all of the sudden. Part two: Go!

After drying my sleeping bag in the sun and eating some chips and a banana, I left southbound again. Two interesting things stand out.

I got pulled over by a cop who passed me, looked back, turned around, and then pulled me over, which was weird. I figured it had to do with some mandatory 'lights on all the time' law (though it was only 2 p.m.), but he asked to see my license from twenty feet away. Confused, I showed it to him. He also asked to see the tattoos on my arms, which was even stranger. Eventually he ran the numbers on my driver's license, and then from his car, he yells, "Oh man, you gotta see this!" Obviously perplexed, I slowly approached and he asked me to sit in the driver's seat while he held my bike, and, on the in-car computer screen, there was an image of a Hispanic dude who looked *exactly like me*, only, well, Hispanic.

"Yeah, that guy right there's wanted for a double homicide—ha! You look just like him!" Wow, yeah, ha, that's really something. He continued, "We've got a description of his tats, and your tats don't match those. Ha! Alright, well, bike safely. You know how drivers are, always hitting people…"

His frequent and annoying use of the single term 'tats' drove the wedge further and further between he and I. Cops that 'get it' or 'understand what I'm all about' are the absolute worst kind, adding revulsion to what was once simple animosity. Furthermore, if you'd committed a double murder, would the *best* option for leaving the state be on a bike? Really? You do understand that riding a bike that far from a town is the only sure-fire way to have *everyone* look at you, right? This is the part where I give a huge A+ to the Washington State Police, since they deserve it for *so many reasons*. Is the sarcasm reading? (I know it's confusing when writing sarcasm.) But seriously, I totally get it: I understand what they're all about. (See what I did there?)

THERE'S A LAST TIME FOR EVERYTHING

The other semi-interesting thing happened crossing the 'bike-friendly' bridge from Washington to Oregon, which is a smaller, less-traveled bridge, though the little traffic that *does* cross is almost all giant eighteen-wheelers carrying logs and downed trees, which, of course, litter splinters, bark, and wood everywhere. (Can you technically 'litter' wood? Or are you considered a roving compost disperser?) This bridge is insanely sketchy, because you're stuck dodging huge wood chunks as well as dealing with traffic spewing debris, swirling dust, and basically ruining a nice bike ride. On the downsloping half of the bridge, I thought it might help to ride on the painted line (since the paint is typically smoother than the pavement), but as I rolled onto it, I immediately realized that it had reflectors painted *into* it, so that every three feet you hit a half-inch bump, and I shouted, "OH-H-H MA-A-A-N-N I'M GO-N-N-N-A-A F-F-F-A-A-L-L-L-L O-F-F-F MYY-Y B-I-I-I-I-I-K-E!" It was tense. Somehow I made it off and managed to bike the next fifty-some miles back into town. I got rained on twice and then also rode alongside a train for about fifteen miles, and the whole time we kept pace with each other, making me think that train hopping would've been a hundred times easier (but not as healthy as biking, which makes this a stupid debate in the first place).

From there, the story dissipates into a 'normal day' as I rolled into Portland. I went to Whole Foods, got some fruit, ate it, called my soon-to-be roommate, and later moved in to a room with three walls. This aspect—the conclusion—is the strangest part of any kind of trip / exploration / lengthy outing, as it all ends so quickly when you arrive at your physical destination. At that point, it's hard to talk to strangers with the openness that you're granted while wandering the planet on your bike.

I think that this has to do with an inferred responsibility of dividing life into distinct 'fun' and 'work' parts. Travel precludes worrying about bills or rent, but when you live somewhere, all of a sudden you shift your sight onto getting things accomplished. What once was a fun bike ride around town has now become 'running errands.' Repetition is the death of excitement.

I don't think that is has to be this way, though. The solution is to fight your tradition of doing normal things in your town. I frequently visit the beach and the mountains when I *don't* live anywhere; yet, when I live somewhere for real, I often don't leave the city limits. How dumb. Many friends have the same predicament: something like 'work' or 'not owning a car' always stands between them and the coast or the old-growth forest an hour away, but if effort is put toward getting there rather than devising an excuse to why you *aren't* going, then I believe that they would make these trips happen.

Determine when was the last 'really memorable day' you had in the town where you live, and then figure out why. It's why going on tour (of any kind) is almost hyper-memorable, because one is in a different place every day and with that comes hundreds of new experiences, even if you realize that people and buildings are more or less the same everywhere you go. The real enemy is habit and routine.

Consider this a plea to leave this writing where you are and actually *do* what you keep meaning to do. Nothing is so far away that you can't accomplish it. Seriously. Travel down new roads (feel free to shout, "New road!" to keep things fun) and unexplored routes. You'd be surprised how far public transit can actually take you from the city center closest to you—and I'm flat out *demanding* that you see how far you can get on two dollars. (That is a zine waiting to happen: *Two Dollars of Distance*. Sure, I thought of it, but I'm burdening you, the reader, with the assignment of trying it out. I'll try it as well, and we can compare notes. Send me a postcard! For real! I always mean for real!)

Or maybe you're injured irreversibly and never have the chance to do those fun things, or maybe you grow old, get married, buy a house in the suburbs, and twenty years from later unearth a box of maps that you once treasured and you're bummed that you never put your hiking boots to use. So redefine the concept of the weekend as 'the time you do fun things'. If you need a job, then try to fit all the hours in on the weekend, so you can have five days off. I assure you that it has the potential to be much, much more fun. And that's what we're after.

In 1960s France, the Situationists would explore the city with maps of other cities, breaking the confines of what a 'map' or even what spacial information meant. If your map tells you that the only way to the river is through someone's house, well, then go through their house. If your goal is to find funny stories, then this is a sure-fire way to do it... I guarantee that it'll be hard to stop laughing, and, to me, that is the whole point. New ways of seeing the world; that's what they were after, and certainly what I'm always chasing, as well.

This has always been about writing your own history while treasuring and admiring personal accomplishments. The dilemma of our lives is the feasibility that one could live a life simply reading books from age seven until an unremarkable death eighty years later. There was no real experience, but an entirety constructed in pure theory. What does this accomplish? If you can't define 'danger' or 'excitement' based on an event in your own life, of what purpose are those words at all? Why live vicariously? Why not simply *live*?

Fun Pages

I was inspired to try this idea by way of *Zine Libs*, a hysterical zine by Erick Lyle (of *Scam* zine fame) that is a spot-on alternative to Mad Libs, exploiting the homogenous nature of the punk lifestyle. I hereby willingly annul my own clichéd creation and present a next stop adventure mad lib. Enjoy.

With summer finally around the corner, and _____ (adj.)-er weather *finally* showing up, I couldn't wait to _____(verb) on my first bike tour! I hadn't really planned much. I mean, I did _____(verb) a book from the library about touring. It didn't really teach me much, since the author _____(past tense verb) in hotels every night, and had a _____(#) dollar budget for each day. I figured, since I only had about _____(#) dollars in the bank, I'd be _____(present tense verb) in my tent every night and probably eating nothing but _____ (adj.) _____ (plural noun) every day. I got a map from an old _____(name of a magazine) at the dentist's office, so that's how I'd been planning my trip—pretty _____(adj.), huh? It seemed like a _____(adj.) idea at the time...

My first day, I managed to bike a little over _____(#) miles! Not bad, right? My _____ (body part) was a bit achy and I could already feel that my _____(plural body part) were going a bit numb, but I started stretching that night to help get my blood _____(present tense verb) again. Not a lot happened on the first couple days, though I did see a _____(color) _____(noun) on the side of the road, followed pretty closely by a(n)_____(adj.) pair of _____(plural noun), and when you think about it, the story is pretty obvious there, huh? My question is: Why would you throw that away? Oh yeah, and some guy driving a _____(type of vehicle) threw a _____(name of food) wrapper at me from his window and had the nerve to yell, "_____!"(exclamation) at me. I grabbed my ____(letter) lock and was ready to bash his _____(body part) in, but instead I laughed it off and yelled, "_____(verb) _____(noun), you gas-guzzling _____(noun)-head!"

In the end, I biked another _____(#) miles, which put me in _____(name of a town), which is where I was trying to get! I didn't even _____(verb) a tire during the whole ride. I couldn't believe it! Bike touring is so fun! I'm already planning a trip to try to ride to the coast of _____(place) this coming winter, and I can't wait. I even upgraded my bike so now I have a _____(brand name) brand frame called 'The _____(verb)-er" and it's got something like seven cages to hold my _____(type of liquid) bottles! I get dehydrated pretty easily, so, you know, having a _____(body part) full of _____(liquid) is really important...I mean, I'd hate to have to drink my own _____(liquid) again...ugh.

When I'm done with the next tour, I'm gonna write it all down, and call it *Next Stop _____(Noun)*!

Two More Hilarious Stories

Well, they might be hilarious. I'm not sure how they come off, but I can admit that having lived these experiences, they were very funny then. One of my favorite feelings is that 'I can go anywhere and do anything!' sensation, which I can only allow myself to fall into when I forget that I don't have nearly enough money to get me *anywhere*, and I certainly can't afford *anything*. However, if a free ride to the North Pole wandered my way, or a ship with 'room for one more, and all you have to do is flip pancakes for ten weeks' called me up, then I would go anywhere. Got it? Right. The world is an oyster, or something. Within the realm of feasible physics, I go anyplace on this earth. Well, almost anyplace.

Trespassing Tale #1: 'You Are Not Welcome Back Here'

There we were: my younger brother, his friend, and myself—three 'fighting off boredom in the suburbs' types, all in our late teen years. I had use of a 35 mm camera for a couple days and we had all communally decided to go check out the abandoned and gutted Burger King that sat out by my old high school. And why not? It would be fun to explore, and I could get a chance to figure out how this camera worked in a weird location. Game on, let's do this!

I'd visited this empty building once or twice in the past week to visit the roof, so I had some idea of what I was getting into. There were windows on all sides, clearly showing the broken lightbulb tubes, droopy wires, and broken tile and brick bits scattered about the floor inside. But here's the rub, as they say: As destroyed as this place was, the doors were still locked and the windows remained intact; therefore, there was no clear entry into this unoccupied wasteland. Smashing a window seemed too barbaric, and picking the lock seemed too labor-intensive and skilled for our meager brains.

"I wonder if the drive thru window is locked," my brother had offered, perhaps knowing the answer. Our three faces huddled around the small glass panes. It wasn't! It was closed but it wasn't locked, so all we had to do was open it from the inside *from the outside*! A quick search of items around us provided a coat hanger we promptly unbent, and next thing you know, all three of us are crowded around this small window, offering advice like, "Yeah! Now turn it upways; no, well, push it both in and up and turn it…no, from the back…"

Looking back, what I recollect most from this time was how excited we all were. It was a perfect riddle of a challenge, with one clear answer and a nearly infinite way of getting there. Brainstorming at its finest! I love this stuff and I live for these moments, and we were getting closer and closer with each twitch and catch of the metal hook we'd fashioned. The hinge was springing towards us, and the lever started moving into place, and…and…and…!

"Well, you wanna tell me what's going on here?"

Before I looked over, I could tell he was a cop from his authoritative voice and his Southern drawl I've come to associate with the cops of North Carolina. Sadly, I was right, as I turned to see two police officers walking towards us, having covertly hidden their car on the other side.

Oftentimes in my life, I am quick to see the humor in a

moment, and this was a great example: three teens trying to politely open a window to take some goofy photographs of a post-consumer fast food shell? None of us drank alcohol, we weren't on drugs, the sun was still very 'up', and, most importantly, we were already chuckling because we knew we weren't doing anything wrong. This was only fun, right?

The next thing I know, I'm getting the "drop the device and step away from the window" treatment, which must have registered on my face. I was quick to over explain that, "No, officers, we're only trying to get inside to take photos," hoping he'd come around to our side and perhaps leave to go deal with real crime. Again, he failed to see this from our angle. "Breaking and entering is a felony charge, son, and we caught you *in the act*! Not to mention *burglary*!" His partner stood, staring at all of us, clearly thinking it over quietly. I appealed to both of them. This was too much.

"*Burglary*? What's there to *take*? It's an abandoned building! How on earth can I *steal* something *when there is nothing to steal*!" This is the problem with our justice system. There's no time for anyone to use critical thinking for even one moment. This guy was freaking killing me.

A dozen more pleas starting with "Look" on my part finally got his partner to see what I was getting at. When he rephrased what I'd been saying for fifteen minutes, I felt like we were finally getting somewhere.

"So you wanted to get inside, without breaking anything, to…to take some photos?" I sighed a great relief. At least fifty percent of these idiots got it.

The most amusing part of the conversation came when Officer #1 had decided to understand, and was now confused about our intentions on some kind of basic human level. "I mean, there's a sunset! Why don't you take a picture a' that?" to which I replied only with huge eyes.

In the end, we each had to sign papers that stated that we were banned from this building and parking lot, not as a 'Burger King', but rather as a 'plot of land'. I clarified, hiding my smile, "So wait, if this building gets turned into a movie store or a gas station, we could still be arrested for walking into the parking lot?"

Emphatically, and evidently quite proud, he barked back. "Absolutely! You need to learn a lesson!"

Another Place I Can't Go: 'A Free Breakfast I Never Tasted'

Some years back, my friend Jake and I decided quite quickly and irrationally to drive his 'dying but not quite dead' car across the country and back. Well, that was our goal, but our reality was 'when it breaks down, then we'll leave it in a ditch and somehow get home.' We actually drove from Georgia to California and back, but one of the better moments happened that first night. If you're adept at guessing my plans, you might deduce that our sleeping plans were even more sparse than our emergency plans. We had none!

So, as we pulled into the parking lot of a quiet, four-story hotel cluster in central Tennessee, we planned to recline the seats and sleep in the car. We parked away from the main doors to the hotel, which coincidentally set us in front of the indoor pool area. All the windows were pitched outward, and we couldn't help but look at one another, silently devisingthe same plan. The next thing you know, we're inside!

We considered swimming, but I almost immediately

thought, *Forget that, we can sleep on these reclining comfy chairs!*, which was true, as they certainly weren't in use. I think the 'pushing our luck and coming out on top' sensation seeped in, because then we're wandering around the inside of the actual hotel. It's around 9:30 p.m., so it's not strange that we'd be returning to our room, and the one lady up front didn't bat an eye as we strolled past.

In retrospect, everything would have been fine had I not seen the conference room door's lock plate glint in the dim light. If I could see the plate, it meant that the door wasn't actually closed! I elbowed Jake and we pushed it open to reveal an empty room with one of those comically big tables on which rich people eat (or do business over), a white board, about fifteen chairs, electrical outlets, pens, tape, and even some plants! The plan was written in paint before it was even sketched out, and we ran to the car for our sleeping bags and snacks, and then came right back to our conference room and locked the door!

I have no clue what I thought was going to happen. Like the dawning realization that the distance runner experiences ten miles from home, we had our own 'Wait, I still have to run *back*!' moment the next morning. Yeah, we got in fine. We even slept fine. But when I heard the lock jiggling at 6 a.m., Jake and I locked eyes and I concocted an airtight alibi in a fraction of a second.

I purposefully spilled paper onto the desk, we both threw our sleeping bags under the table, and I started pretending to work on a 'pitch' that we'd be giving later. Loudly practicing a speech with Jake's watchful, sleepy eyes nodding along and 'getting it', the two hotel owners walked in and jumped in real, actual fear.

"How did you get in here! What's going on? Who are you?!" Ugh. I hate these moments.

No, I don't! I love this crap! We tried calmly explaining that we didn't want to wake our third business partner, still fast asleep upstairs, so we came down to practice in the conference room.

"It was open, so we didn't think anything of it, ma'am." Jake and I shared an invisible smile as the beautiful tapestry of our complicated plan unfurled for all to see.

"I'm calling the cops!"

Ah man! I had thought this would work, too. As if wanting some consolation prize from these two appreciating our made-up story, I couldn't help but feel hurt when she leaped for 9-1-1, her partner guy screaming, "Don't leave! You can't leave! Stay here!"

We probably could have run, but he was blocking the door and I didn't want to leave my sleeping bag, so we stayed. The cops came. I explained. He understood.

"Next time, if you don't have money to stay someplace, maybe offer to clean up or something."

While I see his point (and even appreciate his naïveté), we didn't *need* to stay anywhere. We were fine in the car; it just happened that a better opportunity showed up! It's not like anyone was actually *using* that unlocked conference room from 10 p.m. through 6 a.m. We all knew that! Does anyone *want* to pay for a hotel room? Jeez, people need to relax.

Standing in the parking lot, his sleeping bag folded over his shoulder, Jake turned to me. "...So, should we try to get back in for continental breakfast?"

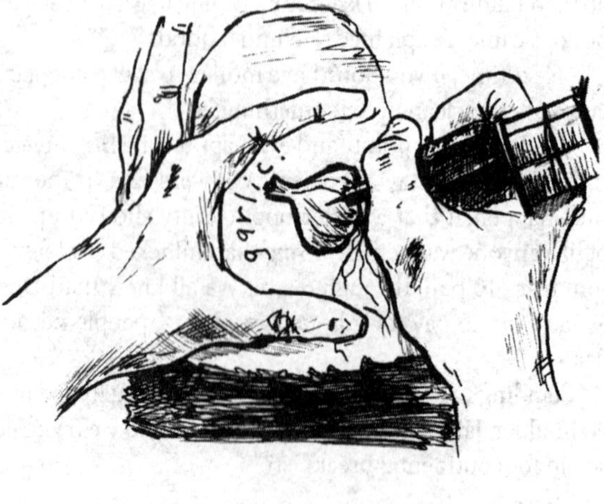
garlic!

NEXT STOP ADVENTURE #5

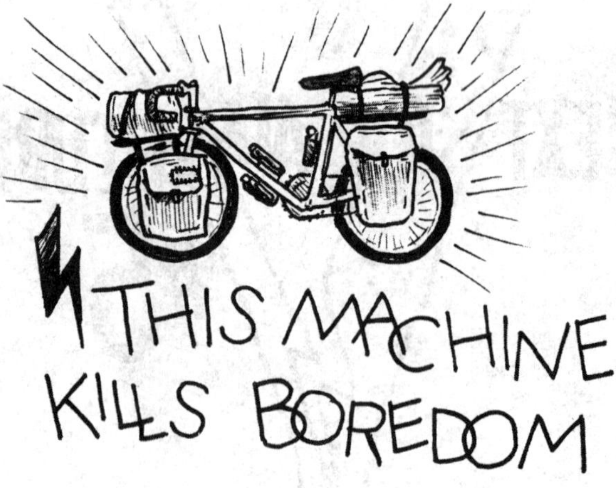
THIS MACHINE
KILLS BOREDOM

Bike Touring In Alaska:
Or 1000 Miles Of Hardship, VHS Tapes, And Rain

> "It's ridiculous to think there's going to be *anything* in thirty years. I don't know what's worse, being blown up in a nuclear war, or having a 7-Eleven on every corner."
> —Christian Slater, *Gleaming the Cube*

PERHAPS IT'S FITTING THAT while biking across Alaska, I managed to find a VHS copy of *Gleaming the Cube*, the seminal skateboarding movie of the 80's. One of its minor themes is that of 'total annihilation versus super-consumption and infinite availability', and had been cycling through my thoughts even before I bought the tickets for this latest bike trip. Human lives have come to this forking path and are pitted with all or nothing extending in opposing directions. Do we allow ourselves to be defined by culture? Even as a nonparticipant, this reactionary quitting of society is still defined as 'what it *isn't*'. From this staunchly black-and-white issue, I found myself wondering about the individual and the ability to further oneself in a third direction. All or nothing...but what about *new* paths? Is there room within our consciousness to push out boundaries that have been ignored? Is a new emotion a step in the right direction? Can I stay *Jung til' I die*?

That need for substance has driven me to strange places: dragging a mattress under a bridge embankment at 3 a.m., crawling on all fours with a flashlight taped to my head under a college campus, the excitement of a sunrise seen 'the right way' by staying up all night (compounded by being alone, with no one to share it with). Personal growth that stems entirely from *you* is more powerful than from an outside source. Change your own mind. Let your experiences teach you things. *Gleaming the Cube* came out in 1989, meaning that in 2014, it's been 25 years. Perhaps in 2019, there *will* be nothing—human consciousness will resemble either a dystopian battlefield, or, more likely, a rapid-fire, beleaguering attack of pop-up windows and information the speed of blast beats, allowing our brains to process next to nothing. My question—no, my *demand* is for you to push life into situations that allow for possibilities in this future to open up.

When I witness friends making creative efforts and accomplishing goals set on their own terms, I feel an undeniable surge of energy and 'something else' that I can't express. Some make music, others paint, some build things, some live in the woods and provide for themselves, and some make boats and sail them in random directions, but they all fall under the banner of 'art'. My own series of forking paths has led me to ride my bike for wildly long periods of time, as well as draw and paint frequently. These are not *the* ways to find that essential strand of life, but they work for me. Everyone can find something—a means of transporting yourself beyond time, beyond space, beyond a world of right angles, the Internet, 7-Elevens, and expectations. A better world exists all around us with access points obscured by piles of 'culture'. I strongly urge anyone and everyone to get out of this world and do some real living. I present this cobbling of words and ideas as my personal blueprint for one such escape attempt.

Over the last nine years of biking that is composed of

nearly 3800 miles of time to think, my advice remains unchanged: If you want to do something, come up with a way to do it and make it happen. I assure you, *nothing* is that hard. Really.

Trapdoor: Or Another Way That The Internet Is Simultaneously Helping Me Through A Doorway While Punching Me In The Kidneys Within The Same Motion . . .

I'm slowly realizing that I'm one of those crotchety old-man holdouts when it comes to technology. Most of the movies I own are on VHS (because they're cheaper that way), I'm not on Facebook (for about a million reasons), and I find myself quietly complaining when the flyers I draw are posted online rather than on telephone poles. I'm not anti-computers, but, rather, a reluctant learner of new things when they already have an approach that I'm perfectly happy with. Furthermore, my current living situation has been Internet free for the last 9 months, and I've never had a phone capable of doing anything internet-ish. And although I'm making rent money from art dealings and mail order patches which hinge on access to my email, I'm still extremely content to stay on this side of the fence.

Despite this aversion to new crap, I decided to take a stab at this wacky contraption the kids refer to as 'Kickstarter', which, to the layman, is a website that provides a simple platform for fund-raising. In many ways, my 'scamming the man' blinders were on as I decided to ask for money to go toward my planned Alaskan bike trip. You see, I'm not one to ask for anything from friends or strangers—really, anyone—as this is an aspect of my personality, an extension of the mentality to use what you got. The point is that using a third-party website as means of fundraising sort of gives the user (me) the impression that the money is actually coming from Kickstarter, like I was grifting them for a couple hundred dollars. I'm sure it's a common joke that "we should do a Kickstarter for that!" It's easy and it's free, so it's hard *not* to see this as a website that dispenses free money.

I pushed ahead anyway with these ideas in place, the justification being that I was going to Alaska with my bike regardless, and that this website involvement only netted me a solid group of people to remind me that what I was doing was interesting to others. It was like a massive pre-order for the text you are reading right now. I had already bought my plane ticket and wasn't looking to re-coop the $450 spent on travel, so I figured that I would ask for only $400, which would be seen as 'a big help.' The crazy part emerged two weeks after the campaign began when donations had already tripled my asking price, which commenced a huge conversation between my brain and me. It's quite hard to come up with answers to questions such as *Is it worth 1200 dollars for me to bike across Alaska?* or *How in the world am I going to use all this money?* Then I realized that $1200 over 21 days is like earning $2.38 an hour for the entire time I was up there! I remember a time when that was a low restaurant wage—something I could have once made *and* been taxed on!

All this information was a lot to take in, but after talking with friends, I was starting to feel more balanced about the entire thing. To me, there are about ten billion more charitable organizations that could do greater good with this kind of money. The argument progresses into banality, though, because what if this particular story changes the life of someone: Isn't that worth more on that personal scale? I remember when punk music and skateboarding changed my life, and that was well beyond economic measure. Perhaps that is the root of the problem, that my life, my emotions, my dreams and ideals are the things that come out during bike trips, during zines, and during creative efforts. Now here I was attaching a number to it, which instantly gave it value you could graph and compare to other lives. The truth to the Kickstarter debate is this: There is a world of difference between what something costs and what that thing is worth. In the case of this bike trip, yes, it costs money—flying to Anchorage, getting food, occasionally paying for campsites—but the *value*, the *worth* of the trip, is a separate concept. Only in some dystopian society could we 'sell' experiences, like in *Total Recall*, but with more meaning. I'd be on team Kuato, by the way.

In short, I asked for money and received a generous outpouring of financial and emotional support from good friends and total strangers. I can say that this trip was not made possible by the donations—it was going to happen anyway—but I cannot express how important it was to think at the top of a four-hour bike climb in the rain, *If they cared enough about my biking here to put down twenty bucks, then the least I can do is get over this stupid hill!* Money means very little to me, but the act of passing forward this hard-won stack of paper, *that* means everything. For all of you who supported and support *Next Stop Adventure*, I hereby dedicate this, and all past and future zines, books, and any story I tell to an excited listener, to you. Thank you.

The Plan

I sometimes fear that I write this nonsense as though most readers know what's about to take place. To remedy this, here's a painfully expository statement about the upcoming handful of paper: I intended to fly with my bike in a plane to Alaska, and then to reassemble that bike and ride it from town to town while camping over the course of twenty-one days. The base concept was that biking is the cheapest way to get around an area while allowing yourself to see the nature that most people speed past. Furthermore, if you're in search of interesting stories to tell, then look no further than your bicycle. I promise that any journey over sixty miles will reveal some bizarre happenings. That's an official *Next Stop Adventure* guarantee!

In buying a plane ticket, I'm forced to consider how the simplicity of Internet purchasing has destroyed what once was a real, human interaction. I don't bring this up because I miss making a lot of phone calls or standing in lines, but there's a heightened sense of importance given to a trip when you have a series of tasks to undertake. With each move toward buying your ticket, you face a real-life conversation that forces you to debate your choices. Given my age, the best comparison I can make is when I bought my first Greyhound ticket, and upon requesting a one-way, the clerk said, "Oh, well, you might as well go to this city because it's just as cheap," correctly identifying my trip as a speedy get-me-out-of-this-town exodus. You simply don't get that kind of feedback while sitting in front of a computer at 3 a.m. as you book a flight. There's no mechanism that springs to life when it becomes clear that you're not renting a car, you're not getting a hotel, and you're staying for three weeks. I love that this is possible. In a world of fences, warning signs, and caution placards all over everything, it's nice to remember that you can still make an epic mistake all on your own without a single person interfering. I booked my ticket for the cheapest days, checking only the sun and moon charts to verify that I'd be getting a hefty overdose of vitamin D (it being July in Alaska), and that was that. I did not check the weather beyond glancing at high and low temperatures, because I wanted to keep the weather patterns a surprise for fear that it would alter my route planning. That, and 'who cares, I'm going anyway.'

Quite unceremoniously I had bought a ticket, and that *immediately* jump-started me into needing to prepare. Our library had a ton of maps and over-explanatory guidebooks, so I checked out a handful and eventually chose two of them to renew on the day of my flight (so that I could bring them to Alaska while avoiding any fines). It worked like a charm! Polite, up-scale grifting! I was a kind con man, running the lamest and most boring con of all time.

If you're planning on a plane-based bike trip, the next thing you need to acquire is a box for your bike. History has shown me that asking any bike shop for one will net you a bike box in a matter of seconds, but I can offer this secondary advice to go with that: Full-suspension bikes (the kind with springs and weird crap adorning them) tend to have larger boxes, whereas track and road bikes have smaller boxes. This matters when you're planning a tour and have things like a tent, saddlebags, and (in my case) a stem that's salt-seized in the fork and a seat tube that is similarly stuck, both which will not go *anywhere*. I took a plumber's wrench to it and only tore the metal around in a blurred circle, which was not the intended result (uh, obviously).

After a quiet moment of frustration, I looked it over with fresh eyes. I had taken off my wheels, turned down my handlebars, and, no matter what I tried, my seat post stuck up out of the box by four inches. In short, everything (see below) fit into the box, but the box bulged around the wheel axles and the top didn't close. I cut out a shape that allowed the box to completely close, but it now had a steel bar sticking out the top. I made a cardboard 'hat' for it, taped it in place, and stepped back in wary contentedness. This was going to work! Kinda! The outline went from a rectangle to a misshapen Tetris piece. I admired it, thinking, "Well, airport security is definitely gonna inspect this…"

Everything: A Math List

➡ 1 bike frame with 2 dents in the top tube (not my fault! Really!)
➡ 2 pair of pedals (one clip-in and one old cage type)
➡ 4 pounds of trail mix and dried fruit that my mom mailed to me
➡ 4 pounds. *Seriously*, this is not an exaggeration.
➡ 1 tent with 7 leaks that I was unaware of
➡ 1 40-degree sleeping bag with …
➡ 1 *very not waterproof bag to stuff it in*

- 1 bike multi-tool thingy
- 2 books on Alaska, containing things like city maps and useful crap like that
- 1 small homemade pillow that I am *so glad* I brought
- 2 pairs of underwear, 1 pair of pants (which I was wearing), 1 pair of socks (ugh, I hate socks), 2 t-shirts, and 1 long-sleeved flannel shirt that I basically lived in for the whole trip
- 4 water bottles (for a bike with 3 cages)
- 24 bagels (I swear to everything that I am not kidding)
- 1 sleeping pad which I *thought* would be comfortable
- 3 pairs of shoes (who *am* I?): clip-in bike shoes, Vans, and some used soccer cleats that I found in a free pile (which are great hiking shoes, so there! [Note: I never used those, so ... well, whatever])
- 1 backpack, which I tend to avoid bringing but I am glad I did

That's about it for important stuff. I brought other little things like bike gloves, a helmet, bike lights, and other intuitive items. Though I never used my bike lights for two reasons: The first is that when bike touring, I find that I'm rarely 'so pumped' about riding past sundown, so it's all daytime bicycling, which is pre-lit by the sun. The second is that the sun sets in Alaska at about 11:30 p.m., and rises close to 4:10 a.m. There's no intolerable heat to necessitate biking late, so there's no reason for bike lights. Safety first! Or in Alaska, safety whenever!

At one point it seemed feasible that a good friend of mine might be coming up to Alaska as well (not to bike tour, though, but to camp and hitchhike around). The concept of seeing a friend around different parts of Alaska was pretty exciting since we'd be able to compare notes on places, so

I'm pretty bummed that it didn't work out in the end. However, to help entice her into coming (and also because I was personally interested in free information), I filled out one of those free-to-mail postcards and requested literature about Alaska traveling. I wrote the contact name as 'Veronica Mars' (a personal hero) and soon thereafter a stream of advertisements for Alaska started bombarding our mailbox. Some of the prices for taking cruises were beyond laughable for someone in my financial position and these pamphlets ultimately provided very little information, beyond the fact that Alaska was looking for me to spend money when I came, while I was looking to spend as little as possible. Well before this trip started, Alaska and I were already at odds with each other....

Well, Here We Are

The next thing I know, this ridiculous trip is becoming an even more ridiculous reality. What the heck was I thinking? There were times when I'd look at my map and intended route and then think that three weeks was *way* too short and my plane would undoubtedly leave without me, and then, moments later, I'd recalculate the distance and think the polar opposite because I'd be done in no time and stuck in Anchorage with no plans. I don't stress over these types of things; I tend to over-think them, capitulate to chance, and relearn what I already know, because something was going to work out.

In the most basic sense, I had everything planned: I had a plane ticket both to *and* from Alaska, I had my bike in a box, and I had some money. For the absolute worst case, this was all I would need. I would travel to Anchorage, put together my bike, ride north for awhile, then ride east, then south, then west, and then fly back. How hard could this possibly be? Simplifying like this may be dangerous, but in this case it made things *way* easier. I'd cross that bridge when I come to it! I gotta get that tattooed on me. That way I can point to it instead of wasting everyone's time by parroting my own catchphrase.

A good friend drove me to the Seattle airport, where it's significantly cheaper to fly from than Portland. I actually drove most of the drive and my friend promptly fell asleep, which is fine, but I couldn't figure out how to remove the New Found Glory CD we had been listening to. Not being able to safely reach the Scholastic Deth discography, I was stuck with NFG for the last hour and twenty minutes. I'll admit that I totally like their first two albums, but the catchiness of their songs would later haunt me like a pop-punk ghost....

At the first sight of airplanes flying toward the horizon, I got this weird feeling in my gut. It's the exact same sensation that plagues me every time I take some adventure-based trip. The problem is that when you don't plan every detail, that allots for virtually anything to happen. Decision-making is totally scattered and random because everything is an option. It's what might be referred to as 'overwhelming freedom', which is like one click away from being an oxymoron. Freedom is the ability to do anything, but the ability to do anything strikes up such anticipatory worry that it temporarily makes me pine for the daily routine I'm so set on leaving. However, as I've proved in past experiences, the feeling vanishes once the theoretical ball (bike?) gets rolling. A more apt metaphor would be to say that once the first domino falls, the trip has officially started, and forward is your only option.

So, planes in sight, my stomach felt weird. Yet the next thing I know, I'm pulling this giant cardboard box out of the trunk, looking at it long and hard, and then hugging my friend. In this moment I felt sincere envy of her role as passive observer. *She gets to just drive back listening to music! Oh man, that sounds so nice right now...* But, as you may have guessed, I lugged my giant bike box into the airport and glanced back to watch the first domino tip past the breaking point.

I sometimes appreciate technical bits of writing woven into storytelling, so here's a little bit of that to help answer questions and round out this tale. I had to pay an extra fifty dollars to check my bike box because it weighed 67 pounds, which I couldn't tell if that seemed light or heavy. Keep in mind that the box was filled with my bike, my four panniers, and *everything* I'd need to stay alive on this trip (save water and more food). In the end, fully assembled and with the water and food I added to it, my bike probably clocked in at about 75 pounds. Including a bear can. But not including me. My backpack and my body added another 155 pounds at the beginning, though that dropped ten pounds by the end. The physics fun will come later, but for now know that my legs would be responsible for moving around 236 pounds of stuff.

My first Alaskan myth was shattered by a brick of total disappointment when I approached the waiting area for my flight. First off, there were a *ton* of people, which I felt was surprising; furthermore, they were completely wrong for this trip. The room was full of sports shirts, lame sports-related hats, children jamming Gameboys or iPhones or whatever down each other's throats, and an overall sensation that Alaska was literally a place you could buy a plane ticket to no matter who you are. Yes, of course I know that's true, but I think that the first check in the ticket-buying process is some interest in your destination— a primal scream culling the pioneer spirit in us all and a beacon repeating 'return to the land…'—yet my immediate surroundings were populated with a great unwashed mass of people who seem to view Alaska and such untamable wildernesses as a giant zoo. I'll be the one weeping quietly in the woods while my compatriots here post Facebook updates about their dinner at the first Taco Bell on the moon. I wince thinking that one day I'll visit 'Paula Abdul presents Denali National Park', but, for the time being, Alaska remains at its core unspoiled, though it's doors are open wide to anybody; a double edged sword, to be sure… Especially if you ask the trees and animals who should come visit. They were there first, you know.

THE WHOLE PLANE RIDE

Day One

The plane landed, I was picked up by a friend of a friend, and I got a bizarre and fairly bright six hours of sleep. I had purposefully chosen July as the time to visit partially for the weather, but more because of the sun's nearly unending display. Even at 2 a.m. there was still enough light to read a book! However, I did not. I slept, instead. Seriously, it's only day one. That would be insanity.

The next morning I woke up, chatted with my extremely kind host, and put my bike back together. I also made three full cups of quinoa and put it in a Ziploc bag (which seemed extraordinarily smart, indicating that it was not my idea but rather my host's). I attached my clipless pedals, put everything in my bike bags, filled up my water, and took a generic-yet-impossible-to-avoid photo of me with my bike posing in the 'before' stance. I had two stops to take before the trip actually started: One was to REI for a bear can and the other was to a grocery store for bananas and apples. Part one of that was a good idea but ultimately unnecessary (read: I was not eaten by bears, so I didn't *use* my bear can), and part two was pointless (though I didn't know it at the time). When are bananas ever pointless, right? It's like a riddle that you'll know the answer to by the end of this… or right now if you guess what happens when you put ripe, unbruised fruit into a heavy plastic container and then proceed to bounce around for a couple hundred miles.

A solid way to feel like an idiot who arrived in Alaska to try his hand at 'the wild' is to visit REI (or any camping supply store) with a fully loaded bike, looking like you're on a lengthy trip. Invariably, the questions come.

"How far have you been?"

"Where are you headed?"

"How long have you been out for?"

To which you dejectedly respond, "Uh…nearly a half mile…I'm going, uh, north…and I've been riding for, maybe, six minutes…?"

It's the equivalent of asking a stranger for their autograph before they've done something to make them seem interesting or famous. What an awkward exchange, right? The reason you ask those questions it to be impressed by the answers, not shocked with disinterest. An avalanche of "Oh…" later, I was gone and eager to complete *at least one mile*.

Anchorage Sucks

Yeah, that's true. I haven't verified it on Wikipedia yet, but I assure you, the first fact you'll read in a bulleted list is that it totally sucks. The traffic is awful, the roads were laid out by some ingenious riddle master (well, at least the crosswalk systems were), and if biking in the barren wilderness of Alaska frightens you, then biking in the city is practically suicide. (Cyclocide?)

The route I'd gleaned from my library book was to travel due west to Earthquake Park and then take one of six bike routes in the city northbound to meet up with the highway, which would ultimately take me to Palmer, Cantwell, and, at some point, the Denali highway. Earthquake Park is a funny little tract of land, dense with overgrowth of trees and moss. I hiked around for a second, took some photos, and was completely enamored by these strange birds that were bobbing around the mudflats. They looked like giant fuzzy herons, like if a heron was molting brown sheep wool. A good writer might take this opportunity to give some real information about what kind of birds they are. Maybe next time.

More interestingly: At mile 2.6 from the absolute beginning of my trip, I slammed my brakes and came to a quick stop only to watch a beautiful gray wolf wander from the woods and across the bike path only a whopping ten feet in front of me. Her back was as high as my heart is from the ground, and she glanced at me for a microsecond, long enough to decide, "…Nope, not him," and then pass silently into the forest once more. Shattering the moment as the wolf disappears, a jock mountain biker pulled off his headphones and called to me, "Dude! You see that?" just as a woman three steps behind me stopped pushing her baby carriage to yell, "Was that a dog?"

I was in Alaska alright. Wolves and breeding idiots are everywhere! I wasn't sure which to be more afraid of!

As I've stated in previous bike-touring texts, writing about the physical act of biking is fairly uneventful. I rode a bunch of miles, stopped occasionally, and ate more bagels than anyone should ever even consider eating. I drank water. I had to deal with riding my bike on the sidewalk a bit. It's not very moving, huh?

Leaving town was complicated, as my map had too small of a scale to be helpful. When the road I needed to bike on started displaying signs reading 'Pedestrians And Non-Motorized Vehicles Prohibited,' I started to worry, as I was technically both of those. I followed the road in the correct cardinal direction and was just 'going with it', which worked until that road gave up. I stood at a corner, ten miles already biked, looking for answers, and all I got was a woman getting out of her car while screaming, "WELL, FINE. If you wanna be a punk and go sleep around, then YOU JUST GO DO THAT," as she slammed the living crap out of the door and the guy in the driver's seat sped off through the stoplight. This was followed with the loudest "OH NO, HE DIDN'T! OH-OH-OOHHH!" that I have ever heard. When looking for cues from life, this doesn't help. So I went straight ahead. But that crap was hilarious. Personally, I'm glad she left him. You can do better!

I found what looked to be a decent bike path (though I had no idea where it went) and when a woman with four kids walked by, I jumped into conversation without even thinking about it.

"Do you know how to get, um, north of here...I'm headed to Palmer..."

My total confusion and lack of confidence paid off! She helped me by pointing out a magic tunnel that set me on the road that I needed. Our brief conversation also netted me an interesting fact that, luckily, would *not* play into my experience up north whatsoever. It turns out that Alaska (whose license plate reads 'The Last Frontier') is the only state in the United States to not require that convicted sex offenders be publicly registered. This means that if your neighbor is a convicted rapist, then their secret will go unnoticed up in Alaska but nowhere else. The obvious result would be that only the extreme criminals might feel compelled to hide their repeated misdeeds by moving to this 'last frontier', so now I was weighing the mental pie chart that was divided into:

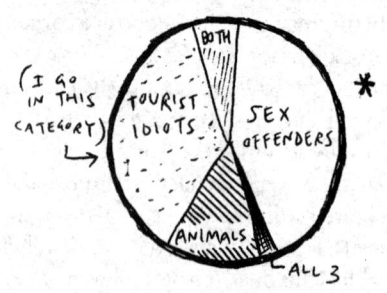

*Pie chart: BOTH, TOURIST IDIOTS (I go in this category), SEX OFFENDERS *, ANIMALS, ALL 3*

I pondered that one for a while and eventually found myself out of Anchorage completely. The side road I had taken ended abruptly and only the highway remained. It just so happened that a cop was sitting in the parking lot alongside me, so I asked him if it was legal to bike on the road in front of me (as there were no signs indicating that I couldn't, though it was clearly a highway with guardrails and everything).

"Yeah, it's legal, and even if it wasn't, I wouldn't stop yuh".

Thanks cop! You're terrible at your job or lazy, but either way I got the okay from the law so there was now nothing standing in my way! Only bears, wolves, hills, and every other non-manmade problem that exists on earth!

After a massive downhill, I stopped to look at the underside of a bridge that I had to cross, and upon hiking to the riverbank I saw graffiti proclaiming that 'Jocks suck cock,' which made me laugh out loud. In the land of unchecked sexual deviants, it was heartwarming to see such vulgar displays of honesty. (Or inappropriate falsehoods, whichever you choose to believe. I skateboarded all through high school and listened to a lot of the Queers and Screeching Weasel, so you can probably guess where I stand.)

Nearly seventy miles had passed and I found myself sitting on what appeared to be the concrete base of a housing project that was either abandoned or torn apart. An interesting thing happened here that was only visible through the glory of retrospection: Of all the amazing sites and incredible surroundings I met in my full 950-mile tour of Alaska, the thirty miles before reaching this spot were somehow the most memorable. I'm confident that it's not because of the sights there—yes, they was beautiful, the Jurassic-Park-esque overgrown plains painted by fading pink light—but my thoughts seemed to carry more weight throughout this part of the trip. I thought of friends whose company I missed and I started making one-sided plans almost immediately. *How have we never gone on a road trip together? That's insane!* and *She is such a great person and I should tell her that more often.* I would say that this was my built-in regret (in the event that I was eaten by bears or killed by Alaska's untamed madness) but that doesn't seem true. I think that sometimes when you're worried, it's extremely comforting to remember who your friends are and why you care about them. Sometimes it takes distance and a bike trip for that to occur. A fun project would be to take a short daytrip and then end it with a hug to someone who deserves a hug. That's basically what I did! I was a hugging *machine* when I came back from this nonsense.

I ate some quinoa with chips and was fairly pleased with this spot as a camping site, but the ever-visible sun begged to continue our race. Sure, it was almost 8 o'clock, but it was still *really* light out! After dinner, with a steady soundtrack of memorized New Found Glory cycling through my brain, I continued on another twenty miles. This would be a twenty-mile stretch involving three strip malls, a giant firework stand with a homemade Batmobile as part of the lawn decoration, and a surprising lack of billboards. The sun started thinking about setting from the hours of 11 o'clock to midnight, so I sort of had a lot of time to think, *Oh, I could camp there... but... nah, I'll keep going*. I wasn't near anything and I had energy, so it didn't matter where I ended up. Further is always better, though I was also getting excited about not moving for a couple hours.

I received a boost of excitement upon realizing that there was a multi-use path that followed the highway for a *long* time. I didn't yet know how far it went, but I was sure that for as far as I could see I wouldn't be dealing with cars! It is also worth noting I only saw a car or two about every five minutes, but still! This path eventually vomited me right next to a church, which I decided would be a perfect camping spot for night number one. I put my tent together, got out food to eat that night, and forced the rest into the bear can, hiding it about two hundred feet away. The odd thing was that I'd find giant piles of poop every time I thought *I'll put it here!*, which was a bit disconcerting. If an animal had pooped there, the chances are that it had walked there, which meant it could walk there *again*, and if you follow the logic, then all of the sudden I've been torn to pieces by some animal that poops strange piles everywhere. The droppings resembled laughably enormous rabbit pellets, somewhere between an acorn and an egg. I would later learn that these are moose droppings, but at the time, hiding my food, I was sure that it was bear poop, and that just by *seeing* it I had officially asked to be eaten.

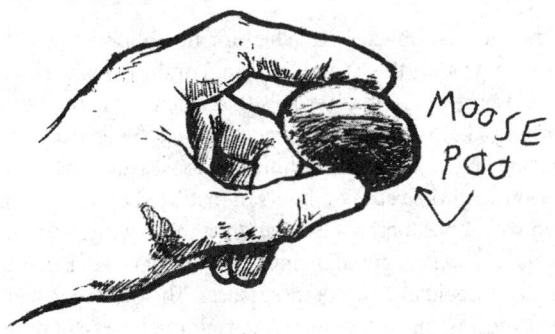

However, I survived the night, only to wake up at strange intervals while incorrectly guessing the time based on the light falling on my tent. "Seven fifteen!" I'd say, as I checked my watch...that read 3:14. This 'light thing' might not be as exciting as I thought it would be.

Breakfast became a standardized ordeal: blueberry bagel with peanut butter, followed by a banana. There was little deviation from this for the entire trip. This meal also doubled as dinner. All told, I think I ate twenty-three bagels and a disturbing amount of peanut butter. *Disturbing*. And I still lost like 9 pounds! The other catch that I had been warned about caught up with me that morning, as the most ludicrous and frenzied mosquitos that I have ever witnessed started attacking me during every bite of my breakfast. The mistake I made was to eat outside my tent, as I had already packed it up and had nowhere to hide. Like most lessons punctuated by pain and blood, you'll only need to learn this once. The mosquitos in Alaska are *terrible*.

Other Things Involving Blood

With breakfast down, I stretched for much longer than I normally would (this is a good thing) and then biked another twenty miles. It never fails that when I bike the next morning, I keep repeating *Oh man, that would've been a great camping spot…* as I pass anything that looks better than my previous night's sleep. Two hours of that later, I arrived in a town with a post office, a gas station, a thrift store and *that is absolutely all*. I figured, being the worldly traveler that I am, that I would use each of these places. The gas station had chips, the post office had stamps and afforded me an opportunity to send some postcards, and the thrift store…well, the thrift store had some quirks.

Allow me to paint you the scene. A homemade, crooked sign remarks 'Thrift Store,' staked in a yard littered with rusty exercise equipment, VCRs, old bicycles, and various car parts. A plastic horse lay frozen in time, springs rusted together from rain and neglect. And it was tipped over. Behind the yard sits a strange fort-looking house with homemade additions and piles of 'stuff' everywhere. I roll up slowly to one of the three front doors and an old man in a rocking chair elbows an even older man while motioning toward me. The older of the two slowwwly ambles forward....

"Whaaa' can I help you with? We got clothes and scarves and books and all kinds of stuff here, you know…" he streams. I admit that I only wanted to see if they had any VHS tapes (a hobby of mine is buying hard-to-find VHS tapes from the 80s for a dollar so that I can watch movies like *Rad* and *Thrashin'* all day while annoying my housemates' friends and anyone else in earshot) and he happily admits that they have a whole room, and why don't I follow him in.

So, it turns out that they had bought all the remaining stock from a video store that went bankrupt and therefore they have a *lot* of movies. This is extremely exciting to me, as this opportunity is fairly rare and typically yields some really good crap from the 80s. I start methodically from the left, pawing over each box, and I notice the old man standing there and staring at me from a whopping six feet to my right. I gathered that his job was to make sure that I didn't steal anything and, being the only customer, I suppose it makes sense to stand and watch. Furthermore, it's a lonely town, so why not engage me in conversation, right? A fun note about his speech patterns that makes this more 'true to life' is that he spoke from his lungs and did so *as fast as humanly possible* with no commas, grammar, or pausing. He was the conversational equivalent to talking to a water hose, pointed at your face and spraying full blast.

"Idn't that different!" He must have said that phrase a hundred times. He'd pick out a movie like *Species 2*, glance at the cover, and say, "There's a real one! Boy! Idn't that different!"

"Uh...yeah...that's a weird one alright..." I tried and tried but failed to handle this well.

"You like jokes? You hear about that new dog they got down there in Anchorage? Oh yeah, oh boy, it's a new dog and it's ILLEGAL! Know what they call it? Ha, yep, they call it a METH LAB! Oh boy, idn't that different!"

At the time this was even weirder, because I absolutely did not understand the joke. The play is on the *lab* part—like, a Labrador. But he accented the whole answer so that I couldn't see the cleverness, which made me think that he was totally bonkers. I still hold that opinion, though, because as I picked out *Altered States*, a great movie about the horrors of float tanks and astral projection, he said, "Boy howdy, I got me a tape of these women, right, and they take these scissors and they just cut off their vaginas!"

To which, with wide-eyes, I shot back, "Excuse me? You have a tape of women performing...uh...self-clitorectomies?"

"Sure do! Want me to run go get it for ya? It's real different!"

I declined his offer, though I feel somewhat torn about doing so. I remain unsure if this was a *movie* he was talking about (like *Antichrist*, perhaps?) or if this was an honest-to-goodness super sketchy video he had acquired somehow. Make no mistake, I don't want to watch this, though I feel like getting it from him and breaking it over my knee may have been the 'right' thing to do. In other moments, I'm certain that the right thing to do was determine if this old guy was a cog in a machine of abusive pornography and literally split his head open with my kneecap and vomit on his brains like an image from the *Garbage Pail Kids* cards. Given my lack of evidence and information, I can't be sure. All I'm sure about is that after I declined, the yodeling started.

"I used to write for the newspaper, I did! Shoot, I also write songs! Here's one now…" and he started in with these epically loud 'fables' that were yodeled like tomorrow was never going to happen. The themes all seemed to be 'she left me so now I'm alone, and I shouldn't never done that thing' types, and I really sped up looking at the tapes while this was going on. "This one's about a job I had, and it goes…" and he'd launch right back into it. What he lacked in talent, he *more* than made up for in loud yodel-yelling. He's also standing six feet away from me the whole time; I hope that part is clear. For good measure, he'd throw in a joke or two between songs, all playing on that standard 'women and men are different for some reason' trope. I don't recall the specifics, but 'How is my wife like than a brick? They both get old and fat!' is a pretty good example.

Ultimately, I left without the potential mutilation porn but instead with some super cheap postcards and a handful of VHS movies. I was also encouraged to pay the 'Christian price', which was whatever I felt like I should pay. I felt like I should pay nothing, though I suppose I was encouraged by his yodeling because I dropped four dollars.

"Boy, it's a good one today! We already had us a customer and it ain't even eleven yet! Idn't that different?"

Yep. Different.

Anywhere Else (Get Me There Quickly)

Things of note this day were seeing another bike tourist (a huge deal, trust me), getting *more* potato chips, and arriving within the bounds of Denali National Park. A tired moment about seventy-five miles in found me resting and taking a 'sitting up, head-bobbing' nap at a completely overgrown rest stop, and I started the great debate with my brain. It's easy to keep biking when you're already *on* your bike, but when you're sitting on the ground and looking at your bike, then picking it back up and continuing on is really, really hard sometimes. Food, weather, and overall resolve are the things that flip that mental switch, and when my resolve went from 49% to 51%, I got up, kept mumbling that same New Found Glory song, and biked a mile only to see a moose walk right out across the road. Unreal! I thought that the wolf was big, but the term was redefined by this hulking brown…thing. A car had stopped and was parked on the side of the road, and the moose's back was a foot over their rooftop. They look like pleasant animals because of what appears to be a smile (though it's not, because it's just the way their jawline is formed, so don't be ridiculous), but when you see one in real life, it becomes clear why they could gore things like your face when you're in front of them. I mean, if you had a seven-foot-wide coat rack attached to your head, wouldn't you feel compelled to rush at yuppies only to watch them freak out? Exactly. Now you are a moose. Go to a fancy hotel and run at people and see what happens.

    I breached the southern border of the Denali Nature Preserve, and to celebrate this momentous occasion, Mother Nature threw a wild party for me by dumping ten billion gallons of water all over every freaking thing for two hours. In the bike touring mindset (or perhaps I can extend this to traveling in general), rain is a massive, wet slap to the face. It's a rare event to feel so hot that a gentle dribbling from the clouds is a welcome change, and no amount of biking in Alaska was going to get my blood warm enough for this scenario. I stopped off at a little lookout place to see the actual Denali Mountain and chatted with an older man who said he's been there for three full days to see the mountain, known for only becoming visible when conditions are perfect.

"I hear you could see it two nights ago between 11:45 and 11:56 at night, since that's the only time the clouds have cleared…"

Wow, that kind of dedication actually freaks me out. It'd be like watching the sky for seventy-two full hours and then missing the one meteor that fell because you were looking at your shoes or eating your boogers. I like to think that, like some forgotten myth from the ancients, that man is still there staring northward, eyes squinted to slits, watching…waiting…bored.

Another two miles of damp dampness dumped me out at a little campsite with bathrooms and a small picnic area underneath a modest wooden overhang. The paradox here was that I wanted only to sit down in non-rain for a moment, but the mosquitos go kill-crazy the second I stop moving. Also, the rain was still coming down really hard, likely enough to fully soak a dollar bill in twenty seconds. If you think about that, you'll think, *Oh, wow, that's a lot of rain*. Trust me.

After looking at my bike and convincing myself out loud to do helpful things like 'Move your hands and legs to set up your tent,' I managed to actually *do* those things. I made camp under a large tree that altered the rain from a strong, steady downpour to intermittent giant drops that fell after collecting in the pine needles above. It reminded me (both in sound and general setting) of that scene in *Arachnophobia* in the trees in the rainforest are being gassed for butterflies and you start hearing weird 'thumps' as giant spiders fall. This comparison did not help me to sleep well that night. Neither did the rain, which was slowly pooling in the corners of my tent. Well, at least it wasn't spiders, right?

↑ THIS IS AN ACTUAL PHOTOGRAPH

One note of interest is that camping in campgrounds (as in official, 'real' ones) provides a strange sense of security that I had not expected. I slept extremely well because a 'legit' situation meant that the back-of-my-head fear of some type of authority awakening me with a gun and the ability to arrest me was quite unlikely. Another note of interest is that when camping in an area where a bear can is recommended, if you get hungry at 7 a.m. and it's still raining, you can't simply find a banana in your backpack; you have to get out of your sleeping bag, put on your wet shoes, and walk a couple hundred feet to where you hid your food the night before. Imagine waking up in your bed in your room and thinking, *Ah, breakfast*... then getting fully clothed in damp fabric only to walk a block over to the patch of trees where you stashed your box of cereal. People don't live like this. Squirrels live like this. Well, I suppose that 'roughing it' includes wet shoes and soggy bagels. Next Stop: Complaining!

The following day was a sitcom of errors, like a disjointed Surrealist play in which I did things in slightly different locations with intermissions that found me riding my bike for about fifteen miles. This is to say I would ride my bike for fifteen miles, stop, take off my rain jacket, drink some water, take a photo, and ride some more. However, the errors were aplenty, so as I rolled to the side of the road to sit down and eat Breakfast Part Two: Bananapocalypse, I began my sucky trend of totally falling over on my bike. It's unceremonious, it's quite surprising, and if you ride with clip-in shoes, *it's going to happen to you, too*. It was actually less my fault than I thought, because the top part of my shoe was separating from the sole of the shoe so that when I turned my foot to snap out then only the top half would turn, but the bottom part with the clip would not. When rolling up a slight incline and steering an idiotically heavy bicycle, you basically get one chance. I failed. In a slow and quiet moment of total melancholy, I tipped over to the right.

As a twenty-nine year old, I rarely found myself in embarrassing situations anymore, as socially I have forged myself to deal with most everything. It then came as quite a shock, you might imagine, to lay there with the bike still stuck to me in the middle of the oncoming traffic lane. I looked like I was trying to ride a bike but didn't understand the force of gravity. It's like all the shame of tripping on a doorjamb with an armload of spaghetti and landing face down in dog poop. Then you're *stuck* there, because your dumb shoes are still latched on to your stupid bike.

Dividing Lines

On this third day, the day of tipping over and beginning a series of small scabs on my knee and elbow, I finally hit a point in which I was running pretty low on water. I had five water bottles, and one bottle was my 'I should never have to drink from this because it's for emergencies only, so fill up *before* it's necessary' bottle, and there I was taking sips from it. With no town for sixty miles and these weird signs reading 'Drinking Water: Boil It First Or You'll Totally Barf It All Back Up' on campground water spigots, I was forced to rely on a stranger. You may have noticed it's absence on my 'list of stuff I brought', but means to heat anything up was something I was not carrying. Cold food for life!

I pulled off at a small lookout where an older gentleman lived for the summer as the campground manager, and I started up a conversation to help segue the 'can I have some of your water because I clearly didn't plan ahead like you did' question. Gleaning from my appearance that I was Luddite-leaning, he confided in me that he was sick of seeing RVs with satellites that pulled two hundred channels to families more interested in watching TV than watching the clouds and the mountains. His irritation was surely merited. The parking lot was overflowing with techno-savvy campers, and then there's me, a filthy, still-damp guy on his bicycle, and then there's him, a guy with a hotplate, a sleeping bag, and enough room in the back of his truck to lie down. Our sides were clear, though the playing field was hazy.

You see, I agreed with everything he said, but as I biked away I was gripped by a horrible thought: Where does the line get drawn? If a family is visiting Alaska, seeing amazing things, and then interspersing them with television, is that really any different than me biking around, seeing the same things (for a longer time), but loudly singing New Found Glory for hours? Was I capable of really enjoying nature without making jokes about it to myself or strumming the guitar parts on my thigh? Were there thoughts left for me to have while staring out at the horizon, or am I doomed to repeat the nonsense I've memorized from movies and songs? How do I show appreciation for a mountain or a forest and make it *mean* something?

This is what the camera replaced: the reflective moments that were once internalized have shifted and we point a small box at pretty things, frame them well, and click a button, and it's supposed to have the same effect. I worry that my brain once took better photos than a camera ever could, but perhaps I've unwillingly replaced that skill. Either nature isn't that impressive or (more likely) my attention is so marred by fast-paced action and memorization that appreciating a tree for a tree requires some relearning. To combat this, I suggest going on walks without a camera. It's a first step, but I believe that it will help anyone who is looking to connect to nature.

Interestingly, the remainder of this particular day found the sun coming out, the clouds whirling apart in formations like oily water, and the horizon totally opening up into sharp browns carving upward into pink and purple smudges. I like to think that nature was offering me a small prize for trying harder to appreciate her, and this afternoon and evening was gloriously welcomed. I took no photos during this time period and I stand firm on my reasoning.

But Apparently, I Did It Wrong

I had rolled into Cantwell, Alaska, which was 210 miles into this trip, and all I wanted in life was more water and something that was not a bagel to cram down my guts. The town's only restaurant was closed (yeah, I know right?), so I went in the no-name gas station instead.

"Oh. Huh." That's me, upon walking in.

Six shelves spanned the room and every surface wore a thin layer of cardboard dust. My options for food were fairly small, and sticking to vegan food dropped it to about three items, each of which I bought. Potato chips, Gatorade, and a giant jug of water! The store gave the appearance that some intense riots went down about two months ago, and the rioters, in the true spirit of equality, left two to three of each item. With nowhere to sit in or near this dumpy gas station, I walked my bike north for a minute and found the good ol' post office—friend to bike tourers and vagabonds alike! That's because you can sit outside of one and you probably won't get kicked out. Well, not quickly, at least. Certainly not in Cantwell!

Allow me to paint a word photo. The entire post office was contained within one trailer that was supported on stilts, with metal stairs sharper than shreds of aluminum cans. (I realize this was to combat the snow, which undoubtedly nets Alaska with a lot of slipping and falling people every winter. If it's not clear, nature hates us and the manner we live alongside her, and this is proof.) I finished my quinoa from the first day and, for no real reason in particular, I wandered in the post office. It was unstaffed (since it was 9 p.m.) and the whole structure was basically a massive PO box, since there was no mail delivery in this town. Interesting as that was, something else caught my eye: a six-inch stack of papers popping off the wall to my left. Evidently, the Cantwell post office has been both prominently displaying (and more importantly, collecting) FBI 'Wanted' posters for the past ten or so years, and here, on this innocuous little wall, was a giant stack of history staring me in the face. Logically, and perhaps excitingly for Alaskan residents, their state seems the ideal spot to run to after committing crimes, so these wanted posters might actually find real use up here. It started innocently enough as I flipped through them, looking for names I recognized or maybe faces I had seen recently, but it soon occurred to me that, having not brought any paper to write my friends, I needed these to send letters. No, I didn't only need them—I would die without them. This mighty stack was the greatest find of my life, and all the events in the past year leading up to Alaska had twisted and turned to put me here in this room, alone and unwatched. It was my duty to take some of these, and when life scribes this path, you don't dare spit in life's eye. You take those FBI posters! You take them no matter what! You take them and you *run*!

Giggling with total madness, I set up my tent in a small patch of forest near the only intersection in town and immediately started reading about my collected felons. I had not given any thought to which posters I pulled off, as I had grabbed only a handful, so this was the first opportunity to see what kind of crime I was dealing with. Of the eleven I had, ten were sizable crimes (larceny, murder, drug running), but the eleventh stood out, as it had way more photos and information than the others.

Five photographs adorned the top and the list of aliases was fifteen names deep. I didn't recognize her by her given name or *most* of the aliases until I got the to second to last one: Assata Shakur! Famed member of the Black Liberation Army *and* a Black Panther. She even escaped from prison! I debated about which of my friends would most appreciate this piece of radical history, and I believe that I did the right thing in sending it back home to Justin.

The lesson here is that if you're ever in Cantwell, Alaska, go to the post office (the door is open all twenty-four hours) and take a good, long look at the history of crime in the United States. If you get overzealous like some of us, you can probably take some of it. And send me one! I didn't keep any for myself.

The Worst Night Of Anything In My Life

When you live life in a way that doesn't piss off Mother Nature, (or pisses her off less, I should say) you find happiness in everything. When you do something wrong, she rears back her fist, slams you in the face, and the tirade of failure rains in endless fall. To prove my point, I offer this as anecdotal evidence:

I had biked up to Denali National Park and spent the entire day hiking, falling over on my bike again (this time to the left!), and enjoying the non-rainy environment that is Denali. Even if you hate hikes, this place is amazing and I would recommend it to anyone. It is beautiful. It looks like what the earth looked like before the industrial revolution got to it.

As the clouds began to gather again around 9 p.m., I figured I could likely bike the twenty-nine miles back to Cantwell to sleep in the same spot as the night before, since I had to go south anyway to eventually cut across eastbound. It rained from the very beginning, and I kept high spirits by reciting every line I know from *An American Werewolf in London*, and then quoting virtually every line from *Clerks*, to follow. It may sound stupid, but sometimes desperation produces weird reactions and I can't even begin to explain them. However, if it'll help you bike twenty miles in the cold rain without becoming deeply saddened by your crappy situation, then by all means do whatever it takes. And really, at this point it was better than New Found Glory. I think we can all agree on that.

The trouble with biking a route that you've already taken in the opposite direction is that you remember all the mile markers and they help you recall that you're still not as far as you need to be. Cantwell was still eight miles away, the rain was getting much heavier, and the wind ramped up her speed so that it was coming straight at my face. My shoes had basically filled with water, my pants were completely soaked through, and my waterproof rain jacket was working everywhere except at the edges, which left my neck, wrists, and waistline literally dripping. I had biking gloves (those cool kind without fingers) so it goes without saying that my hands were soaked. The odometer stared up at me and reflected a mean '9 mph' on its face, because the wind was coming at me so hard that I couldn't even break ten miles per hour. I made the mistake of feeling the bag containing my sleeping bag, and it had absorbed every drop of water that came near it, which meant that my sleeping bag was a proverbial weeping bag of wetness. Yeah, it was that bad. And it gets worse.

After yelling all kinds of mean things at invisible forces wrecking my life, I eventually rolled in to Cantwell, that crummy little city that I'd left once before. I visited the post office only to sit next to the heater and I debated the options I thought I had. Setting up camp in the rain seemed dumb at this point, because I knew that my tent wasn't waterproof enough, and at the current rate of precipitation that would be a real problem. What I needed was somewhere to sleep *under* so that I could dry off a little. In a normal town, this is an easy call to answer, but it is less so in the middle of freaking nowhere. The only overhang in this town was underneath a bridge at the south end, so I got back on my bike, water in my shoes, and pedaled off.

The bridge joined the land over a river about seventy feet in width. It stood about fifteen feet over the river itself, and gravel pits comprised the islands in the river where the feet of the bridge stood. Scurrying down the embankment, with my could-this-*be*-any-heavier bike, I walked over a meager nine-inch stream to the gravel island and made it under the bridge. For the first time in nearly five hours, the rain had stopped pouring on me. Its effects remained evident, but the relief of not getting any wetter calmed me greatly.

I set up my tent in record time, all the while cursing the

biting wind whipping from downstream. The combination of the rain, the river, and the overall lack of sun made for a very cold wind; I'd guess that the temperature felt like 40 degrees down there. I stripped off all my clothes and bungee-corded them to exposed rebar, hoping the wind might dry them overnight, and then I wrung out my sleeping bag, which offered a full puddle of rain that nearly broke my resolve right in half. My sleeping bag was *completely* soaked, inside and out, and there was absolutely no way that I could dry it and sleep warmly tonight. I should also mention how hard it is to think properly when you're soaked, tired, cold, and standing in the middle of a river in your underwear, looking around and saying idiotic things like, "Man, why isn't this river full of amazing vegetable soup?"

The best option I had was to climb in naked, eat as much peanut butter as I could (an old camping trick to keep your stomach working all night to create body warmth), and slide both me and my sleeping bag into my magic space bag, which is a giant tin-foil-looking condom that doesn't breathe at all and reflects ninety-percent of the heat inside it. (It's like the microwave of blankets. Or maybe the solar cooker of blankets, I guess.) The point is that I was in it and I had to try to sleep, since it was 2 a.m. and staying up all night was not an idea I was comfortable with. (But, then again, comfort was slowly being redefined right in front of me.)

As I lay there letting exhaustion take its course on my body, a thought gently appeared in the back of my frigid head: If it was still raining, which it certainly was, could there be any chance that the river I had islanded myself on would, uh, rise? The rain was pouring down at an unbelievable rate, and I understand that while one drop in a bucket is nothing, thirty billion drops is a lot of nothing. So I started to worry. My last thought before falling asleep was that the river wasn't likely to rise the two feet necessary to carry away me or my bike. I was totally sure. Pretty totally sure. Kind of. Maybe. Who cares, because I was tired. I didn't have a plan for that moment, but I was sure I could deal with it if that happened.

I slept in the shape of a comma, later flipping over to the shape of an apostrophe through the rest of the night. Twenty-minute bursts of dreamless, tense sleep was getting me nowhere, but it took my mind off the situation. I had put myself in a MacGyver-Situationist testing zone in which not dying was my only goal and my supplies were my immediate surroundings. The catch to this game is that one can't lose. Even giving up takes effort at this point, and so I lay there, freezing and alive. 'There is no hole so deep that it yields no dirt.' I made that up that night, and if you don't get it, well, go try to sleep in the rain with no cover for eight hours and then reanalyze it. It's genius if you're in the right mindset.

Since the sun never actually went down that night, I decided to get up and leave at about 6 a.m. (which was as bright at midnight, or 2 a.m., or 4 a.m., or anytime at all). For the rest of this Alaskan endeavor, it would be a fair assessment to say that the sky looks like damp newsprint at all hours. Where the power and physical drive to fold up my wet sleeping bag and tent came from, I will never know. I stepped into soaking shoes, slid into damp, heavy pants, and bungee-corded everything onto my bike. It was at this point that I looked at the little nine-inch stream from the prior night, which had somehow transformed into a nine-*foot*-wide river.

The situation I had knowingly put myself in was, in simplest terms this: I walked onto a small island one night, the rain flooded the river around this island so that my island shrank, and the only exit was a nine-foot-wide, eighteen-inch-deep chasm. I could jump it alone, but I had a giant steel bike with me, and while I'm good at pull-ups, I couldn't possible throw an eighty-pound bike that far, let alone deal with the damage it would likely sustain on those river rocks. What is this crap? *Crap is what this is*!

MacGyver's spirit roared over the hills (because it simply *had* to) and I found a giant log on my shrinking island, rolled my bike halfway through the river by leaning as far as I could, and then wedged the log between the ground and the top tube like a massive kickstand. The miracle here is that it held and didn't shift or fall over like I was terrified it would. I took this opportunity to run back, sprinting as fast as I could, then jump the creek, turn around, and pull my bike by the tips of the handlebars over to the non-island side. As the stick fell away, I realized that it had worked!

The avalanche of freezing bullcrap had finally been

dammed! My own personal Alaskan pipeline of misery had ruptured and was no longer flowing! Despite the rain and everything remaining wet, I thought for the first time in hours that I was not going to die from frustration, misery, frostbite, or some other constant problem!

I made it back to the gas station, proceeded to write a lot and sit very still, and soon learned that there were dryers at the RV park one mile to the west. Some quarters and patience later, I was back to being fully dry. Before leaving the gas station, I bought ten trash bags, three of which I used on my sleeping bag to prevent this tragedy from ever happening again. Heed my warning, dear reader: Wrap everything in your life in plastic or else it will get wet, and you will then barrel down the fast track to madness. Trash bags saved my life. I should get that tattooed on me, too. By the end of this, I'm gonna have some extremely regrettable tattoos.

INTERMISSION:
Four Tales, All With One Thread In Common

Somehow writing an intermission seems really necessary to me in this 'bike bike bike bike' writing, so here's a totally different bunch of crap. Try to find the mysterious similarity throughout the following tales of woe and embarrassment….

Four

I can't say for certain if Craigslist has opened up a horrifying gash in our collective culture, but I worry we're close to that point. Whereas years ago one had to *work* for bizarre opportunities, now one can find a hundred on your local

Craigslist site, all waiting for...something. Basically, it's like a 'story generator'—if you're looking to wow some friends at your next social gathering with an amazing tale of reckless abandon and weirdness, just look online and you're on your way. Think I'm kidding? Watch this:

In Chicago I lived with a super rad friend who was without a job and needed money to pay rent and bills. Sound familiar? Ian had been putting in hours on Craigslist each day, emailing everyone and everything that offered money for job-like scenarios. Halloween was around the corner, which meant that the last of the bikeable weather in Illinois was here, and there was no way that I was missing it. I asked Ian to come along and he did. We rode to the waterfront and by the aquarium and planetarium, which is a sizeable ride, and we were hanging out, jumping on rocks, and skipping stones. Ian then got a phone call, and based on his answers it's clear that it's someone he doesn't know, as he answers questions with, "Sure, I can definitely do that...yeah, I have one friend who'd probably be interested..."

He hangs up and explains the following. He'd been called back by a Craigslist poster that was looking for one night's work at fifty dollars for three hours. It was a haunted house looking for 'actors' for their scenes—one of those haunted houses you are guided through and see vignette skits of terror and woe. He then says, "They need a bunch of people, so...you wanna come? It's fifty bucks, dude..."

An hour later we arrive at this sketchy, bro-looking bar on the north side of Chicago and head in. Immediately I realize the mistake, as our 'boss' for the night is wearing a shirt that reads 'My dick ain't gonna suck itself.' I sigh as loudly as I can, and start to wonder if I could kill him and hide him in this haunted house and get away with it, like in a *Tales From The Crypt* comic.

My friend Ian is a pretty big guy and is immediately given the role of werewolf to scare people by yelling and banging on a fence. His job seems enviably simple. The idiot boss dude looked me up and down and asked, "Well... how do you feel about being a demented clown? We always need more of those..."

I muster a, "Umm... uh, I suppose..."

But *right then*, when my stupid fate was almost sealed, this guy wanders in and whispers to the boss. "I can't do the cannibal tonight because my throat is messed up".

I see the opportunity for what it is and scream "OH, OH, OH MAN, I can totally be a cannibal!" The old boss dude gives me the okay and it's done. Clown avoided. *Whew*.

I get this dumb prosthetic mask that covers one of my eyes to make me look like I'm deformed, and the mask is glued to my head. From this point on I can see with only my left eye, rendering the world in two dimensions so that I cannot perceive the depth of things like, say, steps or doors. Then I strip down to my underwear and I'm handed a pair of extra-large tighty-whiteys. I changed into them and they don't even sort of fit. I folded them over at the waist so that they wouldn't fall off, but they're still not really 'on.' For some reason they let me wear my watch, despite being in a scene where I was an island cannibal, which is all kinds of illogical. But then again, you heard the man: *My dick ain't gonna suck itself*.

I'm introduced to my scene partner, a twenty-something girl who is pretend-chained to the wall, the leg of whom I will be pretend-eating endlessly for the night. Our scene looks like this: There's a rocky wall to the back, dead bodies on the ground, and a bunch of hay for some weird effect that I'm still unclear about. We're informed that the scene starts every seven minutes when a new group comes in and we were to be signaled by a flashlight blinked at us from the tour guide.

We do our 'scene.' I yell incomprehensibly, bang some chains, eat her leg, scare people, and that's it. All in all, it was pretty easy. But before the doors open, our Neanderthal boss bursts in saying, "Almost forgot the best part!" while dumping an entire two-gallon bottle of fake blood on my face and chest. I can see out of only one eye, I'm standing half-naked in giant-sized underwear, and now I have corn syrup all over *everything*. The boss moves to high-five me and, because of my one-eye vision, I collide with his *shoulder*. I wasn't even close! Another bad omen!

People arrive, I yell at them, my scene partner screams in agony, and people leave. It was actually fun for the first hour.

"I can't believe we get paid fifty dollars for this! And there's only two hours left!" I say excitedly to my scene partner.

"You mean five. FIVE hours." I'm a bit confused, so I ask when she thinks we'll be done, to which she replies, "Well, I did this last night and the night before, and I was here until nearly three in the morning both times". It's currently 10 p.m. and the math checks out, so I settle in for a much, much longer evening. Then, I 'get it' – it's not three hours, it's *until* three. Ohhh.

In between groups, I take to sitting on a nearby corpse and chatting to this girl. We talk about grad school and I end up giving her advice on universities and the whole of education. It's a fun conversation that was interrupted regularly by frightened patrons of our haunted house. As I sat on the dead body, I noticed that when I bent my arms, more of my hair would tear out because the fake blood is drying and becoming super sticky. My entire chest is coated in it (and I'm a fairly hairy guy), so this is a major problem. My feet have straw stuck to them and I keep tripping on things, because I'm barefoot, the room has a strobe light in it, and I can only seen with one eye.

However, the best moment happens a little after the halfway point, when my partner and I are talking and we see the telltale flashlight blink through the curtain. I stand up to get in position and feel extraordinarily heavy when I kneel toward her leg.

"Uh, you're...you're stuck on that thing," she says, motioning toward my back.

I assume that it's not going to matter, and besides, there's now eleven people to my right all expecting a show, so I jump up only to realize what's happened. The dried blood acted like glue and the dead body I had sat on was now stuck to my underwear, which, upon standing, was now around my knees. Maintaining my 'scary cannibal' guise, I struggle to pull them up, which only brings the dead body smashing into my butt and falling down again with my underwear. I hobble toward the crowd, screaming out noises and thrashing a chain around, but I fear that no one can take this seriously with a corpse attached to my underwear. I look less like a crazed cannibal and more like a contestant on *America's Funniest Home Videos: Adult Edition*. The crowds leaves, terrified for whatever reason, and my scene partner says that it was hilarious.

By the end of the night, she'd fallen asleep for the last six crowds (which was hilarious to me). I eventually made my fifty dollars and biked home with fake blood freezing to my skin, strewing half of my body hairs all about the great streets of Chicago.

An interesting postscript is that Ian had a terrible time, stuck alone in a weird booth while yelling at people. Instead of scaring crowds with the standard screaming, he eventually shifted to horrifying sentiments like "Global warming!" and "Higher taxes!"

For fifty bucks, I got one of the funniest nights of my life, and I think it was *very* worth it.

Three

I was on tour with my friends in the band Circle Takes the Square, and at 4 a.m. we were heading to a friend's house in Athens, Georgia. I had never met this friend, but everyone else on earth assured me that she is super nice and, since you don't have much choice on tour, I went with it. She lived near the college with three or four other people and we got free reign of the living room.

I somehow end up on the couch, promptly getting in my sleeping bag and falling asleep. Everyone else in the band is on the floor or on air mattresses, and as I'm fading off, our host says, "Oh, and if you wake up or hear anything early in the morning, it's my housemates leaving for school," motioning toward a door by my couch. Who cares! We have a place to stay and it's warm. Hot, even!

The next thing I remember was waking up at eight in

the morning to light on my face, only to look over and meet eyes with one of her housemates. I couldn't establish much, but we did see each other and I know our eyes met. She gave a very weird look, but I chalked it up to the mass of smelly people all over her living room floor, as that's odd when you don't expect it.

She leaves in a hurry and I think, 'well, whatever, I'm going back to bed', and I look down only to realize that I somehow kicked off my sleeping bag due to the heat and was laying in only my t-shirt and boxers. Interestingly, though, my boxers had shifted during the night, and there, plain as day, was my junk. It was frightfully obvious and certainly the sort of thing a roommate would look upon with shock. Imagine it yourself: You leave your bedroom at 8 a.m. to take a final exam and see a bunch of sleeping bodies all over the living room, and one is awake, showing off his junk, looking at you in the eye from the couch. *Bad situation*. But it was very funny after the door shut. Very funny. I'm sure I got another 'tour nickname' from this, but I don't remember it.

Two

I once argued that this is the best story I'd ever have. I still think that's true, since it relies so much on chance that it seems totally impossible. However, I assure you, it was real and very strange...it still is, in fact.

I used to accompany my brother to an afterschool daycare where we would wait for our mom to get off of work. This was one of the first days of third grade, when you're super-pumped on school and you keep your pencils sharp, your erasers clean, and you haven't lost your pencil case yet.

I was working on homework at the table for little kids and I got up for some water. When I sat back down in my chair, I heard a loud *SNAP* and thought I saw something small shoot out toward the wall. My first assumption was that part of my seat had snapped off, though a quick look did not confirm that. I shrugged it off and kept working on math.

Around fifteen minutes later, I thought I was going to throw up because my stomach was in a weird pain...not so much pain, but an odd 'off' feeling. I reported it to our counselor and she walked me to the bathroom, waiting patiently while I didn't throw up at all. While walking I had isolated the pain toward my butt somewhere, but she pulled down my pants, and looked at my butt—she even brought in the nine-hundred-year-old owner of the company to look—and there was nothing wrong. I pulled up my pants, went back to my seat, and continued my homework.

My mom picked my brother and I up an hour later and, since I was more comfortable talking with my mom, I began belting out, "Something's wrong with my butt! I don't know what it is, but something's wrong! Ahhh, it's weird! I feel so weird!" We get home, I get my pants pulled down *again*, and I am now laying down face-first on the couch.

I roll my head to the side and see my mom looking quizzically at my butt, but I choose instead to focus on my little brother, whose face I can see poking over my mother's shoulder. I see his face change from confused curiosity to *total shock* as my mom pulls a seven-inch, pointy side down, broken pencil from inside my butthole. The relief I felt was both incredible and instant. But my brother's face was still wide-eyed and full of pure horror.

As an explanatory postscript, it turns out that my brand-new sharpened pencil had fallen onto my seat, one of those children's seats with a sharp curve at the butt-part. The pencil was suspended like a bridge across the dip, if you can picture that (the way a chopstick would look laying across a large bowl). So when I sat down, it cracked in half and the pointy part shot through my Umbro shorts and my He-Man underwear, and then took a one-in-a-million shot and hit *total* bulls-eye without cutting anything! I was totally unharmed except for feeling, uh, weird. The eraser end had shot out and I even found it under a table the next day. Pretty cool, huh? Yeah, right. It was freaking *weird*!

One

At the age of twelve, I was content for soccer to define my life. All my t-shirts were soccer-related and all my shorts were Umbros, so, short of wearing cleats all the time, I was a walking billboard for soccer. My shorts are the key to the outfit here, as Umbro brand's shiny design screamed from miles away, "soccer is my life!"

I went with my family and stepfamily to Carowinds, a North Carolinian theme park that is likely comparable to a Six Flags (though I've never been to one of those). Rides, food, more rides, and one of those log flume rollercoasters where you get soaked. Yeah, you can probably picture it fine.

My brother, two stepsiblings, and I were in line for one of those rollercoasters where riders hang down from the ride. Instead of sitting in a car, you're attached by a super secure vest, so that your feet dangle beneath you as you whip around loops and loud, cranky metal things. It was clearly a newer attraction, and there was a huge line as well as signs reading 'Get your photo taken on the ride! Available afterwards for $10!' (which is stupid, but likely an easy way to make a couple thousand dollars if you're a theme park with a photo printer on hand).

The four of us ended up in the front spots, the only time I've been in front on a rollercoaster, and it was super freaking fun. I tend to yell a lot for effect because it seems to make the whole thing more fun, and this was no exception, even as an ultra-embarrassable twelve-year-old. We get off the ride, I'm walking down toward our family, and I see my stepmom doubled over at the waist, laughing her brains out. I realize that there's a seven-foot wide TV screen flooded with the photo taken on *our* ride, featuring the four of us at the front of the image. It's then that I see what's so funny: The photo snaps at the upside-down part of the ride, and the wind had blown so hard that my ultra-light Umbro shorts have ballooned out and are essentially a focusing mechanism to highlight my twelve-year-old penis. It was literally the *center* of the photo, and at this point the entirety of the riders and their families have all caught on and are laughing.

Anyone who wanted to preserve their memory certainly couldn't buy this photo now—I went and tainted it with my 'clearly obvious, front-and-center, twelve-year-old nudity'. I don't remember being that embarrassed at the time, though I'm sure that I was. In fact, I don't remember anything immediately after that point, so perhaps a damning wall of shame had fallen on me, thereby erasing all memory of the remainder of the day. That seems fair.

Zero

To end this quadruplicate of 'naked stories', I leave you with this wisdom: Being naked is a pretty normal thing. But when you don't expect it, it's pretty funny. I like to think that most stories tell some moral, or inspire the listener, or help to understand the world. But the best stories are the ones that are just plain funny.

Unpaved And Unloved

Back to Alaska, where I'm fully clothed and damp! The next 137 miles were to be on the Denali Highway, a road famous for having not one stop or convenience off of it, as well as for being 95% unpaved. The first ten miles are blacktop, but the pavement gives way to packed dirt with the occasional scattered gravel section for the remaining 127 miles.

I started out in a gentle sprinkling of rain, this time double-wrapping plastic bags around my socks *and* in my socks with garbage bags on anything even slightly important. The following two days presented the Alaska that you hear about in guidebooks and movies, and likely what you've been wanting to picture during this entire text. There is literally nothing out there, save an indication of a road. The biking was surprisingly manageable, given my heavy bike and medium-width tires. I only fell twice! That's pretty good for a guy who's ridden a bike for at least eight-thousand miles over my life. It's like I'm learning.

Unending greenery, enormous expanses of open space, and the biggest optical sky that I have ever seen surrounded me for forty-eight hours. I saw about fifteen cars in that time period, and I did not talk to (or see) a single person. I made camp at what appeared to be a pull-out spot for four-wheelin' types, as evidenced by the tire tracks thirty feet up on the opposing dirt wall. It's hard not to get territorial and just plain upset over these marks of human kind on an otherwise pristine landform. I mean, not that I was doing any better, but at least I was sticking to the unpaved road in this case. Then again, the shrill voice of hypocrisy comes out in me as I think, *Oh man, I wish this hill was paved so that I could skate it…*

I don't have many (or any) stories from the two days that comprised this amazing landscape, but that's only because as a writer I fail to communicate the complex emotions contained within quiet moments. Stories I can relate, but thoughts and muted staring across epic plains and over lush forests, I simply cannot. I will say this: If you wish to unlock a new feeling within yourself and to strip open a dormant, primal emotion, then visit this area. You'll get it.

Ha, I Call It As I See It

That's an Op Ivy reference, by the way. On the end of the second day of gravel madness, the road transformed back into a modern painted-and-paved road again, and, for the sake of the bike riding part of my life, I could not have been happier. Traction and speed had returned, and the risk of falling had dropped back to a normal amount. A small roadside snack, some crazy photos of snow-capped mountains, and a bajillion downhills all rolled me right into the next town on my list of stops: Paxson.

I won't even kid around, because calling Paxson a town

is like saying your front yard is an entire continent. One way to know if your 'town' isn't actually a town is if I can kick a soccer ball *over the entire thing*. And while I'm good at kicking things, the point remains. I passed an expensive-looking RV park followed directly by a (wait for it…) gas station/hotel/restaurant/bar/grocery store. All of these things were actually one place, this one building resembling a more colorful Bates motel. Then the town was over.

French fries were ordered, I visited their grocery store (which was more like a walk-in closet with a lot of potato chips and canned tuna in it), and I filled up my water in the 'cooks only' part of the kitchen when instructed to do so by the manager. This stop did not affect me much; however, the conversation I had with the two French guys in the parking lot did: They were second duo to ask where I was headed and, like the prior couple, had suggested I change my route to ride all the way down to Valdez and take a ferry across rather than bike back through Anchorage. Evidently, the ride to Valdez was overflowing with waterfalls and was the most overlooked gem of the Alaskan highway system. At this point, I was convinced and I thanked them. Their advice elevated my journey into a world of intense beauty and horrific pain, but I didn't know that at the time. For the moment, I set up camp by the river and slept wonderfully, since it didn't rain that night. (It did rain the next morning though, so don't think I'm going soft on you. Still gray, still wet.)

Before I would come close to Valdez, I would pass through Glenallen, which enjoyed a bold font on my map, indicating that it might have some real stuff beyond, say, one entity selling 'whatever was around that day.' My ride was wonderful for most of the morning, with very few cars, rolling hills, and the sun warming my face in bursts when poking from beyond clouds in sharp slits. However, not one to be agreed with for too long, the weather started lookin' all funny pretty soon. One thing that the roads in Alaska allow for is the ability to really *see* ahead of you and determine what kind of weather you're in for. I could see the road and the weather patterns above it for twenty miles quite easily. This means that I knew when I was going to get wet, which is not very helpful information, since it's unavoidable. It's like playing with fate: If someone tells you the day that you're going to die, then death is gonna get you no matter what, so it's hard to fight it with real fervor. The same goes for storm clouds. I can drop gears all I want and really start hammering out the miles, but all I'm doing is getting wet sooner rather than later.

With the Alaskan pipeline to my left paralleling my journey for the next three days, I felt the first raindrop from the graying clouds. This particular storm system had real issues with me and turned on the full-blast sprinkler system within two minutes of breaching the precipitation line. So, after nearly twenty-four hours of being dry and warm, I was already back to being wet and freezing.

The hilarious part happened when I came upon road construction, because this means something quite amusing: The only road to work on was the one I was *on*, so the road stopped all of the sudden and I wasn't allowed to continue (due to heavy blasting, giant machinery, and impassable road conditions). Forced to wait and chat with a very kind woman operating traffic signs, I simply stood in this preposterous downpour with a dull look on my face. 'Unimpressed' was the emotion I was going for. Lighting struck within a mile of where we were and the thunder cracked like a clap of cinderblocks ripping through my skull. I would have jumped had I not ducked so quickly in panicked terror. The good side to this is that the only way I could cross the nine-mile construction was to get a free ride in the control truck! When she rolled up, I threw my bike in the back (which was incredibly hard and you really have no idea) and sat in the dry-ish, warm interior for at least nineteen minutes!

It felt like hitchhiking since I was doing the 'talk-talk-talk-ask-questions-blah-blah-oh-really-how-interesting!' conversation method, though with less need for my feigned interest. At the end of the ride, I had to hoist my bike up and over the edge of the flatbed, mustering every bit of my fading strength to pull this off. It was about as difficult as pulling a mattress out of a dumpster without dropping it, and you're in the rain, and every atom of your being is freezing cold. There was a giant line of stopped cars waiting on me, too, so the whole scene felt like every second counted.

I hope some onlooker saw the truth. "Oh my god, that kid lifted a fully loaded 92' steel Trek over and out of a truck bed on the first try! He should be on *American Gladiators*! What a feat! Someone give him money!" I'm sure the compliments were there… I mean, it was raining hard, so I probably didn't hear them. Yeah, that's it. Cool.

Another Title For Another Thing

Maybe I'm getting a bit abstract, but the monotony of townships in Alaska merits this treatment. It was a full day's ride down to Glenallen, a small burgh that toted multiple gas stations, a grocery store that you've actually heard of, and a full-on visitor's center! The latter wasn't a requirement (as there is nothing to see or do in Glenallen), so it stood more as a clearinghouse of pamphlets about nearby hotels. In essence, I walked into a giant advertising center with a water fountain. I was chatted up by an English couple who were around my age and kept reinforcing how much more impressive I was than they were because I chose to ride my bike. "I mean, we've been *driving* the whole way, but just look at you, man!" It was pretty funny. That dude was pumped.

Potato chips, rain, water bottle fill-up...I reran my personal computer program and settled into a small five-dollar-a-night camping spot. The only oddity of the night was this: I put all my food back in my bear can, moved it all over to the metal box provided at the site, and locked it. *However*, I had neglected one blueberry bagel so crushed by the weight of bouncing water bottles that I didn't notice it at the base of the plastic bag it lived in; therefore, the bagel, bag and all, stayed in my saddlebag attached to my bicycle for the night, all leaning against a picnic table about five feet from my head. Upon awakening the next morning, I was brushing my teeth when I glanced over at my bike and it appeared as though thin sheets of ice had piled up on the top of my rear saddlebag, delicately balanced and cracked in a thousand little pieces. From the distance where I stood, it looked so much like that I had to assure myself that it wasn't *that* cold, so it must have fallen from the tree tops somehow. With an air of total confusion about me, I approached, widened my eyes, and discovered that the plastic bagel bag had been completely ripped to shreds. *Something* came in the night, tore a four-inch gash in my saddlebag, then scattered the plastic shards. As for the bagel, it was still there, which doesn't say much for Safeway brand blueberry bagels. "Even animals won't eat them!" My best assumption beyond it being a bear (which is totally possible) is that one of the ungodly-large crows that patrol the nearby landfill smelled the artificial blueberry and went crazy on it. I lean toward this explanation simply because my tent stood on a gravel lot, and a crunchy, *loud* one at that. A bear would have woken me up. I think. Ultimately, I never saw a single bear over this journey, so forgoing evidence and bending logic to allow this mystery animal to exist as a black bear rounds out my trip a bit better. A bear was five feet from my head! A bear that hates blueberries…? Hmmm. I suppose that bagel was too cold, or maybe too hot. The point is that it wasn't 'just right'…Goldilocks? Over-explained? Also, yes, I know that Goldilocks was the one with the temperature issues, and bears will eat anything, so, who cares; never mind; next paragraph.

Fate directed me to the grocery store down the big hill where I purchased the most exciting Rice Dream chocolate bar that I have ever encountered. Alaska, un-surprisingly, is not known for its variety of consumer options for those conscious of the politics of food. When one sees what was certainly a fluke in the ordering, one pounces, even if one doesn't want chocolate. While buying this and standing in line, I was offered moose burgers that were "right out in mah car, buddy! Shoot dim dong doggies less' go fry em' up right here!" I politely declined, stating that I didn't eat meat, to which I was offered "ahhhh, yur one'a them healthies, huh?" *Heck yeah, I am*! Healthies rule! That's *another* tattoo I gotta get! What is that, three new ones now?

A thrift store around the corner begged exploration, as it literally *just* opened its doors as I glanced that direction, so I nodded my helmet to the VHS gods and entered. I found *Gleaming the Cube* within seconds, which is exciting because it's the only extreme-sports-related movie from the 80s that I didn't own (not that it's an amazing film or anything), and then, thinking back to my hellish night of sub-bridge, sub-arctic camping, I bought some heavy snow gloves, figuring that I'd be able to use them later in winter if not now. (What I failed to do was try them on, but that's another story; I mean, they looked *huge*, so why try them on? It's just like buying pants, huh?) After the three-dollar transaction, I watched as three office-style cardboard boxes were brought in from their porch, all filled with VHS tapes. There were no movies in there, but rather a painfully, eerily detailed collection of tapes, marked with things like '*Donahue*, 7/88' or '*60 Minutes*, 4/15/89.' That was nearly sixty percent of the tapes. The remaining stock offered brightly colored, photocopied covers with exciting titles like 'Personal Protection Vol. 2: Bombs, Bazookas, and Bandanas,' or the heavy hitter

'Using Your Uzi At Close Range.' Now *this* was exciting!

The woman who owned the thrift store was on the fence about whether to sell them or throw them away, so I waited outside until the weeded through box made it to the dumpster and (sadly) took only two tapes, one of which is labeled simply 'Death And Taxes'. Almost two years later, I can say I have watched part of that tape, and it's a documentary. I forget what it's about. Maybe I never knew! I wish I could say that I took the whole box and sent it USPS Media Mail to my house, but I don't have that kind of time. If you regret my decisions here and wish to see these tapes, then put down this zine and go to Glenallen (or any thrift store in Alaska), and you'll find them there. If you agree with my decision that no amount of free time would coerce me *or* you into wasting time watching crap like that, then continue on in this book. Choose your own next stop adventure! Uh-oh, there's an idea. Oh man, that's actually kinda clever…

Welp

From there, I biked south. I saw monotonous forests, giant hills, beautiful lakes, glorious mountain passes, and a terrain that time has carved and shaped over thousands upon millions of years with mankind has barely messing it up (comparatively). If you were to spill brown and green paint on a piece of paper flat in front of you, take your hands (open-palmed) on either side of the paper, and smash them together, crumpling the paper tightly, then the resulting mass would perfectly resemble the land up there. Perfectly. In fact, if you do that, you'll have a completely accurate 3-D map of the Alaskan interior. Do it! Situationist game time!

I spent the night at some little campsite next to a river and it rained again a lot. A shop owner kept offering me 'the greatest pie you ever tried' of which I continued insisting I would not eat because of my dietary choices, which baffled this lurching old fogey so completely that I thought he might collapse. "But…it's real GOOD…", he said as if the quality was what I feared, not the eggs and milk. The look of total disbelief and heartbreak on his face was made somewhat worse when I bought a couple postcards from the gift shop / restaurant / living room. The memorabilia glued to the walls coupled with the glass shelving gave the impression that these two were just waiting for the Food Network to knock down their door and launch this little restaurant into the economic stratosphere, but I didn't see it happening any time soon. However, I'm probably wrong, so keep an eye out. Or not. They have good postcards though!

As I woke up the following morning to pounding rain, I thought I might pump up my back tire, as I hadn't yet and, between the temperature changes and elevation wonkiness, it seemed like a good idea. When I looked at my back wheel, something seemed 'off' about it. I spun it around, only to recoil in horror when I saw a spoke loose on the drivetrain side (the unchangeable one if you don't have this specific tool, which I didn't). Not even loose, but bouncing everywhere because it was broken! Then, to add ten pounds of poo to an overflowing cauldron of 'suck soup', I noticed that four more were broken! Because my flange had cracked! I was down *five spokes* on the same side. Is there a word for a 'bad' miracle? (Disaster, maybe?) Yeah—this was a disaster!

Always one to 'polish a turd', I quickly found the upside. Fact: The spokes didn't break overnight, and they didn't break when I slowly turned the wheel; therefore, they had broken a while back. I obviously failed to feel the difference in my wheel, meaning that, for the most part, the wheel was still operational. It turned, it held weight, and, after a bit of truing, it stayed within the brakes without too much rubbing. To fully illustrate the problem to the non-cyclist, let me abstract this to the point of nonsense. All the spokes on a wheel connect to the hub, which is the metal piece surrounding the axle. (It looks as if you were staring at a UFO landing on a lake, complete with the reflection. Or maybe like a long yo-yo with a bit more room between the two sides. Got it?) Well, the edge of that thing (where the spokes enter in) cracked off, taking five spokes with it. The lucky thing is that because of clever engineering (or chance), the five spokes, though next to each other on the flange, connect to very different parts of the rim; so, the lack of integrity was spread out rather than all in one spot.

A combination of total necessity and the lack of a bike shop meant that I was going to bike on this thing no matter what. So, giving in to circumstance and literally crossing that bridge when I came to it, I continued south toward Valdez over Thompson Pass…

Do Not Pass Go

Sisyphus, the mother who lifted the Volkswagen off her child, the determined Sherpa climbing Everest with someone else's packs, and me standing tall atop Thompson Pass. Can you find the connection?

Follow the thread and you'll see it clearly: We all did something that is the hardest freaking thing on crappy freaking earth. I've never picked up a car, pushed a boulder, or climbed Mt. Everest, but I am *certain* that I am in the right company here. To suffer is to learn, and by this act, I was spitting out PhDs left and right. For four full hours of ten-mile-an-hour pedaling in a fierce, blistering headwind, I was slobbering frothy mist and downpour like an endless series of underwater shotguns pointed at my face. It was cold enough to see my breath, but my blood was pumping fast enough to keep me warm from the inside out. Slowing down to rest for a moment, looking at an ice flow, or punching the ground because it deserves it were all out of the question, as I got cold within seconds. To properly register my disgust, I spat like a licker of toilets might: a determined shot of saliva, sweat, and mostly rain filtering through my beard every couple of seconds. Heated words like, "I don't care for you one bit, State of Alaska!" and similar salty grievances erupted toward everything in earshot. I hated the streams, I hated the air, I hated topography in general—and gravity? There was a solid ten minutes when my one-man chants filled the air, barking with anger. "Down with gravity! Down with gravity!" (Even when I'm upset, I'm still kinda clever.)

Passing tufts of snow adorning lifeless clumps of dirt and weeds, the end became visible: a giant, heavily-stickered sign reading 'Thompson Pass, Elev. 2805 feet' that certainly deserved (and received) a couple photographs. I was not the first, I will surely not be the last, but on this day, I was the only one enjoying that particular success.

However, not unlike the first-time jewel thief, I realized that the end was not yet present; I was at the exact midpoint. To borrow the heist scenario, I just got the jewel, but I still had to get out. I don't know any jewel thieves (though I totally wish I knew Bill Mason, author of *Confessions of a Master Jewel Thief*, go read that book right now, because I swear to everything that it will annihilate your brain with shock and envy that you have never known before) but I imagine they will all tell you the latter half, the 'getting out' part, is significantly harder than the 'breaking in' part. This is also true of biking an enormous mountain pass.

Confusing, huh? All I have to do is ride down it, right? Well, yeah. So I did. Rain, wind, and overall discomfort increased tenfold, and to further complicate things, I was not moving my limbs at all but rather only balancing, so my blood had stopped moving about my veins and seemed to just be sitting there, cooling off. I was forcing a wind chill and it was getting colder and colder. The choices were both pained and paradoxical: either stop, dismount, and try to warm up by jumping up and down, or go faster down the hill to get this whole thing over with while risking getting even colder and wetter. The helplessness was akin to being buried alive; you feel it getting worse with every moment, yet you cannot do anything about it. (Well, uh, except that I wasn't dead when this was over because I was actually out of my predicament, so maybe that's a weak analogy. At the time, it seemed to fit.)

The idiotic signs taunted me with hilarious sayings like 'Valdez, 17 miles,' knowing that ten of those miles were downhill. I was a yelling, insane heap of emotion, barreling down this hill, losing sensation in my toes, and my gloves (which I have yet to explain) fit only my thumb and most of my fingers, meaning my hands were also extremely cold. The problem was that my palm couldn't fit all the way in, so, in turn, the tips of the glove's fingers were limp and appeared extraordinarily long. The gloves didn't fit. At all. *But*, while made for a nine-year-old, they saved my fingers from frostbite.

Like all things that totally suck and are awful, this eventually ended. My empty, frivolous cries of "I'M GONNA STAY IN SUCH A HOTEL TONIGHT; YOU HAVE NO IDEA!" went unnoticed and unrealized, because at the base of the hill, when I had to start pedaling again, I was still nine miles outside of town. Over those nine miles I warmed right back up, and, upon finding the Safeway in town, I thought, "Nah, I'm fine camping. Ha, what was I thinking, 'hotel'...." I have biked up and over some extremely large tracts of country, but this hill, mainly due to weather conditions, was by far the worst.

Go Chase Them; See If I Care

The remarkable, unmissable sights that I was promised en route to Valdez were a series of cliffs and their accompanying waterfalls, a landscape that I was certain would be marred by my near case of trench foot, soggy everything, and frostbitten soul. Just how incredibly must nature present herself to succeed in combatting such a miserable state of mind? Time heals wounds, but can visible beauty? Could a cracked rock face spilling water actually lift my spirits beyond the physical plane and into another realm of post-reality?

I suppose that I had my answer. Against all logic and everything my brain and body were demanding of the other, I stopped to stare four separate times, all during unending downpours. Too inspiring to be termed 'black metal,' and too realistic to be *Lord of the Rings*-ish, I completely failed to properly describe this sight to anyone as of yet. Mouth agape, standing frozen in the frothing, heartless downpour, I had achieved my moment. A clear view of beauty emerged from a pile of crushed hope, and I embraced every second. It's rare to actually *feel* a memory rooting in your brain; this was one of those moments.

As a reader capable of getting on the Internet, you might feel compelled to search out images of these waterfalls, and I fear that photos of them will fail to hold your interest. René Magritte, a noted painter of the Surrealist movement, is perhaps best known for his work titled *The Treachery of Images*, a simple painting of a smoking pipe, with text underneath it reading 'This is not a pipe.' His point was that it was *not* a pipe, but rather a painting of a pipe. Paintings are representations of real things. Furthering this, a photograph of a waterfall is not a waterfall; it is merely a photograph. Images of real things are a weird code to help spell out a feeling without being there to experience it. I think that the logical endpoint to this is to look at things instead of only taking photos of them. Cameras detract from the beauty of reality and have irreversibly damaged the need to travel, see friends and family, and commune with the natural world. Besides, more fun things happen when you're not expecting them to. I can assure you of that.

After destroying any notions of my life as a romantic endeavor by camping right next to a Safeway grocery store, I was back on my bike with 'pretty damp, but not *that* bad' clothing on. I managed to catch the ferry over to the town of Whittier, which was a three-hour boat ride flanked by tall, jagged cliffs with odd varieties of wildlife scurrying around. I saw two orca whales, an entire beach's worth of sea lions, a humpback whale, bald eagles, mountain goats, and these weird fish that I labeled 'pop punk fish' as they did the pogo jump out of the water and then dropped right back in, tail first. My best guess as to this behavior is that they were really, really excited about something. I mean, when I'm jumping up and down, that's always my reasoning.

Whittier is an extraordinarily small place with access limited by one three-and-a-half-mile long tunnel on the edge of town. The tunnel is the second largest interstate tunnel in the U.S., and it is forbidden, illegal, and a terrible idea to bike through it. I was offered a ride by a very sweet younger couple (thanks again Megan and Victor!), who had just finished their first bike tour, oddly enough. Phone numbers were exchanged, and, on the far side, I got back on my bike and kept on going. I passed glaciers at a biker's pace, or perhaps glaciers passed me at a glacier's pace. I don't know. It gets very confusing.

I recall this day of biking being fairly easy, as the sun revitalized my life by upping my vitamin D intake and the wind seemed to be at my back. Another thought that kept running through my head was that, in four days, I would be coming back on this same route and recognizing objects that served as mile markers. There's an undeniable power and safety in this: When you bike (or run, walk, *et cetera*) in a straight line, you're on completely new territory with no sense of warmth or resonance. Doubling back provides a grounding sort of truth, an empowering 'I've been here before!' (however little it may be). To see the passage of time so clearly, to know moments, hours, or days have passed, and my life held together throughout all of it—this was a powerful motivation to continue.

Moose Pass, Alaska was too small to provide me with a safe abandoned campground or anything like it, and after biking ten more miles than I wanted to, I unfurled my tent underneath some power lines a hundred feet off the highway. There was nothing special here, so I went to sleep. I lived through the night, and upon daybreak (well, no, daybreak is three in the morning, so 'when I felt like it') I got up, repacked everything, and did the whole bike thing some more.

At some point during my bike trips, I invariably collide with my idealistic self when I get sick-to-death of riding my bike. Here I am, doing my best to find a more interesting existence, to propel my mind, body, and spirit into a forgotten mode of reality, and all I can do is complain about knee pain, my butt hurting, and how boring it is to pedal up another big hill. Time is a cruel, conniving witch, spinning a wheel of pain and pleasure, hypnotizing me over and over. Forced to repeatedly find fault with my present situation, I powered through, knowing in the deepest part of my being that this is where I want to be. With only a handful of days to go, I look forward with excitement and total fear to the reality in which I can sit on a couch and eat cooked food. Eventually, I will be done with this trip, and I shoot forward with bursts and pleas of wanting this to last forever: my two sides fighting, right in front of me. When I can look past the bike to see the glory of new ideas and uncharted life, in those moments I manage to inspire myself. It's a strange dichotomy and one that I haven't gotten used to.

Tiredness and routine washed over as I entered into the township of Seward, a quaint hamlet with a real grocery store and a lot of campgrounds, all costing something like seven dollars a night and situated forty feet from the water. Perhaps the purpose in monotony and pain is to highlight moments of difference and pleasure. In my own words, I could finally *not* ride my bike, and instead walk around and enjoy life from a slightly different vantage point, which was great. I set up my tent, threw everything I owned in it, and went on a walk. Within moments of locking my bike to a wooden pole, orphaned in a damp, yellowed pile of grass, three crows had taken great interest in my seat and were pecking it like crazy. I don't even sort of know what *that's* supposed to mean…the image of three crows perched on various components of my bike was utterly dystopian, and had I been paying more attention, I should have read it as a bad sign. However, the clarity of this message only appears in retrospect, and I must note that I had a great time in Seward with no bad anything happening. My hypothesis? If life gives you a bad sign and you happen to *miss* it, then you're in the clear. This is further proof that you make your own luck, murder of crows or not.

Actual Proof These People Are Insane

So my case for the general insanity of Alaskans has been, to this point, purely circumstantial. There were videotapes at thrift stores, weird names of thrift stores, and some strange abandoned igloo-looking hut that I saw at some point. However, in looking for a challenging and worthwhile hike in Seward, I found the trailhead to Mount Marathon, a name I was ecstatic about the second I heard it. The backstory on this place is that back in 1905, some drunken guy at a bar bet some other less drunken guy that he couldn't run to the top of this mountain *and back* in less than an hour. Now, not having the ability to look at this rock and hear this legend skews your vision already, as you surely imagine some 'big, but not that big' representation about how tall, treacherous, and feasible this climb would be.

I cannot make this more clear: This is the most ridiculous thing that you have ever seen in your freaking life. It's *really*, really far to the top. This is the kind of dare where one would laugh about it immediately because one wouldn't even think to *walk* it in under five hours, let alone run it in one hour. However, Alaskans being the salty types to grow irritated at difficulty, this hour-long goal became a statewide dare and remains a race to this day.

What's crazy to me is that people *can* run this whole thing in under an hour, something that should speak to the persevering nature of humanity or the spirit of accomplishment within us all…but I honestly see it as incredible peer pressure forcing people to literally give up on their brain for awhile. It's like directing all the blood that should go to your brain to, you know, think, and then sending it to your legs so that you can instead run like a wild person up a mound of dirt and rocks.

I hiked this trail, which is more of a series of snaking paths cutting in all sorts of directions (namely 'up'), and it was really hard. Grabbing onto roots, ripping at mud for traction, and then, once you pass the tree line, tearing across sheets of jagged shale while wind whips around the glacial pass and smacks you right in the face. The view is amazing from the top, and it's clear to me why the summit is the most important aspect to any climb, because everything looks beautiful from that distance. Again, this is why Alaska was the type of place I appreciated—these great moments wait, available to anyone, untouched, with no stairs or guardrails—but in doing so, they make them nearly impossible for anyone unwilling to go through some pain, fear, and an amazing level of both filth and work. For the phrase 'you can't have roses without the rain,' the Alaskan equivalent might go 'you can't have a hundred-acre garden without wading through forty tons of horse crap.'

Coming down was actually quite fun, though, and I managed to embed three flakes of shale rock in my palms and fingers in the descent, which seemed a small price for the ride. One of these remained in the crux of my pointer finger for four more days, as it was too deep to grab with tweezers or a sharp stick or a broken plastic fork. Souvenir! Alaskan style!

Surrounded By Animals

My true stated goal in this entire journey was to see a puffin in its natural environment, and on my last day in Seward, I did just that. I wandered down to the harbor and signed up for a wildlife watching boat tour, and politely declined the twenty-dollar buffet offered for our group. (I know animals are interesting and all, but they're kinda boring if they're not couched on either side by endless wings or mashed potatoes and gravy, right?) I was the only person traveling alone and ended up with a full six-person table to myself. I find these moments happen a lot while I'm bike touring: little blips of loneliness that find me pining to have a friend, or missing my family, but ultimately I'm glad that I don't have to talk to anyone because I'm surrounded by total weirdos and idiots. You see, the great part about the type of people that I meet at the top of a mountain is that they put in the work to get there and value the outcome over the (often) miserable journey. A boat ride, however, is solely predicated on having the money and time to spend on it, as well as simply *being* in Alaska. I sat, walled in by state-college dads, the spazzy, uninterested progeny of spazzy, uninteresting couples, and at least three disaffected teens, to whom a boat ride with whales and the ocean was simply another dumb way to not be on Facebook. It was a sorry lot, and instead of sifting around and finding our common link, I put my hood up and directed all my interest to the whales, the ocean, and the raisins I brought as a snack. Buffets? Ha—I had dried grapes!

The best two moments of the boat adventure were seeing a humpback whale crest a handful of times over the course of about thirty minutes. Our entire starboard side was thick with camera phones and failed documentation of such a rare and hard-to-photograph event. The state-college dad next to me summed the endeavor up well: "Shit, man, this is just as boring as the zoo!" I had long since given up photographing the interesting aspects of Alaska, as I was simply going for 'mood' with my photos. I can sooner pull the memories from a color field than muster up any excitement at the blurry photographed speck on the rock that I swear is a mountain goat. Look with your eyes, not your viewfinder!

The second best moment was the flock of puffins—probably fourteen—bobbing around a small cove. They act a lot like ducks, and are considerably smaller than you'd think. Another fun fact is that they frequently eat so much that it drastically increases their body weight, making them physically unable to fly until they've 'lightened their load.' The amusing part came when one tried to take off, only to sort of 'skip' off the water about ten feet later, and ultimately give up due to overeating. The whole of our boat pointed and laughed. Then our boat's narrator chimed in. "This is the last call for the buffet, so come on down! The dessert buffet will begin in about thirty minutes, so save room for some cheesecake or our homemade devil's fudge cake!"

Sometimes you don't even have to try!

The Bike Trip Is Still Not Over, Even Though I Was On A Boat

Glaciers, animals in their natural environment, and a damp, bitter cold everywhere I went. Alaska. Ahhh, yes. Anyway, back in Seward, I stayed another night then packed up for the second-to-last time. Leaving town was an exercise in memory, as I had biked this exact same road three days prior and could mentally chart my distance based on hills, bridges, and other natural means of navigation. All this really means is that every so often I would say, "Oh man, THAT thing? I thought I was already past that! DANG IT!"

The last ten miles of that day were extremely rainy, which is no surprise to anyone at this point, but I found myself in the midst of a *Seventh Seal* mental chess match for the last six miles. Bergman, from hell's heart I stab at thee! The road evened out, cut across a flat meadow, and was completely straight for six full miles, meaning I could see exactly where I needed to be from six whole miles away. The rain and wind were both coming from this magical ending point, so I was spitting about forty gallons of rain out of my beard and eyebrows every second, and I kept wincing when I'd see out of the corner of my eye the '8.5 mph' on my speedometer. It's *so hard* not to look at that thing, most notably when conditions are really rough, as there's not much else to look at, since everything is grayish-white and freezing. I can't think of a suitable comparison for this state of mind, but if you were told to count down every minute for three full hours while standing in the rain and a clock staring you down, you might have a decent visualization for this torture. Self-imposed, I realize, but still. In my garden of forking paths, I never regret my choices, yet often I wonder what the other side might be like. I imagine it to be less rainy.

At the culmination of those six long miles, the road broke off the to left and immediately the wind was now at my back; that same force that slowed my pace now ran along side me, and I was at a small and totally bizarre camping spot in no time. It was more of a public park next to a library than a campground, and I pitched my tent in this weird 'raised bed' of a camping spot. It was still pouring rain and I was fairly hidden in the shadow of a large pine tree, which kept me less wet than other options I had. The downside proved to be an infinite mass of fleas or gnats or some kind of black speck with wings that kept finding their way into my tent and making me crazy. It wasn't great sleep, but it was the last night I would spend in a tent, and that fact alone makes total misery appear palpable....

So It's Come To This

Ask any bike tourer and you'll get a standardized description of that 'last day of tour.' My personal view is like a scene from a medical commercial, the type featuring someone getting back to that thing they love after taking a pill that got rid of their bleeding rectum or faulty heart or crushing depression. I smile endlessly at everything, nearly on the verge of tears, ready to shout, wide-eyed, "I know, I can't believe it, either!" Absent the narration you might get in the actual advertisement, it appears that I've simply expanded my emotional capacity into literally feeling the joy in every leaf, piece of gravel, and half-decent view of anything. I'm blubbering with excitement, I don't feel ashamed, and it's a great feeling.

Ultimately my last days in Anchorage were spent reading outdoors virtually every day, as the weather was surprisingly sunny and warm. I might even go so far as to quantify it as unfair. However, being one to realign the great wheel, I managed to return my bear can to REI for a full refund, citing the fact that water did, in fact, leak in the top. Mostly, I returned it because it cost eighty dollars, and imagining myself somewhere other than Alaska with a keg-sized plastic jar that can withstand a bear attack seemed ludicrous. With that eighty dollars came some much needed punk points, as these memoirs are wholly devoid of such offenses. Unless you count continuing to bike on a broken back wheel, which I did (and still was at this point). My deepest apologies. Or no, wait, how about "shut up!". Punk! Yeah!

The arch of completion eventually slopes back downward though, as the trip is over. Soon enough I'll get off my bike and I won't have a need to ride it every waking moment. I'll bike around town, sure, but the whole thing will lack the necessity that the last three weeks brought with it. Beyond the physical side of it, I have to wonder about my brain: Did I learn what I was hoping to learn? Was I a different person now, having completed a thousand-mile bike ride? I learned a new word the other day for a commonplace concept—the word 'holism,' defined as 'the theory that whole entities, as fundamental components of reality, have an existence *other* than as the mere sum of their parts.' As with everything, I apply it to myself and my limited history. Sure, I rode my bike a long distance. I saw some crazy things. I climbed a lot of rocks, I ate way too many bagels, I slept in some odd places, and I was too preoccupied with riding my bike to fear any of the billion things that could have killed me, but the culmination of this experience produced something altogether different. My brain is hardwired in math, so it's difficult to picture an equation like $1+1=3$, but that's exactly what this asks of us. To take this experience, pack it away in the folds of my being, only to have it all sprout and expand on its own—late at night, weeks later, the pieces would start to come together.

It was like staring at the stars only to realize that they're not holes in the sky, but they *are* the sky. I do a ton of things on my own, to prove to myself I can, but also because I believe so much in the individual as an amazing entity. It was seeing the creative output of my friends, inspiring *me* to create more, do better things, and live on some larger plane. I feel like my travels have been weird, personalized allegories wherein I find the bits of knowledge that I find I'm looking for everywhere. Like an old samurai movie, I come to forking paths with great frequency, and those clear, distinct choices serve to keep me excited about life. Stability has bred the excitement out of choice: wake, read, bike, eat, draw, paint, sleep—all the sterility of an operating table. Indeed, the question is simple to ask and easy to answer, yet hard to act upon: How do we steal back ourselves? Reinventing yourself is the wrong sentiment, as this great sensation of life never leaves but only gets re-prioritized. Think of it more like hitting your personal 'refresh' button. There are a billion ways to do it, and taking an obscenely long bike trip is only one of them, and I won't guarantee that it will work for everyone. Determine where you want to be and start going there. It really *is* that easy. And when you get there, send someone a postcard. People love that.

Flying back to Oregon, taking my bike apart and stuffing it back in that same aging, weakened cardboard box, I later sat transfixed on the landscape, watching the curve of the earth and the fading terrain that had hid my life for the last three weeks. I'm not sure if I'll end up back in Alaska. There are certainly more things I would love to do there, but there's also a *lot* more dark corners across the globe begging for exploration. With my nose pressed against the window, chewing the inside of my cheeks and debating where I'd end up visiting next and how I would get around—wondering about the size and capacity of life, of *one* life in an expanse of billions—how to do something that matters, to create something of substance. How to bring forward the sensation of excitement and possibility so exhumed from our current state of being: This was my problem, an amoebic, ever-changing task that I would strive to understand in my lifetime. A tap on my shoulder brought me out of this, greeting me, "Here's your complimentary SkyMall catalog. Enjoy!"

The lines are clear; you only have to pick a side.

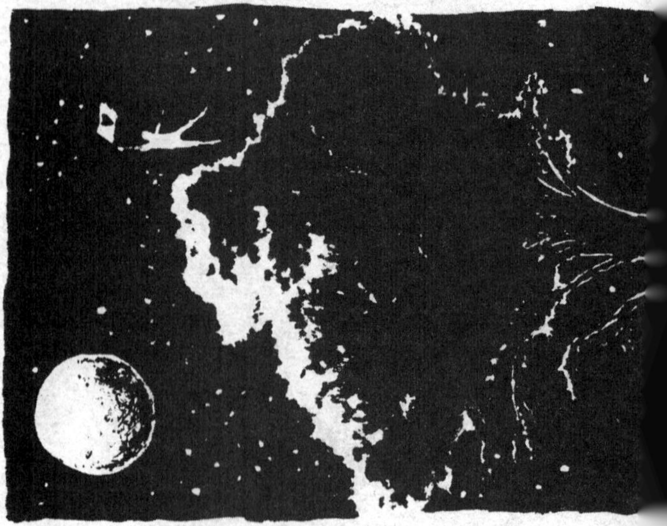

the end breaks my heart
finding life where i leave it
i've been here before

NOW GO OUTSIDE!

THE FOLLOWING PEOPLE ALL DESERVE MORE THAN I CAN EVER GIVE THEM, AND I LOVE THEM ALL: <u>YOU</u>, DOUG, ZACK, DAN, RIO "THE UNSTOPPABLE" SAFARI, ADAM + JESSIE + PIONEERS PRESS, NELLY "50,000!" KATE, MY MOM, MY DAD, DEANNA "THAT'S CRAZY!" MIKHAELSON, BLISS, ANDY "BONYAG!" LYMAN, CHOLAK, WILL T-L.A.L, JAMIE "NO REGURTZ" SWICK, DREW, KATHY, CIRCLE TAKES THE SQUARE, JAKE "BOTH FIRE AND ICE" LOPEZ, STEVE STEVENS, AARON ATTICA!, ISSA + GCF, LONG DISTANCE BIKE RIDERS, COPY SCAMMERS, BILL MASON, McGYVER, NANCY DREW, AND OF COURSE, WITH ALL MY HEART, SARA "SUPER PENGUIN" POWELL.

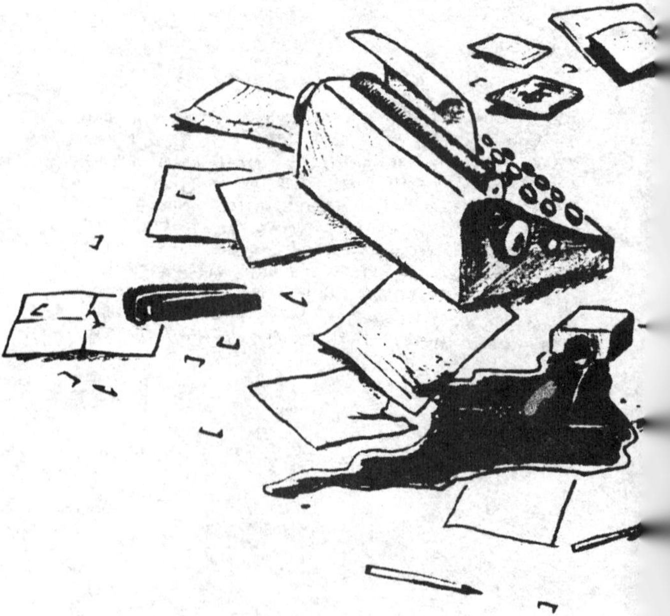

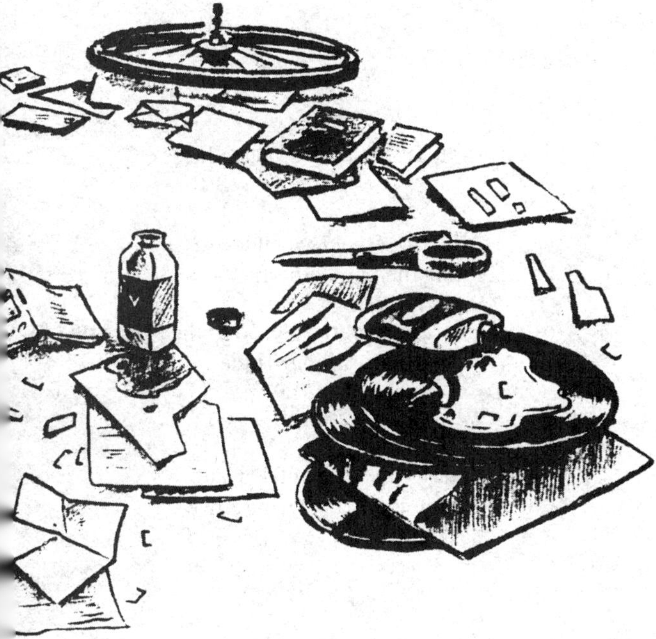

OTHER TITLES BY PIONEERS PRESS

The Do-It-Yourself Guide to
Fighting the Big Motherfuckin' Sad

Under the Radar: Notes from the
Wild Mushroom Trade

Caveworld

Dear Shane: A Mental Health
Resource About Staying Alive

www.pioneerspress.com

MATT SPENDS LONG PERIODS OF TIME ON HIS BICYCLE, AND EVEN LONGER TIMES WRITING ABOUT IT. HE DRAWS + PAINTS A LOT, TOO. HE IS ONLINE AT RETIREMENTFUND.ETSY.COM, + MATTGAUCK.COM. HE LIVES IN PORTLAND, OREGON. HE IS ALSO VEGAN.

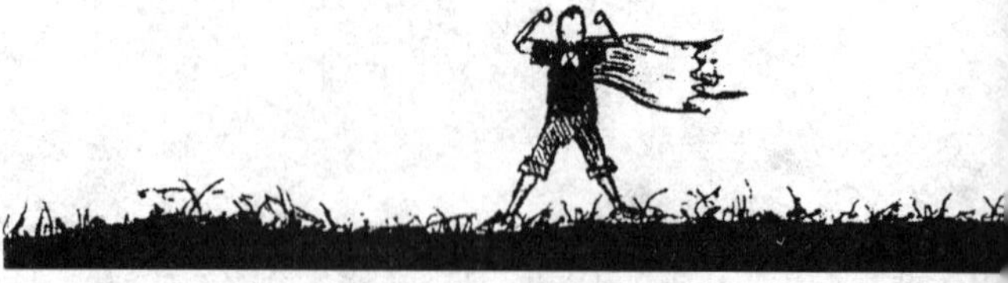